Getting Along With the Chinese

for fun and profit

Twelve months on the *South China Morning Post*'s Bestsellers' List!

Fred Schneiter has written an entertaining and highly informative guide to China, explaining how to work and play with the Chinese. With an unfailing sense of humor, Schneiter offers insights for Sinophiles, Sinophobes, and everyone in between.

Schneiter delves into the lighter side of Chinese psychology and in doing so demystifies one of the toughest markets in the world. He explains when you should and how you can apply pressure, why patience is not quite the overriding consideration it is generally perceived to be, and what to do and what *not* to do when hosting Chinese guests.

Fred Schneiter is the Hong Kong-based Vice President for Market Development in China of US Wheat Associates. Over the last three decades he has worked in *every* province of China, including Taiwan, Hong Kong and Macau, (as well as Vietnam, Pakistan, Bangladesh, Singapore, Malaysia, Thailand, Indonesia and the Philippines) introducing pizza, hamburgers and sandwiches and modernizing the noodle, baking and milling industries.

Getting Along With the Chinese sums up what he learned along the way.

"An essential item to pack in your 'China survival kit'"
The Hongkong Standard
"Facts on China no degree of study can give"
The Shanghai Star
"Offers American readers the chance to understand the Chinese — and themselves — better"
The Oregonian

Also by Fred Schneiter:

The Taste of Old Hong Kong

Getting Along
With the Chinese

for fun and profit

FRED SCHNEITER

Illustrated by Larry Feign

BLACKSMITH **BOOKS**

Text © 1992, 2016 Fred Schneiter
Illustrations © 1992 Larry Feign
All rights reserved

ISBN 978-988-13764-6-6

Published by **Blacksmith Books**
Unit 26, 19/F, Block B, Wah Lok Industrial Centre,
37–41 Shan Mei Street, Fo Tan, Hong Kong
Tel: (+852) 2877 7899

www.blacksmithbooks.com

Typeset with Ventura Publisher by Alan Sargent
Printed in Hong Kong
First edition 1992
Ten printings through June 2010

Second edition 2016
First printing 2016

To see oursels as others see us!
It wad frae monie a blunder free us,
An' foolish notion.
— ROBERT BURNS

It is wisdom to know others.
— LAO TZU

The human nature of people is similar.
— CONFUCIUS

I'm astounded by people who want to "know" the universe,
when it's hard enough to find your way around
Chinatown.
— WOODY ALLEN

To those who sometimes make some effort
to see the other person's point of view.

Acknowledgements

As this expanded and updated second edition takes flight around the world I must express appreciation to those who helped bring it about. First, to Pete Spurrier, publisher of Blacksmith Books of Hong Kong, who came up with the idea for taking on the challenge of a second edition rather than simply going for an eleventh international printing. And to Alan Sargent, Pete's editor, who fortuitously and coincidentally happened to have edited the original manuscript with me some twenty years ago. Alan whittled and polished it after editor Jan Krikke saw something salvageable in my submission. Candy Tong, who helped enhance my *The Taste of Old Hong Kong,* published in 2014, added her welcome and polished touch to this Second Edition as well. Then there's author/journalist Don Kirk who recommended I submit the manuscript to Blacksmith Books. And how could I fail to mention my indomitable wife, The Lovely Charlene, who, after all these years remains my most ardent advocate. She and my resourceful neighbor-gurus Jan Clark, Michael Lie and Bob McQuown, all of whom understand more about computers than I really care to know, helped keep my old Samsung from toying with my emotions.

In acknowledging those—mainly innocent bystanders—whose inputs helped enliven the best-selling first edition, I owe much to Chinese friends, associates, acquaintances and indulgent strangers who graciously, and with candor, put up with all my pestering questions about things Chinese over the decades.

Also I must acknowledge all the non-Chinese who, usually unwittingly, provided ideas, guidance, gusto, and more than an occasional gaffe or guffaw. My indefatigable wife put up with the long hours of seclusion that goes along with trying to convert brain waves into ink.

Distinguished China Hands Donald Anderson, Ambassador Burton Levin and Ambassador Richard Williams graciously reviewed the final draft and shared important insights. So did McDonald's Hong Kong Managing Director Daniel Ng, who opened the first two McDonald's in the People's Republic of China. China hand and author Dennis Leventhal and wife Mary—longtime friends in both Taipei and Hong Kong—contributed invaluable counsel from the first sketchy scribbles and stuck with me all the way through. Asia publishing professionals Mike Morrow and Jan Krikke provided energizing enthusiasm in the project's earliest days. Editor Alan Sargent helped put it on the *South China Morning Post's* best-seller list for a solid year.

Hopefully, bookshop browsers *will* judge this book by its cover, and illustrations, from the pen of Hong Kong's premier cartoonist, Larry Feign, a man blessed with the Confucian quality of seeing both sides of everything. Lam Chung Ying inspired me stoically through it all, a reincarnate and untiring Chinese Socrates to my pesky Plato.

Contents

Prologue

SINCE MARCO POLO came up with the idea of writing about China, we've had all manner of them-and-us books, adventure stories, anthropological/socio-political/economic/historical research works, travel guides, cookbooks and I don't know what all. Sun Tzu's *The Art of War* continues to appear under a variety of guises, almost as regularly as the return of the wild goose. And have you noticed how all books about China seem to tilt either toward the theme of the Wonderful Chinese or the Wily Chinese? This isn't one of those, nor is it a "new management book" dedicated to the wisdom of trying to outwit the Chinese. This is a lighthearted little offering, written in the hope that it may contribute toward a better understanding of the Chinese, and perhaps make some small contribution toward the realization of our largely untapped mutualities.

I've had Chinese classmates, friends and neighbors since the first grade, the year Franklin D. Roosevelt became President. That was an era when Americans knew virtually nothing of substance about the Chinese, aside from what they could work out from the evil doings of Fu Manchu and Flash Gordon's archenemy, Ming the Merciless. Generalissimo Chiang Kai-shek was seen by his wartime ally, Roosevelt, as "the first real Oriental" he had met. Fate afforded me a broader perspective. My high school was on the fringe of San Francisco's Chinatown and the year I graduated, seventy Chinese students—a quarter of the class—received their diplomas. Galileo High likely had more Chinese than any public high school in the country. Most of the rest of the kids were Italians from nearby "Little Italy." (In high school, it was never a question of being in the minority. I *was* the minority.) The past twenty-eight years I've lived in the Orient, working on the development and modernization of the wheat food industry. Most of that time was spent working directly with government and business people under the

Chinese Nationalist regime in Taiwan, and (since 1981) has involved, exclusively, the People's Republic of China. And, before anybody even knew there was such a thing, in 1968 I was one of the world's first distributors of Hong Kong flu.

My hope is the following impressions and recollections may serve as something of your own personal Rosetta Stone to enhance your understanding of China and the Chinese. And while I haven't used a Rosetta Stone, my "romanticized" spelling of Chinese words follows no formal system, but attempts to be consistent with local usage and historical context. This includes famous old brand names which retain their traditional spelling.

The book is intended for homebodies, students, tourists, managers, teachers, backpackers, traders, writers, and anyone else interested in a better understanding of how the Chinese see things. Acquiring a better grasp of the Chinese thought process requires little more than an open mind and an inquiring perspective. If that sounds like you, read on.

A fair amount of space is devoted to the critical business of what offends or pleases the Chinese. While there's no guarantee we can get along better with someone just because we understand them, we can't expect to get far—individually or collectively—if we don't try.

I didn't make up any of this. What I didn't personally experience, was picked up principally from the Chinese themselves and from diplomats, and a wide assortment of friends and associates who have spent years in the Orient. In the event you encounter an occasional contradiction—I'm sorry; that's how China is. As Amy Tan, author, says of China, "pick your truths very carefully."

Despite apparent differences between the Chinese and the rest of us, we surely would be very much like them if our histories had been similar. And, really, the rest of us aren't all that much unlike them.

That brings us to a Chinese proverb about our mutual potentials:

Where there is a stairway it should be used

Who Do They Think They Are?

Seeing the World through Almond Eyes

AFTER TWENTY-EIGHT YEARS in the Orient, I'm starting to get some things figured out. Presently, I'm working on the theory that most problems between China and the West stem largely from the fact that *they* want to do things *their* way while the West wants them to do things the Western way. Sure. It's a bit more complex than that, and while there are more bumps on the road ahead there is some indication that we have started to try to acquire some understanding of one another's point of view. One thing, however, will always remain a puzzle to me. That is, the Chinese breakfast. Where Americans start the day with hot rolls and jam, fruit juice and coffee, in China a bowl of bean curd milk or rice porridge is the star of their morning show. In most parts of the country, the

supporting cast features such (cold) characters as steamed dough, tripe, pickled vegetables, jellied duck feet, boiled peanuts, salty duck eggs, blood pudding and perhaps a sliced, soy-sauced green vegetable.

I can eat just about anything which can be caught, cleaned and chewed. Pickled vegetables are one of my staples, and there is nothing nicer you can do to a peanut than boil it, fresh out of the good earth. Blood pudding and jellied duck feet are OK. But somehow this all doesn't quite come together in harmony at sunup.

Westerners are on a more familiar footing with the Cantonese *dim sum yum cha* breakfast with dainty steamed dumplings with translucent wrappers, tangy little meat balls and yummy custards. From a practical standpoint, the pickles and peanuts breakfast is indeed more of an "eye opener" and Chinese friends insist they couldn't contemplate facing their immediate future without this Sino smorgasbord. The mere suggestion of buttermilk biscuits and gravy would be so unsettling they'd have to go back to bed until they got over it.

Having met myriad Chinese dawns in the company of friends over countless cold jellied duck feet, I've recently evolved a new regimen. I just say "no" to breakfast feasting with the group. Instead, in my room, I have cookies, tea and fruit (acquired earlier at the street market). That's plenty, as at sunup the standard non-Chinese digestive system will still be working on the previous night's banquet. Chinese don't grasp the Western inclination toward dieting, but it helps to tell them that avoiding a big breakfast keeps your weight under control while riding the Chinese banquet circuit.

The foregoing is less a critique of cuisine than it is an endorsement of the theory that aside from the peanuts and pickles at daybreak, just about everything else in our sometimes sputtering East-West melange is malleable. While China and the West are closer today in many ways than we give ourselves credit for, most foreigners have a muddled view of the Chinese simply because foreigners haven't taken a close enough look at them. Given a choice, it's far better to be a *befuddled* foreigner than one who has "been to China a couple of times" and come away convinced they have the Chinese figured out.

Initial incursions into Beijing (Peking), Shanghai, and Guangzhou (Canton)—the usual places foreigners go—do afford some opportunity to learn a little about China. (Certainly more than friends, neighbors and the home office staff may ever know.) But this smidgen should be kept in perspective. In the beginning, much of what the foreigner "learns" or assumes is wrong. Or—at best—not altogether correct. But a start is a start.

Someone's having "been to Beijing and Shanghai" is not quite the same as having "been to *China.*" Initial impressions, often acquired at the gallop, could be described as being the tip of the iceberg. They could be, but that's not quite how it is. In the case of China it would be more accurate to say, it is like a snowflake which is *about to fall* on the tip of the iceberg.

Simply asking questions about how the Chinese see things has its limitations. Throughout the Orient people tend to give an answer they think will please, or which they think may benefit them. The wrong question can only result in the wrong answer.

"When I want to return, I buy a ticket from the conductor when the train arrives?"

"Yes."

That's not the right question. It should be, "Is there any assurance there will be a seat available on the train when I want to return?"

Often, frustrations which foreigners endure result directly from our not saying what we mean. Weekending in Macau with my wife we found we had no water in the bathroom. Charlene is a good sport and a good traveler but having water in the bathroom is something she's picky about. I phoned downstairs.

"We have no water in the bathroom."

"Yes?"

Of course. Sloppy communication. It needed a replay.

"We would like to have some water in the bathroom."

Having said what I meant, the matter was quickly resolved.

Tuning in on the Chinese wavelength comes more easily if you follow the advice of the baseball great and sometimes philosopher, Yogi Berra, "You can observe a lot just by watching." Good advice. When you are not sure what you should do next—Watch and wait. Look and listen. It's an unbeatable combination that can get you out of a pickle faster than Dorothy's ruby red slippers got her out of Oz.

One day we stopped for lunch in a hot and remote region where we hadn't seen a foreigner for three days. This wasn't a fancy restaurant but it was the best place in town. I was with old cronies who knew they could count on me to do something a little silly once in a while, if only to perform the primary function of foreigners in China; to provide comic relief. (This is recommended, if for no other reason than it helps them figure out that you aren't stuffy, which rates even lower than silly.)

In this context when the waiter approached with a bottle of questionable-vintage local brew, I extended my empty rice-bowl, and he filled it, to the group's amusement. Taking a sip, the stuff proved to be so bad it could only be swallowed with the most firm resolve. There was nothing on the table to pour it into. I was hungry and wouldn't get any food as long as whatever-it-was remained in the bowl.

Also, there were implications of "face"—my friends', the restaurant's and my own. The only option was to watch and wait. The person next to me wrung a giggle from the group by having his bowl filled too. He took a mouthful and his eyes rounded noticeably as his eyebrows fluttered. In a single motion he turned, sprayed whatever-it-was into the atmosphere, and emptied his bowl onto the floor. With the group's encouragement, mine followed his onto the floor—a demonstration of the wisdom of paying attention.

In wandering around the rice-eating Far East, I've found you can tell a lot about the wheat market potential of some new place without even bothering to ask. If the local bread looks bad, smells bad and tastes bad, it's obvious the people there don't like bread. And, the baker who baked it doesn't like bread either. That spells market *potential* for good bread. If you rely only on asking questions, in this case the answer would be, "We don't like bread." That's not it. They don't like *bad* bread.

With the Chinese, always pay attention to the little things. Little kids for example. Kids have a litmus quality which affords instant insights into the nature of a neighborhood.

Chatting with children made my first trip to the remote northwest frontier city of Urumuqi particularly memorable. Talking over my shoulder to youngsters who were trotting along beside me, I fell smack-dab into an open manhole. Happily, as foolish as one may appear in these circumstances, there is absolutely no social stigma attached to a foreigner's falling into a manhole because it's not that uncommon. (The *China Daily* reported a few weeks later that 135 manhole covers had been stolen in Beijing in the first eight months of the year. Where they went, the authorities didn't say, but a manhole cover would make an ideal grill for a Mongolian barbecue.) After three stitches with black silk thread, administered by the head of the Xinjiang Medical Institute Hospital First Branch Outpatient Section, with his entire staff looking over his shoulder, I felt relatively reconstituted. Though I had some trouble convincing my overly-attentive hosts that, while their concern was appreciated, I absolutely did not want to be sear-sealed with the laser the hospital reportedly had tucked away somewhere.

Probably no one shows more concern for an injured visitor than the Chinese. No matter what assurance you give that a little blister or scratch "is really nothing," within minutes someone (whose departure you'd missed) suddenly reappears, with pockets and hands full of pills and time-honored potions to hasten your recovery.

In *Riding the Iron Rooster,* the engaging and mildly masochistic tale of train travel in China, Paul Theroux tells how he narrowly missed toppling into a deep hole in a factory in Langxiang. He was so rattled by the experience he "had to go outside and take deep breaths." As a learning experience, simply being rattled by what *nearly* happened can't compare to actually toppling into a hole in China. Foreigners should abide by the code of the ancients . . . walk or gawk, but don't walk *and* gawk. There are doorways, perhaps three floors up, opening out into space. Now and then there's an open elevator shaft. Uncovered manholes, unexpected and unrailed drops and broken curbs and sidewalks are common. Public liability coverage remains a foreign concept, not because Chinese are callous, but because they don't go around falling in holes.

On another character-building trip, my flight landed several provinces off course without enough gas in the tank to dampen a doily. We had to take a bus from the middle of the field where the plane rolled to a stop. During refueling, none of the passengers expressed any curiosity about the navigational error, because it was understood the answer would be designed to make everyone feel good, rather than to shed light on the situation. While the curiosity of less-traveled foreigners might be piqued over such an incident, Chinese are inclined to discount it with, "What difference does it make?"

An authoritative view of how we've arrived at where we are today with China was shared in Hong Kong by Han Suyin, whose book *A Many-Splendored Thing* deals with the mingling of East and West in a romance set in Hong Kong. I asked her why it has taken so long for China and the West to come at least this close together.

"Has it really been all that long?" she teased.

"Not the way China looks at things, of course, but it *has* been several centuries."

"Perhaps," she replied, "it has something to do with the way the French fight wars. They always fight a war the way they fought the one before. With China, the West has perhaps had too many Sinologists who are more preoccupied with ancient dynasties than they are with the future."

Another point Westerners generally miss is that Chinese are more like us than we imagine. And, many of the dissimilarities are not all that different. Where we get "goose pimples" they get "chicken skin." If you sneeze, they say, "Longevity." They have heartburn and henpecked husbands. Their youngsters make mud pies, play hide-and-seek and jump rope. Where we cook birds and walk dogs, they walk birds—with cage in hand—and wok dogs. They make doughnuts that are long and straight and others the size and shape of a tennis ball, and hollow. Bridegrooms pay the wedding bills. At funerals they wear white, instead of black, and it's a tradition to give red eggs, instead of a cigar, to announce the birth of a son. Where we talk of a man in the moon, they speak of a lady, and a rabbit. Where we see the face of a fanciful monster in the variegated and animated blossom we call "snapdragon" they see gulping lips and call it "goldfish." They wave when they want someone to come nearer, while waggling your finger at someone in the Western come-hither style is, in many parts of China, a particularly obscene gesture. The major difference between Worcestershire and soy sauce would appear to be the fact that there are countless versions and brands of the latter. Where we bake bread they steam it. In earlier days they had drawbridges too, but theirs were designed to sink, rather than to be raised. Chinese toddlers don't wear diapers. Instead, they are outfitted in trousers which are open at the bottom so their little undercarriages are unencumbered. When I suggested an apple a day keeps the doctor away, a friend in Beijing responded, "Hey. An *onion* a day keeps *everyone* away."

It was not Confucius who said, "Without our traditions we would be as shaky as a fiddler on the roof." But he surely wouldn't have disputed the idea. Foreigners, who may know that Chinese are traditionalists, remain pretty much unaware of just how *intensely* traditional they can be in their day-to-day doings. An example of this can be seen on Hong Kong's beaches, which are elbow-to-navel during the hot and muggy summer season. With the Mid-Autumn Festival, the Chinese conclude that the seaside season has ended. However, the best beach weather comes after that, with dazzling and balmy sunny days, particularly in December. Aside from a few year-round exercise enthusiasts, Hong Kong's beaches in winter are pretty much left to the enjoyment of privacy-relishing, less-tradition-bound Westerners and Filipinos.

Coming to terms with contradictions has a lot to do with how the Chinese see the world. As a Ministry of Agriculture official expressed it, "A bad harvest is a problem, and so is a good harvest. How do you move it? How do you store it?" What is China's great blessing? Children. What is China's great problem? Population.

When you get two different answers, it doesn't necessarily mean one of them is wrong.

Despite their monumental consistencies, Chinese have the capacity to be wondrously inconsistent. Problems developed when a delegation we were taking to the US insisted we use their interpreter, rather than someone we wanted to take from our consulate. That was resolved by our taking their interpreter *and* our interpreter. Shortly after that the next delegation threw a curve by insisting *we* provide the interpreter. That complicated things as we hadn't budgeted for it. But we got the money and worked it out.

An essential element of working relationships in China is that if it is at all possible for you to do something they want, you should do it. If it is not possible, you are expected to find a way to make it possible. Flexibility is one of the best allies you've got and you should always employ it with a smile. If something is indeed beyond the realm of possibility, you need only say it is "inconvenient" to put the matter to rest with no further explanation required. The word "inconvenient" conveys far more finality to the Chinese than "impossible."

Trying to figure out who the Chinese think they are is less a science than it is an art form. But, like a lot of art forms, if you're interested and make the effort, it will enhance your understanding, broaden your vistas, and for those involved with things Chinese, perhaps ensure a better night's sleep.

Willows planted at random spread a pleasant shade

Inscrutable? That's Disputable!

How to Read (the) Chinese

THROUGH SEVEN CENTURIES OF COMMERCE, contact and conflict since Marco Polo's odyssey to Cathay, the West acquired no substantial concept of how the Chinese think. And much—perhaps most—of what the West takes for granted about the Chinese is wrong.

Since the establishment of the People's Republic, one of the better backgrounded Americans to go to China was Fox Butterfield, the first *New York Times* correspondent in Beijing. He studied Chinese language and history at Harvard. After graduate work he studied in Taiwan on a Fulbright Fellowship. He began reporting for the *Times* in Taiwan in 1969, before going on to other Asian assignments. On his arrival in Beijing, with impeccable Asian orientation credentials, what was one of the first things he came to grips with? In his words, "I had to unlearn many of what I took to be facts about China."

One thing all foreigners seem collectively sure of is the idea Chinese are inscrutable. And they're wrong about that too. But the idea is so ingrained in our thinking that the phrase "inscrutable Chinese" has somehow managed to become both hackneyed and redundant with the adjective defying almost any other application.

Chinese don't find each other inscrutable. If *they* don't, why should we? If luncheon conversation with a friend in China begins to lag, an effective stimulant to getting it moving again is the question, "Did you know foreigners find Chinese ways strange?"

Typically, the response is, "*Really!?* But, foreigners are the strange and unpredictable ones!"

On a number of occasions Chinese acquaintances have confided (to our shared consternation) "You know, I don't think foreigners understand China." It's true, and the agony is compounded by the fact the Chinese don't understand foreigners either.

To act un-Chinese amounts to the unthinkable, "acting like a foreigner." A Hong Kong businessman, relating a problem he'd had with someone born in Shanghai, lamented, "That's not the way *we* do things. He's obviously part Russian."

Youngsters assimilate the spoken and signaled pressures of peers and parents and they get the message when things go unsaid or undone.

Two of the more subtle acquired arts are innuendo and indirection, which are applied masterfully in dealing with foreigners. These mask a basically direct and unswerving style.

To illustrate, here are some random observations:

- Chinese are easily offended. If a transgression, embarrassment or indignity is perceived to be of consequence, they are likely neither to completely forget nor forgive.
- If greatly displeased, they'll not miss an opportunity to even things up. They're never in a rush about this and when it happens it's done with the utmost finesse, like a triple-cushion pool shot.
- They are most unlikely to give any outward indication of genuine hurt or offense. A broken arm is kept inside the sleeve.
- If displeasure *is* shown, it's likely being done for effect.
- They are not particularly offended or surprised when foreigners breach the bounds of their view of civilized conduct, such as flailing cameras in the faces of "quaint and colorful" passersby. The reasons unruly outsiders were seen as barbarians hold true today. Foreigners who are sensitive and savvy enough to circumvent this ancient expectation please the Chinese and come across as a happy surprise.
- If you ask a question a second time about something you wish to pursue and they again say, "It is under study," or, "It is not a convenient time," you can conclude that the subject is closed, or very nearly so. If you can, drop the subject.

- If you raise your voice in anger, the louder and more upset you become, the less you are heard. They have the capacity to tune you out altogether in such circumstances.
- In hosting they will pamper you to pieces, having been working at banquet graces since the time when, outside China, people were sitting in trees sucking raw eggs and discovering that apples taste better than pine cones.
- A real Chinese friend will go to almost any lengths to help you, well beyond what you might expect from anyone else you've ever known.
- Appearing unexpectedly at the front door of Chinese friends, with your suitcases, you never will be asked how long you plan to stay. Each day they'll presume you'll still be there the next, and meals or entertainment will be planned accordingly. An early sage noted that your best chickens should be killed to serve guests, but it isn't polite to ask guests if they mind if you do so.
- In business, Chinese will strive to get the upper hand and expect you to do the same.
- A courtesy or kindness will be returned.
- In China, youngsters do not complain about what's on their plate.
- Chinese tend to subscribe to the philosophy, "Old ways are best," so a foreign manager in China can expect more problems than elsewhere in getting employees to adopt new procedures. If incentives are attractive or the employees have had a fair degree of exposure to foreign managers, introducing change is much easier. Face is part of the problem so any such efforts should be enhanced if you can get employees to understand the *reason* for a new procedure, while emphasizing that the way they were doing it before was not *wrong*.
- The Chinese who jostle you on a crowded Hong Kong street do not mean to be impolite. They simply feel they have as much right to that space as you have. Little old ladies jostle harder than anyone else, perhaps because at their age they feel they don't have as much time to put up with people getting in their way.

- If a mother is contending with a cantankerous toddler, and you smile and suggest, in Chinese, "I'll give you five bucks for the kid," her reply will be, "Just take him. No charge." Further, the youngster's deportment will immediately improve.
- You will get more done in China through personal relationships than you will through any institutional or contractual loyalty. It's unlikely this will ever change.
- If you meet a new business contact who seems rather dull, who says something along the lines of, "I'm just a simple person," be prepared for a memorable and perhaps costly lesson in Chinese business administration.
- Chinese are not by nature violent, and contrary to the widely-held foreign view, few are good enough at slam-bang Kung fu to hold their ground against a reasonably good boxer. However, Chinese do practice *Gung fu*, a variety of disciplines for toning both muscle and mind. "Gung fu" translates as "outstanding achievement," conveying the idea of exercise and is a generic term for all the so-called "martial arts." (Chinese friends assure me that the term "Kung fu" is strictly movie terminology.)

Gaining a better understanding of the Chinese is easier if you think of them as born actors. They are not as unemotional as foreigners presume. They fret, fear and fume the same as anyone else. Westerners expend a fair amount of energy in communicating feelings, but Chinese society doesn't work that way. Take my advice: never teach a Chinese to play poker. Westerners, who use facial expressions and gestures to augment communication can be unnerved by people who generally refrain from doing so at all. To compound our predicament, a smile or a chuckle from the Chinese, rather than indicating agreement or amusement, may signal nothing more than quizzical lack of comprehension. If some misfortune or accident occurs, Chinese laugh or grin out of embarrassment, which foreigners generally interpret as an inclination to mock adversity. Getting into an embarrassing situation is not what

Chinese are supposed to do. When it happens they laugh because they don't know how else to handle it.

Then we have those almost subliminal stirrings which we call "body language": such things as the shifting of one's bottom in a chair being a sign of boredom or annoyance. Chinese understand this international language and are highly skilled at affecting or suppressing these signals themselves. Their mastery in this affords them a comfortable edge.

Doing this even moderately well is not easy. Try sitting through a long, dull, frustrating encounter without the slightest glance, nod or furrowed brow and you'll better appreciate this skill. Being clearly outgunned, if you are involved in a particularly important negotiation you can make it a bit more difficult to read your expression at critical points if you take a chair with your back to a sunny window. (Providing they haven't already staked out those strategic seats.)

When Chinese choose—for effect—to use gestures, facial expression or tone of voice to make a point, to gain an upper hand or to put someone at ease, it is done with the smoothness of polished jade. Don't misread this as duplicity. These are no more than the basic skills employed by all diplomats, negotiators and parents of teen-age children. When we do this, we see it simply as technique. When they do it, it fuels our conviction of their inscrutability.

Reading the Chinese is like reading music or an electrocardiogram. You have to understand what the squiggles mean. To do well in fishing a trout stream, you have to understand what the water is telling you. Without some knowledge of water reading, you won't know where the biggest fish will be feeding. Golf requires some skill in reading grass. Catching more fish, playing better golf and understanding the Chinese requires you to learn to read the signs. What astonishes me is people who agonize over their nine iron will swing giddily into China without acquiring any knowledge of how people there think. And while we're at it, have you ever heard a golfer refer to an unruly nine iron as "inscrutable"?

It's well established that in foreign countries, students from traditional Chinese homes will be in the top of their class. Bringing home a test paper with a score of ninety-five, they will be asked why the score wasn't 100. Where American parents praise a child, a Chinese parent is critical. But, in testimony to their adaptability, studies of families which have moved to the US show that by the third generation, students are more interested in "courtship and cars" than in school. Despite this ethnic back-sliding, important insights are provided by family values in traditional Chinese homes.

Traditional Chinese self-reliance and industriousness is legendary. Chinese-Americans' median income is the second highest after the Japanese. It's estimated that Chinese own more than ten percent of San Francisco. That just didn't happen by chance. Lee Kuan Yew, Prime Minister of Singapore for more than thirty years noted, "The Chinese mother is a great force for education. She will nag about homework and keep the television off." Chinese parents endorse the Confucian respect for education. They make considerable sacrifice to provide the best possible schooling for their children. In our early days in Taiwan I was surprised to hear people of fairly modest means say they had youngsters in high-paying technical or professional jobs in the US, after the parents managed to put them through one of the better universities. Nearly half the doctoral candidates in American graduate schools for science or engineering are Asian. Sociologists have explored this willingness of Asian parents to sacrifice more for a youngster's education than most American parents of similar means would do. The "cohesion" of the Asian family unit is cited as the underlying factor. But there's a filial *quid pro quo* which must be taken into account to understand the forces at work. The greater the parents' sacrifice for a youngster's education, the more comfortable are the parents' later years when the children traditionally provide for them. It isn't unusual for Chinese to save thirty percent of their income for investment, a child's education, or something else equally sensible. Frugality is a paramount virtue. Children are taught not to waste money on non-essentials.

The complete uniform of China's Young Pioneers, the equivalent of the Boy and Girl Scouts, is simply a red neckerchief worn with street clothes. Without a closet full of toys, youngsters entertain themselves for hours with nothing more than a puddle, a twig or a bug. Farmers pass an idle hour moving and capturing broken bits of straw and pebbles on a "playing board" scratched in the dust. Laborers fashion a Chinese chess game with bits of broken tile. Improvisation is clearly a Chinese characteristic.

Back to the inscrutability factor. You can learn a lot about this from Hong Kong tailors, who I've gotten to know pretty well since arriving in 1964 because I long ago gave up trying to buy a suit off the rack there long enough for my six-foot-two frame. The important thing to remember in having a suit made is: never haggle. It's OK to *ask* the price. When it involves something already made, haggle. But never when you're having something made. They can make a suit about as cheap and shoddy as you want.

Unless you've gone to the same tailor for years, his general approach—while charming—can be rather like that of an itinerant rug merchant trying to make the money for a train ticket out of town ahead of the police. They have every reason to believe they have you where they want you, because you'll probably be back in New Jersey before the zipper falls out, and the casual customer (particularly a tourist) doesn't often know a whole lot about tailoring or the quality of cloth.

The only disadvantage to using the same tailor is that it isn't as entertaining as going into a shop where they don't know you. One day, at my wife's suggestion, I ventured into a new shop and ordered a suit. Returning to try it on, the tailor predictably oozed, "Perfect. That looks really great." When a tailor says that, study the merchandise carefully in the mirror. Tailors, remember, live by their wits, much the same as gypsies, itinerant roofers, riverboat gamblers and writers. Some tailors would say "perfect" if the suit hung on you like a sumo wrestler's mattress cover. Studying the warps and ripples, I gripped the jacket and pulled it forward leaving a foot-and-a-half cavity between it and my belt buckle.

"Fix this," I suggested.

"You prefer it *snug*?"

"I prefer it to fit." He agreed he'd take care of that.

"Other than that, it really is perfect," he purred.

"The sleeves are too short."

"Oh! Let me tell you. That is the difference between a tailor made suit and one you buy off the rack. With the ready made suit, the sleeve is always a bit long. The short sleeve is the *mark* of a tailor made suit."

This guy was good.

"I didn't know that about ready made suits," I said.

"Few people do."

"The reason I don't is because I haven't been able to buy a suit off the rack here for nearly thirty years," I replied, with a James Bondish icy stare.

He pondered a moment. "We'll fix the sleeves."

There is no crash course for getting acquainted with China or Chinese tailors. The learning experience rides China's timetable. The answer (or something close to it) eventually surfaces. For years a business associate, on his occasional trips to the Far East, pondered on the tasty little dried shrimp with which Chinese embellish a variety of dishes. "My, these are good," he would exclaim on discovering some in his soup. "I wonder how they make them?" Aside from being dried and salted no one could offer further details, although he never failed to exclaim and raise the question each time he came across them. They're often quite small, not much larger than a pea and, for lack of a better reference, he began referring to them as "pea" shrimp. Finally, holidaying one Sunday in Hong

Kong on Cheung Chau Island, we paused for a cool sip in the shade of a large flowering tree. Just across the lane, lay a newspaper on the ground scattered with shrimp, drying in the summer sun. "There you are. Pea shrimp being processed," I said, pointing to the little pink pile. "Yeah . . ." he said wistfully. "But there's got to be more to it than *that*."

As we relaxed over our drinks, a boy of perhaps four, toddled out of a nearby doorway. Marching straight to the newspaper, he paused, fumbled briefly with his britches, and suddenly launched a manly saline arc over the shrimp with a flourish which suggested he might be writing his name in Chinese. Wow. My associate looked as if a dead mouse had gone down his gullet with the last gulp.

Our conversation dwindled through the remainder of the afternoon until I came up with, "Things are not always what they seem in the Orient."

"If you're talking about the shrimp, I'm *sure* that's not how they do it," he grumbled.

"That's what I mean."

"I suppose you're going to use that in your dumb book."

"I won't use your name." He brightened considerably.

Few foreigners have a better grasp of the difference between reality and illusion in China than American James Veneris. Taken prisoner in Korea in 1950, he later joined twenty-two other prisoners of war in refusing repatriation and has been in China ever since. James is now a retired factory worker and teaches English at Shandong University. When I asked his views on Chinese "inscrutability," he laughed, "There's nothing mystical about the Chinese."

The world is different from what it was in those distant, dark days when James and I were swept up into the Korean War. As our global village shrinks in resources, clean water, breathable air and living space, it seems important that we try to become better neighbors.

A good neighbor is a treasure

Absolutes Don't Compute

Assorted Contrasts and Contradictions

SPRING FESTIVAL IS CELEBRATED in China's mid-winter. Winter melon soup is eaten in the summer and fall. The succulent, skinny, snow peas which Westerners associate with Chinese stir-fry are called Holland beans in China. The game of Chinese checkers is not Chinese but, rather, evolved from German and American roots. In Tibet doctors take a patient's pulse with both hands. Within a few miles, the name of Beijing's major east-west street, which passes in front of the Forbidden City, changes five times. What we call the Yangtze is known in China as either Ta Jiang, "Great River," Chang Jiang, "Long River" or, in its upper reaches, Chin Sha Jiang, "Gold Sand River." Curling through Shanghai, the Wusong River becomes Suzhou Creek (but only in the English version).

Chinese venerate age but commonly dye their hair to appear younger. The massive, ornate tomb of Genghis Khan in Inner Mongolia does not contain the famous conqueror's remains. In the north, "rice eating" Chinese eat three to four times as much wheat as "wheat eating" Americans. The rickshaw was a Japanese import. The abacus was developed in Babylonia about 5,000 years ago, was used by early Romans and Greeks and found its way into China in the early Ming Dynasty.

Chinese parsley (coriander) originated in the Mediterranean region. New Zealand's kiwifruit is native to China. South China's lichee nuts are a fruit. Bonsai, the miniature tree culture which has long been a national art form in Japan probably started in China before the 11th Century. The national game of Japan, Go, was learned from the Chinese during the Tang dynasty (having probably evolved out of divination rituals 3,000 to 4,000 years ago). The Japanese paper-folding art *origami* originated in China as *che chih* after China's invention of paper. Cantonese, in the south, prefer fish or shrimp. Northern Chinese prefer meat. North of the Great Wall lamb is preferred. In the south, on Hainan Island, coffee—rather than tea—is the drink of choice for many people.

China is a merrily-bubbling cauldron of contrasts and contradictions.

* * *

Better understanding of a country can be enhanced if you listen for the words or phrases which keep popping up throughout the day. In Germany, an example is *arbeit*. That means "work" and it says a lot about how they look at things. (During the Occupation of Germany we could tell from three blocks away whether youngsters were German or American because the German kids would be working while the American kids were playing.) In the Middle East you constantly hear *insha'allah,* which means "if Allah wills it to happen." Americans have their "OK." There's Mexico's *mañana* for "tomorrow" and the Philippines' *bahala na,* which can be taken to mean "tomorrow maybe."

China's entry in this word-clue game would have to be the ubiquitous *chabudoa* and its cousin *meiyoguanxi,* both of which attest to the national disinclination for exactness. *Chabudoa* vaguely translates as "more-or-less" while *meiyoguanxi* means "it doesn't matter." They are used interchangeably and are encountered with about the same frequency as "OK" in America. There are several other ways to express inexactness in China, though you get the feeling that none of them conveys quite the same sense of urgency as *mañana* does in Mexico.

Chabudoa literally means "gap not much." It can be used to respond to any number of statements or questions, such as "Nice day" or "See you at eight?"

For the foreigner, the concept says a lot about the nature of things. The first time I encountered it head-on was during one of my early trips to Hong Kong. I was looking for a shop to copy a small leather camera bag. I found a little leather place on Nathan Road where the shopkeeper said they could reproduce it exactly. The "exact copy" turned out to be twice as large, of a different shape and color, with a clasp rather than a zipper, and was made from hard, rather than soft, leather. This wasn't the result of poor communication. It was simply a physical manifestation of *chabudoa*.

Near the ancestral home of Sun Yat-sen in South China is a museum which, among its exhibits, contains a world globe which he is said to have brought back from one of his travels. I had a close look at and found it showed Brasilia, the capital of Brazil, a city which didn't exist until thirty-five years after Dr. Sun's death. It could be argued that the globe on display is probably pretty much like the one Dr. Sun owned and visitors enjoy viewing it. It would be indelicate to call it to the attention of the museum staff. While not a bull's-eye, it's close.

The Chinese may do or say things which make it appear that you're on target but often this is more illusion than actuality. It has more to do with *chabudoa* than anything else, so don't take it personally when it happens.

Will you settle for light brown walls in your living room after specifying they be painted off-white? Are you comfortable using a business card with the letter "l" instead of "t" in your office address? Within the *chabudoa* ethic it can be argued that the walls aren't really very dark and that people will figure out that "streel" means "street." Just how *meiyoguanxi* a style you choose to adopt is up to you, bearing in mind you can have the walls and the cards redone but you aren't going to change *chabudoa*. In some cases a preoccupation with exactness can be perceived as outright rude.

One of the more memorable experiences I've had with this involved what Arthur Conan Doyle might have called "The Case of the Disappearing Noodle Plant." This plant was a joint-venture facility, designed to serve as an example for the modernization and expansion of China's wheat food industry. The story started on a bright, sunny afternoon in Shanghai. An official from the Ministry of Commerce mentioned "this is the day" the equipment for the instant noodle plant was to arrive in port. Several days later, back in Hong Kong, I learned that the $200,000 worth of equipment had "disappeared." Checking by phone and telex on its route from the factory in Japan, the trail went cold at the Shanghai docks.

But in China it isn't easy to lose anything for long, even a noodle plant. So I avoided the "Western" approach, whereby I would rush to Shanghai and beat about the bushes and byways.

Taking the Chinese approach and sitting it out, the plant reappeared within a month, as mystically as it had vaporized. The happy ending is, seven years after it went into operation, it was credited with stimulating the construction of more than 200 similar noodle plants around the country. (Most of them now locally made.) It followed that we became heavily involved in responding to Chinese requests for assistance to help modernize and improve the production of traditional dry noodles, a product they invented in the first place.

*　*　*

It sometimes seems there is a slight *chabudoa* twist or a story behind the story to almost everything in the Orient. Take Hong Kong history. The guide books explain that England's acquisition of this little enclave involved three separate treaties. The first applied to Hong Kong Island, and the second to Kowloon peninsula across the harbor and a number of outlying islands. The third treaty involved the New Territories, a rolling, green larder and buffer which thrust the British flag another sixteen miles north into China. More than 235 islands made up the rest of the package. The New Territories' lease was to run for ninety-nine years, expiring in 1997 while Hong Kong and Kowloon were to remain under British rule forever. That's was the historical fact understood by everyone. Everyone except the Chinese.

When I first arrived in Hong Kong in 1964 it was suffering a serious water shortage. Signs in hotel bathrooms asked guests to leave water in the tub so it could be reused for washing floors, sidewalks and cars. Restaurants did not serve water unless requested. Hong Kong was, and is, dependent upon mainland China for an adequate water supply. You needn't be a political scientist or a cattle rancher to appreciate the implications of having someone with their hand on your water tap. China also supplied a great deal of Hong Kong's food, then about thirty-five percent in dollar value.

If China had been inclined to reappropriate Hong Kong at any time in recent decades, an ad in the paper indicating when they were coming would have about done it. "The People's Liberation Army Invites You To Tea At The Peninsula Hotel At Four On Wednesday."

A few years ago a cartoon in the Hong Kong press showed a half dozen British soldiers on a field exercise atop one of Hong Kong's little outlying islands. Their officer, swagger stick thrust northward, is saying, "I suppose you chaps are asking yourselves, just what we might do if five Chinese divisions attacked from, say, oh ... somewhere over there." The look on the troopers' faces made it clear that was exactly what was on their minds.

The Japanese in less than three weeks in December 1941 established that British Hong Kong was too small and exposed, with supply lines too extended and a defending force too small to put up much more than token resistance. As if that weren't enough, as in the fall of Singapore, the Japanese were too unsporting to come from the direction which the fixed gun emplacements faced.

A key point which seems to have gone unnoticed is that China abrogated all treaties when the communists took control of the Mainland in 1949. In effect, these three Hong Kong treaties had not existed for nearly half a century. The People's Republic had always claimed the area as part of its territory. But there was no real opposition to British rule. From its establishment in 1949 until 1964 when France became the first Western nation to recognize the PRC, Hong Kong was the only window China had to the West. The economic health of Hong Kong was long seen as essential to China. Even in the worst days of the national insanity of the Cultural Revolution, Beijing made no moves against Hong Kong. And when Hong Kong's business community finally became openly apprehensive about the expiry of the ninety-nine-year New Territories' lease, it was the British—not Beijing—who raised the question of renewal.

Prime Minister Margaret Thatcher went to Beijing in 1984 and the Chinese—sticklers for form—graciously joined her in formal discussions on the future of treaties they didn't recognize. What should have been clear to everyone was, that once the question was raised, a firm position toward repossession was the only option the Chinese government could take, without losing face and enduring the wrath of its entire constituency.

Despite the earlier success of the legendary St. George, the British were about to learn that no matter how firm the resolve or inspired the endeavor, sometimes the dragon wins.

When the British asked about renewal of the New Territories lease the Chinese said they were taking back everything. Their position was that the first two "unequal treaties" had been imposed on a crumbling Qing dynasty and were, well ... unacceptable. Britannia conceded and the process was thus set in motion for the return of the entire administrative region.

Richard Margolis, the Foreign Office's Deputy Political Adviser to the Hong Kong government at the time, and a participant in the negotiations reflected, "I've spent a great deal of time thinking about whether, if things had been done differently, we would have got a better deal, but the answer is no."

Among the details to be ironed out was establishing just where the China–Hong Kong boundaries are. The border was drawn in 1898 and the *South China Morning Post* reported that officials "have no idea where the New Territories end and China begins." Confidential talks were launched to work this out.

Portuguese Macau reverted to Chinese control in 1999, two years after Hong Kong. This treaty, too, is more fable than fact. One authoritative reference, *Discovering Macau*, by John Clemens, states: "There is no known documentary evidence to support the Portuguese contention that an official grant of land was made by the Chinese Emperor in 1557, but certainly in that year the Portuguese were allowed to set up their factories and houses. It seems probable therefore that an agreement was made on a local basis with the

Cantonese mandarins. . . ." Whatever the arrangement, the Chinese gained the comforting support of heavily-cannoned Portuguese ships in the strategic Pearl River delta while neatly containing the barbarians in a tiny enclave far away from Beijing.

In its creep toward modernization, the future—through most of the 1980s—seemed less a matter of China going to Hong Kong than of Hong Kong going to China. For decades, modernity crept north from Hong Kong Island, up through the peninsula and across the once rural countryside of the New Territories. It slipped across the border a few years ago, turning the sleepy town of Shenzhen into a *de facto* extension of its throbbing neighbor to the south.

The Prime Minister's Beijing experience demonstrates how even national leaders, with all their influence and high-powered expert counsel, have just as much to learn out here as we do.

*   *   *

Another example is General Douglas MacArthur. After leading Allied forces in the Pacific in World War II and then guiding Japan's rise from the ashes of war, he was confident the Korean War would be won by Christmas of 1950. With United Nations troops sweeping through North Korea toward China's Yalu River border, most Allied commanders shared MacArthur's confidence. Though Premier Zhou Enlai twice warned the United Nations through the Indian Ambassador not to press all the way to the border, the general flew the river to reconnoiter. Seeing no sign of Chinese troops—who were moving by night and observing strict camouflage discipline by day on the snowy north bank—he reached the unfortunate conclusion there were none. He pressed his troops on. In November 1950, 300,000 Chinese troops swarmed into North Korea. For the next thirty-two months, bloody battles raged up and down the peninsula, grinding to an icy truce in July of 1953. Chinese and North Korean dead, wounded and missing totaled some 1,600,000. South Korea lost 58,127 men. Other United Nations units lost 3,194.

American dead in Korea totaled 54,246 in just three years, compared to the ten-year toll of 58,135 Americans in Vietnam. In William Manchester's *American Caesar,* MacArthur is quoted: "Asiatics love a winner and despise a loser; they respect aggressive leadership." What MacArthur missed was, nobody likes to feel threatened. Further, China couldn't appear to be a loser either, as Zhou's warnings should have made clear. The Supreme Commander wasn't the only one coming up with incorrect Asian inferences in those fateful days. As late as November 24, 1950, the CIA saw "no evidence" that China planned major offensive operations. Two days later, the Chinese pulled the plug, streaming down from mountains which MacArthur had seen as too precipitous to shelter troops.

MacArthur's massive miscalculation attests to the Chinese mastery of making things appear different from what they are and illustrates their capacity to do exactly the opposite of what may seem logical or expected . . . at least to those who don't know how the Chinese feel about things. Approaching China with an open mind, President Nixon arrived at Beijing Airport on February 21, 1972. Thawing a relationship which had been in cold storage more than twenty years, he called it "the week that changed the world." A Western political cartoon at the time captured the spirit. A supervisor was depicted watching a workman putting up a banner in Tiananmen Square which read, WELCOME IMPERIALIST RUNNING DOG. The supervisor's reaction was, "Not bad Wong, but give it another try."

The Nixon-Mao conciliation was momentous, particularly, given Nixon's rock-ribbed, right-of-center credentials. The stage was set for the Nixon visit through "Ping-Pong Diplomacy." The East-West dialogue was initiated informally by Chinese and American players at the 31st World Table Tennis Championship in Nagoya, Japan in April of 1971. Mao Zedong and Zhou personally approved the Chinese team's participation in Nagoya and Mao approved inviting the American team to visit China. While Americans tend to see the thaw beginning from Nixon's initiative in going to China, actually Nixon was invited to come. Specifically, by Zhou Enlai.

*　　*　　*

While the direct approach and a concern for absolutes are not things the Chinese normally dwell upon, they're gracious enough to allow us to draw them into our pursuit of specifics. Not having all the answers doesn't seem to reduce their willingness to try to help us understand.

Some years ago, prowling the dark and dusty recesses of a little shop in one of the twisty back alleys which were then common in Taipei, I happened upon a stack of unusual wood carvings. Selecting four of the most interesting ones, I negotiated a price and that afternoon they were on the wall at home.

Years later in Hong Kong, a guest noted that these were likely from an old temple, and reminded us that such things were considered unlucky. Working in China can be tough enough without courting bad luck, so I pursued this question with Chinese friends. Answers always fell a little short of clarity. One evening, an electrician who had come by to replace faulty wiring, paused a moment in front of the tablets.

"What do you think?" I asked.

"Nice."

"Maybe not so good?"

"Nice."

"Not bad luck?"

"It's OK," he said firmly.

"I give them to you and you can put them in *your* house," I probed.

"Nice. No thank you." And he scurried out the door.

I related the ominous story to a Chinese friend the next day. "But you have excellent *feng shui* at your place, with the mountains behind you, the sea in front with islands that look like dragons on the horizon," he said, adding that the hills bordering the bay below were like the jaws of a tiger which make the location particularly auspicious. It was a classic application of the basic aim of *feng shui*. That is, setting at ease the mind of the mere mortal. That evening I shared the good tidings with Charlene.

Confronting *feng shui* head on with her free-style Presbyterian Positive Thinking, Charlene (who'd taken a particular liking to the carvings) concluded that our *feng shui* was indeed in control of things and the tablets would remain right where they were.

* * *

A classic example of the problems foreigners face in trying to get a straight answer involved a time in Taipei I was having trouble locating an address, because—as often happens in Asia—they didn't run in sequence. I stepped into a little shop to inquire. There were two people behind desks, writing, with their heads down. I asked if they knew that address. Neither looked up and both pointed at the same time . . . in opposite directions. It was one of those rare occasions when there was no question that I was dealing with folks who wanted to be polite, but who had not the foggiest notion what the correct information was.

A foreigner can go for years, or forever, unaware that they don't have the story quite straight. Dropping in on American friends in Singapore, the hostess served a spicy appetizer, saying that a Chinese acquaintance had given her the recipe and that it was called something like "sitwan."

"Sichuan?"

"Yes, that's it. You know what it means?"

I explained Sichuan is a province, and a cuisine. To say a food is "Sichuan" is almost as vague as calling it "Chinese." Her friend had given an answer which was true, while totally missing the point.

These sometimes variations in the way we describe things tend to muddle understanding. For example, if you asked someone in South Asia how large a family they would like to have, they might say they would prefer to have a small family. But the answer lies in finding out what they consider a "small family," which might well be five children. Foreigners frequently arrive at the wrong conclusion because they don't understand the context well enough to know that they have not arrived at the final answer.

When I arrived in Taiwan, a major university was completing a thirty-five-page wheat food consumption survey for my organization which involved 915 households. A key market development question related to the consumption of wheat among those people from all parts of China who had come to Taiwan in 1949 with Chiang Kai-shek. Since people from the south are traditionally rice eaters, we wanted to know—in their new surroundings—were they switching to wheat? I was confident the study would show that they would eat about the same amount of wheat as northerners if it were available, economical and of good quality.

I was shocked when the survey leader later told me that the study had established that people from the south *did* eat less wheat. If correct, that would have shattered a long-held conviction and require a re-think in our industry's Asian market development strategies. When the study reached my desk I checked the numbers. People who had come from North China consumed 75.71 grams of flour per day, compared to 72.91 grams for those from South China. That's about a teaspoon.

The numbers proved to me what I'd felt all along, that in Taipei, Chinese who had come from the north and the south, were eating about the same amount of wheat. In North China today, a person consumes 300 to 400 pounds of wheat annually compared to as little as ten pounds in some rural areas in South China. Those numbers represent a significant variation. But the difference cited in the study is just enough to thicken a bowl of lentil-frankfurter soup.

This is more than an example of the difference in the way that an academic statistician and someone in market development may view numbers. It involves a subtle difference in perspective which the foreigner often encounters in the Orient.

In other places, it often can be something of a frustration to discover that what you'd previously heard or understood was wrong. In Asia, it's often a clear sign of progress. Work at it. All the time.

Doubt what you hear and believe what you see

Just Like Learning Your ABC's

A New Look at Old Ideas

THE UNITED STATES isn't the only "Great Melting Pot." China has fifty-five ethnolinguistic groups which differ in language, physical features, customs, religion, and historical backgrounds. They include the dominant Han, and such diverse and scattered cultures as the Mongols and Miaos, and the Uygurs, Kazaks and Kirgiz of the Western frontier. Most foreigners have relatively little contact with these various varieties of Chinese and the general foreign view—if spoken—would come out something like, "That guy looks Chinese. Acts Chinese. Must *be* Chinese. They're inscrutable y'know."

If I defer to local custom some might say I am "acting Chinese" but that isn't what's involved at all. And doing so doesn't make me more Chinese or less American.

The world is full of people who look very much Chinese but aren't. And I don't mean ethnic Chinese who happen to be Thai, Malay or Filipino. In a sombrero and serape many Chinese could easily pass as Mexican. Brown-haired and red-headed Chinese are not uncommon along the Silk Road. In Macau some have a round-eyed Iberian look while in other regions you find Russian, Korean, Turkish, Persian, Pakistani and even (occasionally) Irish features.

On the other hand, some Chinese do indeed look alike. This stems from common gene pools which, in the early days, were fairly restricted to particular regions, valleys, deltas or even villages. Anyone who has spent much time in India or the Philippines, for example, can usually tell which region someone is from simply by their physical appearance. Early Chinese immigrants in the US came from only a handful of areas in South China, and Americans in those days did have some cause to think that Chinese did look very much alike.

That rusty old saw that "all Chinese look alike" can be said only by people who have seen relatively few of them or have been around twins a lot. It works both ways. Chinese have the same trouble when it comes to Occidentals. As recently as a decade or so ago in some of the less-traveled byways of the Orient, a routine-looking American male attracted stares, not so much because of the curiously large nose he followed about, but because people were trying to figure out which movie star he was. Having seen few real live foreigners, the strays who did wander into town seemed to the locals to look like the folks they'd seen in the movies.

All this illustrates a key aspect of the old dichotomy—whether it is the East looking West or the West looking East, cultural astigmatism can run high.

So the Chinese do some things a little differently and we don't look quite alike. So what? Rather than it being a question of how they look, or act, being Chinese boils down to how they feel about themselves, other people, and things. That's what makes them Chinese. And, that's what makes us what we are.

At dinner one evening in Xinhui (near Hong Kong) with seven local industry officials who were natives of that city, the subject got around to their close relatives outside China. How many in Hong Kong? Ninety-one. In the United States? Eight. In Canada? Eighteen. I was so shocked I failed to ask about relatives elsewhere. Xinhui claims to be the "hometown" of Overseas Chinese. The nearby community of Jiangmen, with a population of 216,097 claims 600,000 sons and daughters living outside China. In the Foshan district of the Pearl River Delta area in Guangdong Province, half the families have relatives overseas, which perhaps explains why half the Overseas Chinese investment in China goes into this province, and half of that into the Foshan region.

Overseas Chinese who have emigrated, or were born elsewhere, are known as *huaqiao*. The degree that a huaqiao becomes involved with foreign culture depends largely on the community and the degree of clannishness, or racial discrimination, involved. Chinese in the California Gold Rush hung together and flocked to any theater offering Cantonese entertainment. Today, their descendants in San Francisco are found in front of the TV, or at the disco or a football game; a reflection of Chinese adaptability.

In the official vernacular of Beijing, Chinese living in Taiwan are "compatriots," reflecting their different political and filial status. Younger, internationally-oriented Chinese refer to an American-born Chinese as an "ABC." A recent arrival in a new country is an "FOB"—fresh off the boat. FOB's, or Chinese who have lived for some time in almost self-contained pockets of Chinatown, are more likely to have maintained their traditional customs and way of looking at things. At the same time they become caught up in acquiescing culturally to the West. The offspring of such individuals, say, in San Francisco, likely will be about as American as the Fourth of July. Growing up among little big-nosed peers they are more likely to have a jack-o'-lantern at Halloween than to carry a paper lantern during Mid-Autumn Festival.

*   *   *

A Chinese lesson in Taipei afforded some insight into how traditional Chinese see themselves. We were practicing some free style conversation when the teacher said, "You're German, right?"

"The name is Swiss, but I'm American. My father's parents came from Switzerland."

"That makes you Swiss, then."

"No. My father and I were born in America. If you were to get married and go to America and had children there, they would be American."

She replied coolly, "If I have children in America they will be Chinese."

Then there was the young lady who phoned our Beijing office inquiring about a job. Her distinctly Chinese first name seemed oddly out of synch with her last name, which was as old-English as lavender. It had a nice ring, and I asked if she was Chinese. "I'm married to an Englishman. I used to be Chinese," she replied. I'd never heard it put like that before. "Aren't you still Chinese?" I asked. "Well, yes," she chuckled. "I'm still Chinese."

The Chinese have a deep-seated concept of roots stretching back through the ages. Historically they really didn't move around a great deal. Lives were lived out pretty much in sight of where they were born, often in the same house where the family had lived for generations, each year plowing alongside the graves of their ancestors. If you ask a Chinese in China or Hong Kong where they are "from" the answer invariably will refer to the ancestral home.

My assistant, Pansy Lam, was born in Macau, and brought to Hong Kong as an infant, where she has lived ever since. While it might be said she is from Hong Kong, or Macau, that's not how she sees it. She considers herself a native of Xiamen, a city on the coast of Fujian where her father was born and where the ancestors are. That's typical. But a third or fourth generation Chinese accountant in Seattle may tell you his family is from Boise.

Shortly after we moved to Taiwan, I announced on my return home one evening, "I've been invited for a dog lunch next week." My wife assured me I had gotten that wrong. That was good news, as I was looking for a graceful way out and admitting to the Chinese you're henpecked is a *carte-blanche* to get you out of virtually anything. My host countered with the suggestion we go to a place just outside town where we could have another suitable seasonal specialty. That meant something you won't find at McDonald's, but which surely—according to centuries-old tradition—would help keep us warm during the approaching winter. The specialty turned out to be snake wine which was ceremoniously placed in the middle of the table in a huge glass jar. Inquiring about the contents, I learned that what we had here was a rather large cobra and a bamboo viper. The snakes had marinated for a year, along with various herbs in two gallons of something-or-other that will pickle a snake. And it's expensive. I managed a time-out after the second toast, with the observation that costly vintage stuff should be savored slowly, preferably over a long period of time.

Someone asked, "You like turtle blood?" The host was talking to me. I was afraid of that. Asking how it was prepared gave everyone a chuckle because they don't "do" anything with it. It's direct, from the turtle to you, in a bowl. And it tastes rather like you might imagine. Later, into the meal, I was surprised to see that the fellow next to me had touched neither his snake wine nor his turtle blood. I whispered, "How come you didn't drink that?" He explained that some Chinese do drink snake wine and turtle blood, while others do not. Had I known that I could have been a non-snake-wine-and-non-turtle-blood-drinking American.

At a banquet we were hosting in Beijing, it was a shock to see a platter of cooked scorpions suddenly appear on the table. Each sneaky, snaky-eyed little creature, somehow deep-fried into a perfect strike position, was perched on a sort of potato chip. I turned to our secretary and asked how they had found their way onto our menu. She said she'd been told this was a sort of "mini-lobster." This in no way enhanced their attraction and I found myself seriously pondering what undigested snack the scorpion might possibly have snared just before its demise. A woolly worm perhaps. Surprised at the degree of our Chinese guests' ravings over this unusual delicacy, I whispered to the waiter to bring a second serving. When that platter appeared, our old friends, who had been so ecstatic over the first serving, blanched. "Oh!" "Ech!" "Not again!" "We *had* those already!" With the exception of three of the people who were from Shandong, where they really do like scorpion, the others had found them as challenging as I did and their display of delight when the little creepies first appeared was pure theater. That scorpions have been used for centuries for the treatment of arthritis, high blood pressure and heart disease has not spurred an inclination to order them again. Chinese say that mosquitoes won't bite you if you eat scorpion, which sounds reasonable to me.

On that note, a few summers ago my wife Charlene and I were enjoying a holiday on the Oregon coast, when a young Asian happened along. On the possibility he might be an exchange student or tourist, I greeted him in Putonghua, the national language of China, which foreigners usually refer to as Mandarin.

Startled, he said, "Oh! I'm not Japanese."

"That's Chinese," I replied, equally startled. "It means, 'Good morning.'"

"My folks are from Canton," he offered weakly. "Cantonese."

"*Jo-san*," I replied.

"What's that?"

"That's 'Good morning' in Cantonese."

"I don't speak that either," he shrugged as he continued up the beach with a smile and a wave. What might his ancestors have thought of that little exchange?

After all these years I'm still mortified by well-intentioned Westerners on hiring committees, chief executives and boards of directors who wax ecstatic over the hiring of a third-generation Chinese-American as their Beijing representative. They dismiss the possibility that the individual may not be particularly qualified aside from, well, looking Chinese. These hiring exercises should perhaps be carried out in Denver, where you need only walk through the airport to be reminded that all are not cowboys who wear the boots. Ever hear of a second or third-generation American of Belgian extraction being sought to head-up an office or to escort a delegation to Brussels?

A Chinese in the home office, tapped to tag along on a business trip to China, can be beneficial providing you've got the right one. A Cantonese or Taiwanese may not hit it off so well in Beijing. They may not hit it off at all. It depends. A zippy extroverted ABC who fits in well with the Cincinnati crowd probably isn't exactly what you need to handle things in the more reserved atmosphere of Beijing. Caution should be exercised to avoid the mistake of going into something like that willy-nilly. ("Joe's Chinese isn't he? Looks Chinese. Let's take him along.")

While the people in China will provide interpreters for a business mission which is of some consequence to them, it may help to have one of your own. Be sure the individual speaks Putonghua. (Or, Cantonese if you're working in the area near Hong Kong.) Look for someone who has spent considerable time in China. Don't consider someone particularly well qualified simply because they were born there (and left as infants) or because the *father* was born in China.

An example of where that kind of thinking can lead you is illustrated by my chance meeting with an American friend at the former Pan American lounge at Tokyo's Narita Airport. He was headed for Beijing with a trade delegation. It was their first foray into the Middle Kingdom. Introduced to the group, I circled their coffee table handing out my business card and, when I got to the Escort-Interpreter-Guru-Chinese-American they'd acquired for the trip I presented the card with two hands, in the traditional, courtly style. He took it with one hand which I took to mean he hadn't expected me to do that and I'd caught him off guard. He was still fumbling for his card when I sat down and, finding it, he flipped it across the table as you'd toss a peanut to a bear at the zoo. I have to admit the guy made an impression on me as I'd never seen that done before (or since) anywhere in the Far East.

Lumping the Chinese together without regard for their individuality reveals a disinclination to see, for example, how much ABC's differ from their native counterparts. It's exactly what old Mr. Wang has on his mind in Rogers and Hammerstein's *Flower Drum Song* when he lyrically laments in San Francisco, "I am puzzled by the attitude of children over here." Perhaps my most memorable encounter with this took place in Beijing. Entering the gate to the US Embassy annex, an excited ABC tourist approached me. He was easily identifiable by his uninhibited approach, hair style, accent, designer jeans and supporting embellishments. He blurted, "Scuse me! You American? Gotta problem. Lost my passport. Wow!" Thrusting a thumb toward the two impassive People's Liberation Army guards at the entrance he added, "These dudes won't lemme inna gate." He hadn't explained the problem to the guards because he couldn't speak Chinese. I told the guards what the problem was and arranged for someone to come out to escort this not-so-very-Chinese past the billowing Stars and Stripes and into the building. Back home in the United States, someone taking notice of this young man would simply have perceived him as "being Chinese."

Probably all foreigners, from childhood, have had their perceptions of China somewhat fuzzed by a variety of seemingly innocent and innocuous forces. Back in the heyday of American radio a mystery series featured the crime-fighter, Lamont Cranston. Known to the enemies of law and order as "The Shadow," Cranston had the power to make himself invisible. How did he do that? As the announcer explained each week, Cranston used a strange and mysterious hypnotic secret he'd picked up years ago, "in the Orient." Well, of course. Where but in the Mystic East would you expect to learn a strange and mysterious hypnotic technique to make yourself invisible? Liverpool? Not likely. That's definitely something you might pick up in China.

The fictional detective Charlie Chan, in the popular American film series in the 1930s and 1940s was simply a caricature of how movie-goers thought a Chinese detective should act. That the role was played by a Westerner and that Charlie's proverbs made him sound like a walking fortune cookie didn't diminish the "celluloid reality."

As for the Chinese, they love to learn American tribal customs relating to what we do—or don't do—at a cocktail party or barbecue. They manage somehow to suppress their giggles when we tell them how the Easter Bunny lays colored eggs and hides them in the grass or how Santa lands on the roof in a reindeer-drawn sleigh and slips down the chimney. It's the ultimate in one-upmanship over their Chinese associates if they can say, "hold the anchovies" when ordering pizza with Americans.

But have you noticed that as Chinese begin to pick up on these things we are quick to label that as *Westernization*? If Americans choose to go to a Chinese restaurant, no one suggests they're becoming *Easternized*. (If anything, Westerners who pick up a few Asian preferences or inclinations are likely to see themselves as becoming more *Cosmopolitan*.) But "Westernization" is something we read and hear constantly in reference to modern Asians. How can we not apply the standard in both directions? (Is it perhaps because people—in looking at the other guy—are disinclined to take that broader perspective?) If it doesn't apply both ways, it's chauvinism.

Chinese in Asia are less inclined to want to be like someone else than anyone. To them, being Chinese is the best thing that could have happened to anybody. A basic problem for the country's modernization program has been trying to resolve the sticky question of how they can move ahead and still remain culturally

Chinese. But, they need only look to Hong Kong, Singapore and San Francisco to see what a remarkably good blend that can be.

Shortly after the opening of the country's first new international hotel in Beijing in April of 1982, a small standing sign was installed near the entrance to direct traffic to the right as it came out of the driveway. The written instruction to drivers, in both Chinese and English, was "Turn to the West." The innuendo was not lost on visiting Westerners, and it became standard practice for hotel guests to pose rather gleefully alongside the sign for a snapshot. After a few weeks, the patience of at least one Chinese ran out. The signboard was broken off and carted away. All that remained for some time was the upright post, a mute reminder that humor is in the eye of the beholder. The signboard was never replaced.

That brings us to another major misunderstanding. It's said you shouldn't joke with Chinese. But Chinese enjoy a good laugh as much as anyone else. What we are dealing with here is simply the basic rule of humor: you can joke about just about anything providing you know your audience. While a favorite comedy form in China is "cross talk" in which two glib comics regale the audience with rapid-fire innovative mispronunciations of words, you should never tell jokes that depend on innuendo, slang, or word play,

because they don't translate. Similarly, Chinese enjoy earthy humor, but under no circumstances should an off-color joke be attempted—because it won't be recognized as a joke. If you casually ad lib about something, in good taste, which you find amusing, they'll probably get a good giggle out of it. One of the safest devices, anywhere, is joking about yourself. The Chinese language affords us a particularly fertile field to amuse with the unexpected wrenching of a familiar phrase. For example, the Cantonese New Year's greeting is *kung hei fat choy* which translates literally as, "I hope you get a lot of money." At one office New Year's lunch I offered the toast *kung hei baak choi* (I wish you cabbage). The staff was so taken with its silliness that I continued to use the fractured phrase through the long New Year holiday. Surprised Chinese strangers got a giggle out of it because the blatant mutilation made it clear that I knew that Westerners are generally seen as a source of amusement in our attempts to speak Cantonese. Waiters rarely stifle a grin if, on asking you how many people are in your party, instead of replying in Chinese with, "two people" you say, "two big noses." That's the expression which *they* use.

The phrase "*kai wan xiao*" is always used by interpreters when translating a humorous remark. The literal meaning is "open play laugh." A device long used by astute interpreters when called on by a visiting company official to translate "a joke" is—after the "joke" has been told—the interpreter explains in Chinese, "Our esteemed visitor has just told a rather amusing story which really doesn't sound funny at all when you translate it but if you all just give a polite little laugh we'll get on with dinner." (On cue, everyone gives a polite little laugh and they get on with dinner.)

When it comes to whimsy, it helps if your audience knows you. Crossing the Yellow River in a remote reach of Qinghai Province, I was struck by the river's gunky brown consistency: rather like a cup of strong coffee with a tad too much cream.

"This river must be only about seventy-five percent moisture," I suggested. Our escort apparently took that as a scientific observation, and with local pride, insisted: "Oh, no. The moisture content of the Yellow River is much higher than seventy-five percent."

"*Kai wan xiao,*" I said with a smile and gentle nudge. That conditioned stimulus wrung a practiced, but not perfected chuckle out of him. I decided not to say anything about a "dry humor" because that wouldn't translate at all.

Another important point foreigners seem to miss . . . if a Chinese laborer, ankle deep in cold mud, sees a group of foreign tourists, his thoughts don't tilt toward, "I wish I could be like them." If he gives them any particular notice it more likely will be along the lines of, "Nice cameras. Great boots. Strange looking women. I'm glad I'm me and not one of those poor guys." While they might fancy your camera, they don't envy your non-Chineseness.

The multi-millennial romp through history has afforded the Chinese much time to dwell on how we all fit into the scheme of things. They seem to have arrived at the cozy conclusion, "It's a pity you can't be Chinese too." They don't seem particularly stuffy about this. It's more as if they just inwardly feel terribly good about it—like wearing long underwear on a cold day—*you* know what it is that's giving you that warm feeling.

In China, individuals would be disinclined to become Western-ized at the expense of losing their Chineseness. It isn't the thing to do.

Are Chinese women who have cosmetic surgery, to make their eyes more round, an exception? Not so, says Dr. William Shaw, a prominent Chinese plastic surgeon. Born in China and a professor of plastic surgery at the University of New York, he says, "To say Chinese have cosmetic surgery so they look more Western is not quite correct. You cannot take an Asian face and make it look Western. The double eyelid operation makes the eyes more attrac-tive, makes them look bigger and more alert."

The interest of Chinese in acquiring things from the West which provide more comfort or convenience simply reflects the basic human inclination to have things more comfortable and con-venient. Pearl S. Buck's *The Good Earth* and John Steinbeck's *The Grapes of Wrath* both tell of people struggling to improve their lives in a harsh environment. It's a universal theme. The Joad family didn't head out of the Oklahoma Dust Bowl for California because they wanted to be more Western.

Prior to the US military drawdown in Taiwan in the mid-1970s (so quietly effected that hardly anyone took notice) we had in our neighborhood a number of US service families and at Halloween quite a few costumed trick-or-treaters came to our door. A smat-tering of dolled-up Taiwanese youngsters also came by. They didn't do it to be Western. They were in it for the candy.

Part of our problem in getting this Westernization thing straight seems to be our basic Western Ethic which compels us to want to help others to be more like us, in the conviction this is, after all, what they really want. Or, at least what they *should* want if they know what's good for them. And if not that, it's what we know is best for them. If nothing else, it would sure make things easier for us if they would only do things *our* way. All this suggests fairly heavy condescension on our part. It's certainly an impediment to better understanding.

* * *

In introducing pizzas, hamburgers and the like to Asia, the US wheat industry would have had a problem if the approach had been, "*eat* like *us*." We said, "What do you think of this?" They said, "We *like* that" because it affords a more varied, versatile, convenient and nutritious diet, which is generally more economical and it beats eating 300 pounds of rice a year. (Also, it tastes good.) The idea has become so popular, Asian youngsters visiting the States today are surprised to find that America has McDonald's too.

East-West vistas were broadened when Beijing Journalist Liu Zongren turned the tables on the Gosh-I-Visited-China school of American writers and came out with *Two Years in the Melting Pot.* His book is an engaging account of his experiences in the United States. One of his comments caused me to look him up one weekend in Beijing and invite him to lunch. Heavily into an exchange of our theories and experiences, as dessert arrived I said, "I'm writing about this thing foreigners call 'Westernization,' taking the position that someone's acquiring a refrigerator has nothing to do with their being less Chinese."

"Exactly."

"Well, you wrote about being invited to a little party in the Chicago area and the feeling of being at ease with the group, summing it up with the statement, 'I was becoming Westernized.'"
He grinned and kept chewing.

"I think that was just an easy way of saying you had become more comfortable with foreigners in that kind of social situation." I took a big bite and smiled.

"Of course," he replied. "America made me feel all the more Chinese. Doesn't foreign travel give you a keener sense of being an American?"

Good point. Having spent close to half my adult life outside the United States I get weepy when the Stars and Stripes flutters up a pole and *The Star Spangled Banner* is played, and choke up a little just *thinking* about it. (Can untraveled Americans fully appreciate what it means to live in a country like the United States where you can say what you think . . . without thinking?)

My chat on this subject with Liu (and many other Chinese) suggests that Westerners should forget the idea the Chinese want to be more like us. Consider this encumbrance we call the Western business suit. This type of suit is growing in popularity in China, though it's not as practical as what people wore before.

I spoke with Dr. Marjory Joseph, former editor of the *Clothing and Textiles Research Journal* who was involved in studies specifically related to what they call "apparel psychology." She agreed, "The business suit is a type of uniform and a means by which people of all racial backgrounds and sexes seek to fit into a 'business' pattern that is international in scope."

Regardless of what it's called, faded photographs from a century ago show government and business leaders from the far reaches of the world wearing this type of suit. No less an authority than *National Geographic* calls it "the uniform of the working world."

Turn this Westernization around and view it from an Eastern context. Take the britches worn by the king of Siam in *The King and I*. These are quite similar to the knickers I wore on my way to the Charlie Chan movies. My American bathrobe, which carries a "Made in Turkey" label, has a distinctly Japanese *Yukata* cut about it, as robes often do. Our oversize, casual winter wear is styled along lines similar to the uniforms of the 2,000-year-old terracotta soldiers at Xian, which brings to mind the two American matrons I overheard in the Forbidden City. Nodding toward a display containing the Marco Poloesque uniform of an early Ching dynasty officer, one of them remarked, "That uniform shows a distinct Western influence."

Such lopsided inferences are made by the Westerner who orders Chinese noodles in a Hong Kong hotel and, noting how many Chinese are eating spaghetti, somehow infers the Asians are becoming Westernized.

I had occasion to reflect upon this as Charlene and I holidayed on an azure-splashed crescent of bone-white beach on Bali. As we relaxed in the shade of a fragrant blossoming tree, a barefoot local couple came slowly toward us, laden with baskets of native handicrafts. As they eased into casual negotiations with us over bits of shell jewelry and wood carvings I nodded at the man's watch and asked the time. "Watch not work," he said, as if he found particular pleasure in that fact. I glanced at the girl's watch. She shrugged and grinned. Her watch didn't work either. At that, the man pointed at the sun and said with conviction, "11:30." Dropping his aim slightly toward a large sea bird in flight he said, "one o'clock." Another, almost horizontal adjustment of his aim and it was, "five o'clock."

"Thanks," I said. "I think I've got it," making a mental note to order a light snack at about half-past the sea bird. Motioning toward his attractive partner I asked, "Wife?"

"Yes," he replied. "She twenty-four years old. Maybe twenty-one. Something like that."

These Balinese were obviously onto something pretty good and we had a great week on that wondrous beach. But it's hard to imagine ourselves, or that couple, comfortably trading places and cultures. Chinese see things that way too. A bit more intensely perhaps. Trying to see the Chinese more on their own terms, rather than through the historic haze of "inscrutability" will help identify our common ground. If we don't understand how they feel about themselves, how will we ever begin to understand how they feel about the world . . . and us?

To know people you must listen to them

Keeping Your Face in Place

The Ancient Art of Getting Along

O NE OF THE LEAST UNDERSTOOD and most elusive of all Chinese concepts is "face." Explanations usually oversimplify the way it works, suggesting it basically involves someone becoming embarrassed about something. Any foreigner who has no better understanding than this will not only *lose* face, but contacts and contracts as well.

You may note in approaching a door with a Chinese host, he always gestures for you to precede him. The foreign guest invariably smiles, nods and plods through. That's the old international guest/ host tango but it's not the way it's best done in China. There the guest should resist and gesture for the host to go first. After further exchanges of mild protestations, the host gestures a third time, when the guest should proceed with some show of reluctance. A good technique is to invite the host along with you as you finally proceed through the door. When you're hosting, to go through a door before your principal guests is poor form except when something like a factory tour is involved. In that case always say that you'll "show the way."

Punctuality is one of the many forms which face takes. Always be on time and if hosting lunch or dinner, get to the restaurant ahead of your guests.

What you wear is a function of face also. If you dress less formally in calling at an office than you do when your boss is in town with you, Chinese may read something into it.

Escorting a departing visitor all the way to the elevator is a standard way of giving face. On occasion a visitor may be seen all the way to the front door of the building when particularly high esteem is involved.

The number of tables at a dinner, the seating arrangement, the menu, and at which table a person is seated all relate to face.

In selecting food for an upcoming function at Chengdu's Jin Jiang Hotel, the food manager suggested sea slugs. Banquets invariably feature these bland, gummy, gourmet blobs, which Chinese males look upon as a marine form of ginseng, with the same reputed tonic effect. Personally, I suspect they are about as nutritionally beneficial as swallowing your pride. Even when called "sea cucumbers" Western guests remain squeamish. I'm not, but if shipwrecked on an island sea slugs are absolutely the last thing I would resort to eating. But I included them in the menu knowing that the guests would appreciate it. Even an ungainly, primordial sea slug—which is actually a worm—can give face.

The ancient concept of face surfaces in the most unlikely forms. While shopping around Hong Kong's fast and flashy Wanchai district for a pet bird, a perky little black and white warbler in a cluttered back lane caught my eye. But the shopkeeper could not be talked down to a reasonable price. A passerby paused to watch the negotiations, and sizing up the situation explained, "That is such a fine bird he wants to keep it. It gives face to his modest little shop."

If a craftsman repairs something for you, such as a shoe or a chair, give the thing a little close study before paying the bill and show your approval rather than treating his skill casually. He'll appreciate your appreciation. That's face too.

Hands have a lot to do with face also. Anything offered to you with two hands should always be taken with two hands. When handing anything of some consequence to a Chinese it's a nice touch to use both hands. This applies to business cards, gifts, brochures, or whatever. It elevates the presentation out of the ordinary. Holding a glass with two hands during a banquet toast is more polite than using one. If your host pours you a drink from a container held with two hands, hold your cup or glass with two hands as it is poured. If you smoke and someone extends a pack of cigarettes held in this manner, take a cigarette with both hands. Presenting a contract with two hands gives it a little flair. (When drawing up a contract, the line for your signature should appear respectfully below the names of the Chinese.)

If someone extends only one hand in taking something you offer with two, that means they've been caught off guard by your doing something they didn't expect or they're perhaps deferring to the international one-handed style. Or you've encountered someone disdainful of the old courtly style. Regardless, the two-handed technique is recommended because it's hard to make a bad impression when you're trying to be nice.

Applying the principle on a broader scale, in the People's Republic of China, if you are introduced to a large audience or enter a crowded conference hall and the group applauds you, it is polite to discreetly and slowly clap for a moment or two with them to return the courtesy. It's part face. Part egalitarianism.

Always work at being aware of when you're given face or when you have an opportunity to give it. In general, the application of face grows with the degree of formality involved in a situation. A pleasant "hello" when you pass the hotel floor attendant may seem to you a routine courtesy but by simply acknowledging someone's presence you are giving face. On entering a meeting room where there are a few dozen people, don't greet only those nearest you. Make an effort to establish eye contact and exchange a nod with everyone in the room. You may later learn the inconspicuous person in the corner is actually in charge of the whole shebang. When visiting a factory, nod and smile at the equipment operators. They appreciate knowing you know they're there. On departing, acknowledge everyone with a handshake, a smile, a nod or (at least) a wave.

Face is equally important in dealing with Overseas Chinese. Politeness and consideration help develop a good relationship with just about anybody, whether or not they even know what face is.

Until you've gotten the hang of its finer facets, there's little chance of your being aware when you have lost or been given face. Giving face is not something you deal with now and again. It floats about all day, every day, transcending the foreigner's usual cursory concept of what it is.

Friendly high-ranking businesspeople or diplomats on an initial or rare visit to China are largely immune from the consequences of any serious breach of this protocol. With such visitors the hosts will be more concerned with substance and results than with the foreigner's understanding of the nuances of their culture. But, of course, the high-ranking visitor who *does* know how to deal with this will be particularly well regarded.

In the early euphoria of the New China Trade, although it was cumbersome, awkward and unwise, Western corporate chief executives rather relished the idea of personally leading the company's initial foray into China, something like a caped cavalry officer thundering ahead of the dragoons. It's best for the foreign official not to appear until the work is done and understandings worked out, at least reasonably well, to lessen the risk of someone losing face.

Richard Nixon made some mistakes, but going into China before things had been made ready for him was not one of them. While he had not spent a great deal of time around the Chinese, he understood the importance of drawing counsel and support from those who had. As the Chinese say, "If you wish to know the road, ask those who've traveled it."

Business people should think thrice before deciding to take along a spouse on an initial trip to China if business is, in fact, the purpose. Unless the spouse is a business associate or has some substantive reason for going, the Chinese will infer that the trip is really a holiday. A businessman traveling without his spouse will be urged by his hosts, "You must bring your wife next time." They're just being polite. (They have been using that pleasantry less since they learned the foreigner takes it seriously. It's then necessary to provide the spouse daily with an interpreter, transport, problem-solving, sightseeing, meals, shopping and entertainment … an all-expenses-paid vacation.) Such invitations do accumulate, and after the same individual has extended the invitation a half dozen times over a number of visits, and your face is established, do take the spouse along to meet your friends.

Overwhelmed by the pleasantries and platitudes of the brief initial sojourn, foreign VIP's have trouble later in understanding how staff in Beijing could be having problems with things which the boss settled so genially over a cup of tea with those great folks back in Beijing. We don't hear many of these stories since the word started getting around. Chinese can be gracious hosts but they also can be very tough negotiators. Transient executives have begun to learn that the folks they drink tea with are rarely the same ones with whom the local representative grinds out the details. Second or third echelon staff people may not like their boss, their job, the project, foreigners or whatever, and this gums up the local representative's best efforts. This perversity isn't limited to Chinese, but they have fine-tuned it. A number have confided, "If I can't succeed at it, I don't want the other guy to succeed either."

Long-time friend, Sinologist, and hands-on China Hand Dennis Leventhal has a good grip on the concept. He says, "Face is defined by a person's social connections. You're not an 'individual' in the Western sense of being defined by your personality and character, but rather you're a locus within a social context. You're X's parent, Y's spouse, Z's friend, and Q's employee. Thus, you lose face by violating the propriety of a relationship. That is, you are defined out of social existence." At least, for a time; directly proportional to the magnitude of the indiscretion. One can lose face for an hour. Or forever.

Family relationships are an overriding consideration in the scheme of social existence. A Wong from Chicago on meeting a Wong from Shanghai will feel a family bond on the premise that perhaps 1,000 years ago their ancestors tilled the same field.

In social relationships, the face factor is evident in the Chinese language which, in the written form at least, dates from about 2,000 BC. Where English has just over thirty words to express basic family relationships, Chinese has about 120. The status of a cousin is expressed in sixteen different ways, from "eldest son of one's father's brother" to "elder daughter of one's mother's brother." A reference to a brother or sister in Chinese always expresses the ranking of the relationship. Brother-in-law is expressed ten different ways and nephew and niece in six different ways, depending upon the individual's position in the family. It's common throughout China today to use, before someone's name, the word *lao* (old or experienced) or *xiao* (small). A Mr. Ma, the senior member of the bureau, will be addressed as "Lao Ma" while the younger Mr. Li will be addressed as "Xiao Li."

Since the 1949 revolution there's been a shift in traditional ideas of family and face. "A teak door does not face a bamboo door" hardly promotes an egalitarian society. Today, a high-level official will wait patiently to use a phone in a restaurant while a waiter chats with a friend. However, in that vast realm where face relates to being courteous, considerate, and reciprocal, it surely enjoys as much following as it did in the old days. It remains paramount in the role of the considerate host and the responsive guest.

Things become a bit more complex when you get into the area of constructive criticism; what the Chinese call, "medicine for the ears." In China it is difficult to offer a critique without sounding . . . well, critical. The trick is to say what you have to say in a manner which does not cause the other person to think they've been doing something wrong. Put the emphasis on the fact you simply want it done differently.

An extreme example of this problem, reported in the *China Daily*, involved a farmer working on a tree-planting project who, when asked to replant a seedling, considered it nitpicking and hit the supervisor with a shovel.

*   *   *

It seems that hardly anyone in China knows how to drive, apart from full-time assigned drivers. Private cars are a rarity and drivers—tooling around in a shiny air conditioned car—hold one of the country's most coveted positions. Every bureau has drivers and when you go someplace they drive you. Drivers usually seem quite surprised when you tell them that you, too, know how to drive. (I refrain from telling them I've driven for nearly fifty years as that would be intimidating.) Drivers are usually young and spirited. That's worrisome. That there are so many bold, but so few old, drivers has clearly ominous implications. (It probably would be a good idea to check drivers' palms to see if they've got a long life-line before riding with them.) The problem is that good driving is equated with fast driving; something apparently inferred from the fact beginners drive slowly. When scheduled to travel around the country by car I always ask with a smile, "Is it possible for us to have a beginning driver, preferably one who took his drivers' test this morning?" A "good" driver typically rockets down back roads at eighty miles per hour in small (often moderately maintained) vans, and while we've never been clocked, we've surely set several adrenalin-charged land-speed records across China. Drivers are always pleased when they hear how little time elapsed during the trip, although foreign passengers may be in a state of shock with shreds of car upholstery under their fingernails.

It can be established within a matter of seconds whether the day's driver is going to be a problem ... in driving from the hotel courtyard to the street, if he honks the horn more than ten times, don't count on him to overwork either the brake or his brain. I once monitored this over a span of ten minutes in which our driver honked eighty-two times, and (at sixty to seventy miles per hour) shifted into neutral and coasted fifty-six times. Counseling a driver on how to operate a car safely on the highway is difficult and Chinese never presume to bring up the subject. (As they see it, how can you tell a *driver* how to drive?)

I got out the "ear medicine" on a stretch of new highway when our very young driver chose to pass a five-ton truck loaded with wet gravel just as another huge truck was coming from the other direction. All three vehicles in that steel and meat sandwich were hurtling along at full throttle. Only a breath of air separated our fragile little van and those two menacing, monstrous machines. Not knowing a lot about physics I have to presume that the annihilation implications of the collision of three vehicles going that fast in opposite directions must be roughly equivalent to an elephant sitting on an ant and twisting about. I had a brief vision of friends passing that spot in later years and saying, "This is where Fred met his fate. Right here. And over there . . . and in that rice paddy up the road. And part way up that hill." It had been a dangerous and stupid maneuver, though perhaps not all that uncommon anywhere you put inexperienced aimers of automobiles on new highways.

The officials who were with me—typically—didn't know how to drive and seemed unaware of what had occurred. Such life-and-death decisions are routinely left to the driver. However, whenever it comes to a choice between saving the driver's face or saving my neck, my neck takes precedence.

Applying "ear medicine" is a delicate operation as the critic can lose face along with the one being critiqued. In a situation like this, cloak the criticism in a compliment.

"I've noticed you are a good driver," I fibbed. "But you know, back there between those two trucks . . . you can't tell about other drivers . . . maybe crazy. Maybe their tires blow out. Maybe they want to commit suicide on your hood ornament. Be careful around them. OK?"

Newcomers or visitors who are learning face on the job need not be particularly apprehensive. None of us gets it right all the time. But *trying* to get it right all the time is what it's all about. The Chinese can tell when you're making the effort.

If you sense that things are beginning to go less smoothly than before and the reason isn't apparent, it's possible you've erred in this sensitive area of face. At the first opportunity engage one or more of the principals in casual conversation. If the responses are proper, brief and clearly detached you've probably stepped in something.

Play over in your mind recent events and remarks. If you can deduce what little thing might have been done or missed or misunderstood, set out patiently and graciously to try to smooth the situation, preferably without referring to it specifically. If it stems from an imagined slight or criticism this usually can be put to rest by applying little demonstrations of regard. Maybe you've been coming on a bit too strong or fast, or missed the significance of a key point that was brought up. Or perhaps the interpreter has inadvertently set things on edge by using an inappropriate synonym.

Wrapping up arrangements on a million-dollar project in Beijing, Chinese counterparts expressed concern over delays in our acquisition of equipment. This was years ago so it was necessary to explain how Western business competition works, before going on to say we were dealing with competing suppliers to get the most for the lowest possible price. The interpreter used the phrase, "cheap equipment," which was a bad choice of words. Apologizing to the interpreter (to give him face) I explained "what I had meant to say" was that we wanted to get the best possible price so we could get more equipment for our money. Face for them. Face for us.

Boiled down to its basics the concept of face probably exists in one form or another in all the world's cultures. Pierre Boulle's *Bridge on the River Kwai* is not so much a story of prisoners of war building a bridge as it is a story of an epic confrontation between Japanese and British face.

In its Chinese application, face is more intense than what we have in the West. With its chameleon characteristic, face can seem a formidable challenge to the foreigner. But it needn't be if you relax, use common sense and keep in mind that the other person's feelings are important.

A textbook example involved a group from Shanghai visiting the US. Invited to dinner by an international company which was keenly interested in the multi-million-dollar sales opportunities the visitors represented, we were driven in a gleaming stretch limousine to an opulent hotel with one of the firm's young executives. Top company officers flew in from headquarters. The cuisine and libations were memorable. All the right things were said. Farewells at the table after dinner were the ultimate in cordiality. We were escorted back to the limousine by the young executive and waved warmly on our way. The window dressing was all in place but the Americans didn't understand face enough to realize that by failing to make the final polite gesture of walking the guests to the front door they missed the opportunity to demonstrate that this was something more than just another business dinner they were obliged to attend. Gestures of goodwill lose their punch when delegated. The personal touch of walking someone to the door is what face is about.

My most remarkable encounter with face occurred at a funeral south of Taipei. It took place in a small community with the Buddhist services held in the town's little movie house. The walls inside the old wooden building were hung from ceiling to floor with condolences in bold black characters on long white paper banners. The only foreigner among some 350 mourners, I was seated with friends and my assistant, Mr. Lu, smack in the middle of the theater. Toward the end of the service a small fire broke out on stage amidst the array of candles, traditional offerings and paper banners, and began to spread impressively in little rivulets of flame.

Theater fires are fraught with hazard and their capacity to panic a docile audience into a screaming stampede is noteworthy. People kamikaze out of balconies onto a surging, stumbling crowd, trampling others underfoot and piling up in blocked exits. That could be difficult to ride out.

The immediate order of business was to tally survival options. It might be possible to stand our ground until the crowd thinned and then, if we could get through the flames on stage, we might perhaps get out through the stage door. But there probably wouldn't be a stage door and if we could find one it surely would be chained and padlocked. Scratch that. It might be better to hold our ground, drop to the floor behind the crowd and try to crawl out beneath the smoke. Those were the options. Wait. There was one more.

"Mr. Lu," I said. "This place is on fire."

"Yes," he replied casually.

"This could get serious."

"Yes," he agreed.

"How about we go to the bathroom? Do you have to go to the bathroom?"

Mr. Lu said he didn't have to go.

With the outlook dimming in the thickening smoke, my resolve to depart at the instant anyone else rose was thwarted by the fact that no one was stirring. The Chinese were just sitting there without a murmur or change of expression! Of course. It would have been a monumental loss of face to be the first to stand up with all those Chinese sitting stoically without a word or a twitch. They were simply unwilling to let a theater fire, at that point anyway, diminish their decorum. Fortunately, attendants brought the fire under control.

Not only was this terrible tableau a monumental display of the discipline of face, it also demonstrated the Chinese commitment to the axiom, "An emergency should be taken leisurely."

Chinese rarely lose their cool. You seldom see them display anger because face is lost in direct proportion to the degree of anger exhibited. Losing one's temper is not the thing to do. However, if a cab driver has an emotional outburst in the middle of the street or a civil servant is silently but clearly fuming behind a counter it's a safe bet that face is involved. Heated histrionics involving shouting and arm waving usually don't really involve anger. These manifestations of firm resolve are a ritualistic device designed to attach blame, fracturing the other party's pride, while hopefully swaying the opinion of the onlooking jury.

Along with the knack for appearing angry when they really aren't is the ability of Chinese to be civil—if not actually pleasant—when they are angry or highly offended. A foreigner in this kind of situation might see nothing amiss. But with some sensitivity to face you can tell when things are beginning to get out of balance.

Slow to take offense if you use common sense and discretion, the Chinese have the most amazing memory for things people do which please them and they respond readily to courtesies or favors.

If you receive a peach, give a plum in return

Everyone Hums "Chinatown"

Strolling Through the Beaded Curtain

ONE OF THE MORE IMPORTANT Chinese characteristics is "single-ness of purpose," a mental set where things tangent to a given situation are simply disregarded. This tenacity prompted their forebears to decide to build a wall clear across the top of their country, to move a mountain or to dig a canal 1,100 miles long; and then to go out and actually do it.

A classic illustration of singleness of purpose involved Tom Gorman, a Hong Kong-based business consultant, who was escorting a group of Chinese visitors through the US. Coming from one of the more remote provinces, the Chinese had never been far from home before. Swinging into eastern Canada, the visitors asked to stop to cash a bank draft. Tom located a bank and before he had the car locked and the meter fed, the visitors dashed in ahead of him. Moments later, as Tom entered he suddenly remembered that it was Halloween. He was reminded because one of the bank officers was wearing a brilliant orange fright wig that looked like an explosion in a spaghetti factory. Another employee sported a bulbous red rubber ball where his nose should be. The next employee wore a silver lamé space suit. This bank was really into building a folksy image. When Tom caught up to his Chinese visitors they were talking ever-so-casually with the Wicked Witch of the West, complete with a green chewing gum wart on her nose.

"This draft is drawn in favor of whom?" WWW inquired.

"That's me. Chen."

"This draft is made out to Mr. Fu."

"Chinese names backward. I'm Mr. Chen," he said with assurance.

"Do you have some ID, Mr. Chen?" (Despite the Shredded Wheat coiffure and the green gum, this was one efficient witch.)

"Chinese passport OK?"

That's how it went, with Mr. Chen casually negotiating a bank transaction with someone who looked like she'd fallen off a broomstick. It was quiet in the car as Tom drove them out of town. Tom didn't say anything. The visitors didn't say anything. Tom couldn't stand it.

"Ah . . . did you notice anything . . . unusual back there?"

"Back where?"

"Well, in the *bank*," Tom suggested.

The long silence was eventually punctuated with a chorus of wide-eyed histrionic "noes," the sort a youngster uses when asked if he knows where all the cookies went. Tom explained Halloween, the costumes, acting silly and bank public relations. The visitors said they found Tom's explanations very interesting and were sorry that they had missed it. It's true Chinese really don't always take note of things or dwell on them as we might. In this case, while Tom was engrossed in the costumes, the visitors were knee-deep in the much more important business of cashing the bank draft. (Wanting to be good guests, Chinese are disinclined to comment on matters involving deviant behavior in your culture.) While Tom was mulling it over in the car on their way out of town, the visitors were very likely more concerned with when they'd stop for lunch. That's one way singleness of purpose works.

This coalescence of concentration takes root at a very early age. A toddler, playing alongside a busy street is typically watched over by a youngster who seems hardly a year or so older. From the attentiveness it's clear the concepts of responsibility to family, discipline and singleness of purpose have already taken root. In China with mama and papa probably both tending the field or the shop, it's the practical way to handle it. Similar examples will be seen many times a day during a trip through the countryside. The water buffalo—upon which the fortunes of the farm largely depend—is often left in the care of a pre-schooler who may be barely knee-high to the animal. These youngsters seem entirely engrossed and totally in command. Itinerant butterflies, tadpole pools or approaching playmates seem hardly noticed.

China's invention of gunpowder provides another example. Apparently satisfied that the principal application of this volatile stuff was for festive fireworks and exorcising demons, it was left largely to others to pursue and perfect more barbaric uses for this Chinese creation. Though the Chinese were first to use it in warfare, in incendiary arrows, small mechanically-projected grenades, and to frighten the enemy with noise and smoke, they barely dabbled in its real potential. By the 17th Century, Macau, the minuscule Portuguese colony on China's South Coast, was the leading pro-ducer of cannon in the Far East. This was 1,000 years after the Chinese began manufacturing gunpowder for fireworks and 500 years after gunpowder became known in Europe.

To maximize their food resources over the millennia, the Chinese have pursued the purpose of contriving more ways to prepare more kinds of food than anyone else in the world. They've even done it with turnips. As the host suggested over the braised something and the lizard soup at a rural banquet, "We'll eat anything with four legs, even a table properly cooked."

It's not essential for foreigners to be preoccupied with this concept. Just be aware of it so you recognize it when you encounter it. A difficult negotiator or a truculent ticket agent might well be pushed over the threshold of acquiescence if you can identify what single little hook they're hung up on. When you find yourself getting nowhere after suggesting a number of possible solutions, remember . . . one of the most important questions you can ask in this part of the world very often is: "Well, then, how would *you* resolve it if you were me?" It's amazing how often that simple little device works.

*   *   *

Understanding other traits generally acknowledged as "typically Chinese" affords insights. For example, the word "pragmatic" has been liberally applied to the Chinese. You can read it into almost everything they do. During a stop in Honolulu I dropped into a little shop with my old friend Harry Wong, the "Noodle King" of Hong Kong. Spotting some brightly colored plastic sand castle molds which I felt would be a hit with the grandchildren, I picked up a few and headed for the cash register. Harry took them at first to be flower pots, a reasonable inference considering that's what they looked like. And that would be a more practical use for them, rather than the trivial pursuit of building sand castles!

It's easy to sometimes misread this practicality as being something else. That is, something may not appear practical to the foreigner . . . but it makes sense from the Chinese perspective. Examples are legion, if sometimes obtuse. One occurs several times a day at the railway border-crossing between Shenzhen and Hong Kong. There are usually only a few foreigners among the hundreds of Chinese who erupt from the trains. On alighting, the Chinese are waved past the quarantine station while foreigners are required to present their health forms and answer questions relating to their possible contamination. The system makes sense because the arriving Chinese likely aren't stricken with anything which China hasn't already seen a lot of. *More* practically, it would create a massive bottleneck and long delays if they were to run everyone through the process.

Consider the cleaver. If you find one in a Western kitchen, chances are it is used only for chopping. But the Chinese also use this versatile implement to slice, peel, dice, shred, mince, and julienne. The back of the blade can be used to tenderize meat. The blade also serves as a scraper to clean a cutting board. The flat of the blade is used to crush garlic and to lift and carry chopped food while the handle is used as a pestle. In a Chinese kitchen the cleaver is a multi-purpose food processor. (In a Jiangsu bakery, I saw a particularly innovative model with a bottle opener cast in the back of the blade, an ideal accessory for a barbecue recipe I picked up on Guam which reads, "First, drink one bottle of beer.")

*   *   *

"Ethnocentric" also lies near the top of the foreigner's China Bag of Buzzwords. While Chinese do seem inordinately proud of who they are, having pride in your country and culture is a fairly common human trait. But Chinese *are* unique and they're aware of that. Who else could have put their mind to it and come up with more than 100 uses for bamboo? For starters, bamboo chopsticks are used to eat the tree's succulent shoots and they drink bamboo liqueur from bamboo cups. These are the folks who came up with a system for lifting one kernel of rice with two little sticks or for carrying two baskets of rice with one big stick. And, who but the Chinese could have come up with a way to make you feel better by sticking pins into you?

With barely four score English words beginning with the letter "X" we have managed somehow to apply one of them to the Chinese. The word, of course, is "xenophobia." Considering China's limited exposure to the outside world over the centuries and the grim nature of some of the encounters over the past century-and-a-half, some apprehension toward foreigners should be expected. As Omar Khayyam contemplated on another subject, "if a curse—why then, who set it there?" The "give em a whiff of grapeshot" mentality of the 1800s dismayed Sir Frederick Bruce, Britain's first Minister to Beijing, who was moved to write, "I should get on much better with this government and make more progress toward a better order of things, were it not for the idea entertained by admirals and consuls that they may use force whenever they deem it expedient."

I suspect that foreign misconceptions of Chinese "qualities" have been nurtured largely by our disinclination to consider that we might be wrong. This theory evolved out of my ukulele, an unlikely medium, but perhaps no more so than Archimedes' bathtub was in working out his theory of displacement. In high school, parties and outings rarely got going before the ukulele did. One of our sing-alongs was *Chinatown* and as time went on, it became apparent that while everyone was familiar with the tune, no one (including me) knew the lyrics. (What made that all the more curious was the fact most of these parties were held only a few blocks from San Francisco's Chinatown.) Over decades of strumming and humming on three continents, a dozen islands, and assorted seas and oceans, I've never met *anyone* who knows the words. Coming across the lyric only recently, it was a surprise to find just what a monument to simplicity it is. Single syllable words make up three-quarters of it. But, striking up the song on the ukelele, after the opening "Chinatown, my Chinatown," everyone just hums and la-di-da's.

In later years, in Asia, I began to see a distinct analogy between that song and the casual approach foreigners too often take with the Chinese. (The comfy old stereotyping/pigeonholing routine.) We seem inclined to just "hum along with the music" when it comes to things Chinese as if there really isn't any more to it than that. And, if there is more, well, let's not fret about it. They can just learn to do it our way.

Kicking this idea around with Chinese friends, a clear consensus emerged. They agreed that inexperienced foreigners getting off a plane accept the fact that they have absolutely no comprehension of the flood of written and spoken Chinese swirling about them. It's as if they'd suddenly been struck deaf and illiterate and they clearly understand they don't understand.

However, meeting someone in a business suit, speaking English with a dash of American slang, who orders eggs over-easy with hash browns for breakfast, they think "Now, *this* guy I *understand.*" They don't of course, though they are comforted by the delusion.

There's another form of the syndrome which manifests itself in the foreigner, who, having ordered a bowl of chop suey in Chinatown seems to see this as a qualification to launch into higher levels of business and social dealings with the Chinese. As a Chinese confided, "We are part of more than 5,000 years of culture and people who don't understand how we feel about that will never understand us."

A friend advised, "The time to call on a Chinese is when you don't need their help or involvement. That keeps the threshold warm for the time you need them." I was amused to recall that counsel following a visit with an old friend in Hong Kong. Our association goes back twenty years but our paths hadn't crossed for some time. I found myself in the neighborhood of her office in Mong Kok one morning and dropped in just to chat. After my departure, she phoned a mutual friend and said, "Fred was just here. What does he *want?*" A predictable Chinese reaction . . . and while I didn't want anything it did warm the threshold in the event something does come up.

It's ongoing experience and chewing the pulp of personal relationship, which fuel the Great China Learning Machine.

A successful China Trader in Hong Kong sums it up, "My home office people now are coming to China just a bit unsure of themselves and that's great, because it shows they're beginning to understand they're out of their element. It wasn't that way before and we had serious problems."

Another friend in Hong Kong relates this little story about an American visitor.

"An old buddy on his way to China stopped by. It was his first time in Asia. I asked if he had any questions about how things are, and aren't, done up north. He brushed that off saying that wasn't a problem because he had one of their 'top international people' with him. I asked if the guy had any China background and he said he hadn't, but he'd spent a lot of time in South America and Europe and knew all there was to know about working internationally."

In China, you had better soon learn that "working internationally" has little application. While the foregoing incident occurred several years ago, the culprit has yet to close any of his (typically multi- million-dollar) deals with China, despite ongoing jabs at it.

Often, the uninitiated sweep through China seeing people who, though prestigious, lack either the authority or funds to initiate anything. What is perceived as enthusiasm on the Chinese side often stems from a predictable desire to get something from, or sell something to, the foreigner. Typically, such visitors return home happily, but eventually wiser for the experience. It doesn't have to be that way.

It was refreshing to hear an American executive in Beijing give his view of what might lie ahead for his company in China.

"We aren't kidding ourselves," he said. "We know our product and we know how to merchandise it. We are known all over the world. But we don't know China. Developing some understanding of that is a top priority." Even with their no-nonsense attitude it took them nearly five years to get into production in China.

Approaching China realistically does not automatically ensure success. But it's the only way to make headway with a minimal loss of face, funds and time. Happily, there are fewer foreign fannies being scorched today than was the case in the earlier years of the "New China" learning process. People are now more inclined to head home from the second or third visit with a distinct impression they aren't quite as sure of what is going on as they previously believed.

Spreading the gospel of getting-along over the years, I've participated in a number of briefings for visiting groups. One, a state governor's delegation enroute to China through Hong Kong, seemed particularly unprepared. Chatting with one of the staff members after the briefing I said, "I'll give you the name of a book and if your people will just scan it before you leave it'll provide some helpful insights." I mentioned it again the next day on seeing him at lunch and again a few days later when I ran into him in their hotel. He smiled quizzically and replied, "You're really pushing that book. Have you some financial interest in the publishing company?" I assured him I didn't, returned the smile and wished him a whole bunch of luck on their trip. Years later, the results of their mission remain—to put it gently—nebulous.

"Fact finding tours" into China too often turn out to be anything but that. The exercise isn't quite the same as going to the park to see if the tulips are in bloom. An American businessman stopped by my Hong Kong office after one of these trips. He confided he'd been told in Beijing his bid on some equipment for a joint venture was "very competitive." He was unaware that the European partner in the venture was handling the purchase, and the officials he'd met in Beijing had no idea of the prices. He felt quite good about what he thought he'd learned. But it was wrong. He didn't get the contract.

I had a visit with an action-oriented Kansan who had just arrived in Hong Kong from his first incursion into China. This was some years ago, before China's travel industry had given much thought to amenities. He was critical of some of the problems he'd encountered in his travels and his mood wasn't moderated by my suggesting this basically reflected the glitches of an evolving system.

"Well, it seems to me they should do it *this* way. . . ." he snorted, and proceeded to share his theories on streamlining things.

I confessed, "It seems to me it should be that way too. But it's their country and they aren't all that interested in hearing our critique of their way of doing things. They aren't all that crazy about how we do a lot of things." He seemed to buy that. To his credit, he has been back since and, seemingly, is much more comfortable in taking things as they come. His experience illustrates that you can develop a more open-minded attitude if you realize you don't have one.

Fishing off the Baja California coast, one of our group philosophized, "When I was young I used to come down to Mexico and I'd get terribly annoyed over little things. I finally realized that's how Mexico is. I started to relax and now I have a great time."

That should be an international law. Particularly when it comes to the impatient foreigner in China. Remember, basic Chinese values aren't all that different. Chinese have long honored the ethical concepts which form the building blocks of civilization: virtue, patience, diligence and piety. Family and the role of their country in human history are held in high regard. A quality which they particularly esteem in individuals is what they call "the human touch." It relates to consideration and face. There is a widely held view among Chinese that it's a trait more common to them than to foreigners.

We have to be aware of these things because the Chinese are. But don't hold them or China in awe. If that happens, your glasses fog up so you are unable to see things clearly. The important thing to the Chinese is that you have some understanding of their past and who they are today. When they show a visitor a priceless piece of art or a spectacular monument to human endeavor, there is no hint of "Isn't that the most wonderful thing you've ever seen?" Rather, if you pay close attention, what they are saying is simply, "This is something we did."

Good drums do not require hard beating

How Now Ding How

Speaking Cross-Culturally

I BECAME AWARE OF ONE of the world's major communications pitfalls while traveling the back country of India, Pakistan, and what is now Bangladesh. Settling into old Victorian hotel rooms—with a pitcher of drinking water on a side table—I was careful to ask the floor attendant if the water was potable. The response typically involved a slow bow and a solemn, "Yes, *Sahib.*" Despite the assurances, my digestive tract and I grew more skeptical with each trip. For emphasis, I began picking up the pitcher, saying, "*This* water *okay* to *drink?*" The response remained, "Yes, *Sahib.*" Inner rumblings continued to enhance my doubts. Finally, one day up in the Punjab I said firmly, "I drink this water I get sick. Right?" The bearded face solemnly intoned, "Yes, *Sahib.*"

Never presume that the command of a few job-related words means that someone has mastered your language. Sometimes the tip-off comes in the form of a your favorite wool suit coming back from the laundry rather than the cleaners. Even in the better stores in cosmopolitan Hong Kong, when asking a clerk where you might find a particular item, it's important to know that "We don't have that," actually translates as "I don't know what you're talking about."

It's been a source of some wonder to me how it sometimes is virtually impossible to find clear answers to simple questions about the most mundane things. (Let alone how tricky it is with the really *critical* stuff.) Take the phrases, *"chin-chin," "ding how"* and *"gung-ho."* If you've only heard a few Chinese expressions, it's likely it would be one of these.

We'll disregard our most common adopted Chinese word, "ketchup," which is Cantonese for their invention of "tomato sauce." *Chop-chop,* a pidgin expression which goes back to the 1830s, won't be addressed either. It meant "Hurry it up" in Colonial Sinospeak. It isn't used today, even by first-time tourists. The same goes for *joss,* and *washee.* They're the stuff of old movies and period novels. About the only place you're likely to encounter *taipan* is in an occasional nostalgic headline in Hong Kong's *South China Morning Post.*

Chin-chin aroused my curiosity years ago, but asking around about it, I couldn't find anyone who knew what it really meant. Chinese friends in Manila, Hong Kong, Bangkok, Jakarta, Singapore and Kuala Lumpur didn't have the foggiest notion. One day in Hong Kong the sign "Chin-Chin Bar" caught my eye. I checked with the bartender. He didn't know. No one in the place did.

Years later, after occasional casual assaults on the question, I concluded there just was no answer. Then, one evening at dinner, a Chinese friend from Shanghai held up his glass and said *"Qing qing."* I asked what it meant.

"It's Mandarin. You know, 'Please, please . . . join me in a drink.' "

My recently-acquired five-and-a-half-pound *Dictionary of Slang and Unconventional English* concurred. As a toast, it dates from the late 18th Century. It came into use in the Royal Navy a century later and by 1909 was common in club society.

Ding how meaning "very good," is another curiosity. In the *lingua franca* of World War II in Asia, it was a popular expression amongst American servicepeople. A number of American military people were stationed in Taiwan when we arrived in the early 1970s and you'd occasionally see someone in a T-shirt with DING HOW and a "Number One" thumbs-up picture on the front. But I noted Taiwanese locals never seemed to use the expression. I started asking about it. A few locals said it was simply "US Air Force talk . . . canned World War II Chinese." Others simply stated, "We don't say that." Some time later at dinner in South China, not far from Hanoi, something which sounded like it popped into the conversation. At the first lull, I inquired and (no matter how the tone was inflected) the responses wobbled somewhere around "that-wasn't-exactly" what was said. The dozen people at the table—who were from different parts of China—agreed they *don't* say *ding how.*

Firmly hooked on my own halberd, I continued the quixotic quest. While some said it was a term used by "people up north," others suggested it was used "down south." Others said it's a "Chinglish" term used mainly by tour guides and shopkeepers.

The consensus which eventually emerged was that this Anglicized GI word is northern Chinese, properly rendered in the official Pinyin phonetics as *ting hao,* meaning "excellent." Northerners did admit to an occasional use of *ting hau,* which to the Western ear sounds about the same.

The stereotype that all Chinese say "flied lice" is due to the fact that *some* Cantonese can't distinguish "r" and "l." Cantonese speakers also occasionally have trouble with the "th" sounds, saying (for example) "feory" in place of "theory."

While foreigners who know only a few words or phrases might be inclined to impress tourist friends with an occasional *ding how,* I've never heard it used by those with a good command of the language. It's unlikely you'll hear it as Chinese chat among themselves. Chinese really are not much into superlatives. They're more inclined to be low key and the overworked *bu cuo* illustrates the point. It's the equivalent of "not bad." If you comment on something being particularly good—say, the weather—the usual response is "Not bad." A Cantonese might say "*Gei ho,*" meaning "quite good." Unless it's something such as a compliment directed at you, Chinese don't often suggest that something is outstanding. That would put their judgement on the line, risking a loss of face. Saying that this or that is "very good" is just not their style, unless they're trying to sell you something.

When on a train to Beijing, two people from that city sat next to us to share the fourteen-hour ride, I decided to monitor their usage. On arrival, my tally revealed that while they'd used words for "good," "fine," and "quite good" roughly thirty times each, they each uttered *ting hao* only once. Generally speaking, Chinese probably use this expression somewhat more often than a Marine Corps drill sergeant says "gracious."

"Gung-ho" is another sort-of-Americanese oddity. A battle cry of US Marines in the Pacific, it now conveys the idea of a sometimes naive, aggressive spirit. It *is* Chinese and it means "work together" or, more exactly, "industrial cooperation." It dates from the 1930s when American Edgar Snow, author of *Red Star Over China,* and New Zealander Rewi Alley helped initiate the Gung Ho industrial movement to supply Chinese troops in the war against Japan. When the *China Daily* reported in September, 1987 that the International Committee for the Promotion of Chinese Industrial Co-operatives had been officially re-established, the headline read: GUNG HO COMMITTEE RELAUNCHED. However, this phrase is not something you'll hear on the street. If you use it, be prepared to explain what you mean. Lt. Col. Evans Carlson is credited with bringing the term into Western usage during World War II when he commanded the 2nd Marine Ranger Battalion. He'd picked it up in the late 1930s as an observer to the Communist Chinese 8th Route Army.

The trials one encounters in trying to nail down linguistic usage apply equally to the pursuit of other information. If you ask a question once or twice, you're still likely some distance from really arriving at the answer. Tracking down the more simple curiosities is not undertaken as one would research a thesis. The process can be an entertaining diversion as well as an effective social device. A particularly rich resource of information is a dinner table with a dozen or so relaxed Chinese from different parts of the country. Always have a few cultural questions handy for these occasions. If things begin to lag, try asking about *ding how.*

* * *

Of all the areas of culture, the one which perhaps affords the deepest insights is the language. The rule that a grasp of the language gives you a better understanding of the people who speak it holds particularly true for the complex and antique Chinese language and culture.

I've come to grips with Latin, Spanish, German, Japanese and Chinese and have managed to get around in taxis and get three meals a day with a smattering of Urdu, Thai, Malay and Tagalog. Believe me when I say that (outside the African Khoisan language which uses a clicking sound) Chinese is about as far as you can wander from a European tongue. Latin, not one of the happier recollections of my high school years (either for me or the teacher), is basically one of the grandfathers of English. Spanish, once you get the conjugations, seems largely a matter of remembering whether you put an "o" or an "a" at the end of a word. Communicating in German is not so tough providing you don't take the grammar seriously. Japanese syllables sound something like English played backwards, and there is a simple phonetic script which can be mastered in a short time with relative ease. No matter how you inflect, for example, *sashimi,* it still is understood as "sliced raw fish." Loosely intoning Chinese in that fashion can result in a startling array of different, if not outright embarrassing, meanings. Chinese grammar is almost nonexistent, with no conjugations, plurals, tenses or masculine or feminine forms, but it is monumentally challenging for those who didn't grow up using it. After my first few lessons at the Taipei Language Institute I had serious misgivings about ever being able to use the language. After a few weeks of laborious lessons I phoned an American acquaintance who lectured regularly in Chinese at one of the universities.

"How long does it take to get this language right?" I asked.

He laughed, "You never get it right. Just try to come close. The Chinese will figure out what you're trying to say."

In the case of Cantonese, its eight inflections include one which is described as a "high, light, throw-away tone," so you can appreciate how rare the foreigner is who can make much headway with this dialect. Compounding the problem is the fact Cantonese has three separate branches in Guangdong Province ... and each of these has variations.

China's national language consists of words of single syllables—such as *ma, wo, li, xin*—accented by one of three tonal dips, blips and flips, plus one flat tone. The combination conveys the meaning of the word. Nearly fifty different meanings can be extracted from various applications of the syllable *xi,* pronounced "she." Used as a prefix or as part of a phrase, it conveys a couple hundred different meanings. Then there's *shi,* sounding something like "sure." Its meanings cover more than twelve pages in my dictionary.

Speaking Chinese isn't simply a matter of learning the words. You have to learn the words *and* the music.

The trickiest word of all is innocuous little *le.* The dictionary gives only two meanings for it. "Happy" and "sloppy." But the sound has a wide range of other wispy applications. In just a few of its functions, at the end of a sentence it can signal a changed state, habitual action, completed action, indicate progress up to a point, signal something can now take place, or indicates a speaker has ended the conversation. Used with verbs, it performs entirely different functions. In Singapore, people seem to use it as punctuation. Steven Kerr of Ogden, Utah, actually wrote his master's thesis on this one syllable at the University of Hawaii.

One sound may appear any number of other ways, as a prefix or as part of a compound word such as white-heaven-goose, which means swan. Electric-brain is a computer. The language is full of this sort of thing, and once you have a working vocabulary, and some experience, it becomes fairly easy to work out the meaning of a term you've never come across before . . . such as hit-word-machine: the word for typewriter.

Because of the lack of tenses, expressing the passage of time in Chinese requires some adjustment to your perceptions. For example, in China, conceptually, the future can be behind you. The day after tomorrow is expressed as "the behind me day." The day before yesterday is "the out in front of me day." In the case of weeks and months, the passage of time is conceptualized as moving from underneath you to above you. Next week is literally "underneath me week." Last week is "above me week." And last year is simply "gone away year."

Foreigners may have trouble with the simple declarative sentence: "Hu's on the phone."

After establishing that Hu is a name and not a pronoun, there is the problem of establishing exactly who Hu is. In a single day, one might be involved with Hu Wan Fu, Hu Chi Fu, Hu Yuan Ming and Hu Zhen Quan.

Thus the nickname comes into play, which gives you "Good Drinker" Hu, "Fatty" Hu, "Gold Tooth" Hu, and "Bald" Hu. Unlike nicknames in America, where someone may go by "Red Eye" or "Shorty," Chinese nicknames are more a secret code. They are generally used only by a relatively few people in a given group. Individuals are often unaware they've been codified.

In struggling to attain a passable grasp of the Chinese language, you may take comfort in knowing that the Chinese have just as much trouble learning English. My good friend from the Chinese Embassy in Washington, on a summer stroll, stopped at an ice cream shop and asked if he could buy some to "take out." The clerk said he could, adding, "but not sundaes." It happened to be a Sunday and (not being familiar with what Americans call ice cream in a cup with goop on it) my friend thanked the clerk and went on his way empty-handed.

*　　*　　*

When it comes to the written form of the language, as arcane as Chinese characters may appear to the uninitiated, there is even more to it than one might suspect. Written with brush and ink, it is an art form in itself. One of the country's most popular hobbies is calligraphy, the pursuit of writing beautifully. While it's believed the first Chinese ideographs appeared about the 16th Century BC, recent studies suggest they may go back 1,000 years or more before that. Chinese characters can be written from top to bottom, right to left or left to right. A glance at a page reveals which way to go because there's only one way it makes sense. All characters are created from a set of thirteen basic strokes, written in a specific sequence. First a horizontal stroke, then vertical, then left-falling and so on. If the sequence isn't followed correctly, the word won't look right. No wonder that more people can read it than can write it.

The written language is the same all over China, regardless of the dialect and it remains one of the most cohesive elements of Chinese culture. People today can easily read and understand things which were written thousands of years ago. We readers of English have some trouble unraveling Chaucer's 600-year-old:

> Whan that Aprill with his shoures soote
> The droghte of March hath perced to the roote,
> And bathed every veine in swich licour. . . .

Chinese characters are basically pictures of ideas: concepts rather than sounds. Nearly all characters have evolved by combining two ancient ideographs. (Similar to an international highway sign which might show two cars side by side, superimposed with a red circle with a diagonal slash through it. We understand the combination means "no passing.") Being able to read 3,000 characters is enough for general daily usage, such as reading newspapers. About 500 more will carry you comfortably though a novel. Well-educated people read about 6,000. Scholars learn about 9,000 and it might take twenty years of study to learn all 50,000. Adult literacy has increased from twenty percent of the population in the early 1950s to just a whisker below 100 percent today.

Being visual rather than phonetic, you can't "sound it out" as you usually can with alphabetic scripts. And Chinese does not lend itself well to Romanization.

Despite the limitations of the endeavor, the Chinese language has been rendered into various Roman alphabet phonetic systems, one of the more imaginative being Gwoyeu Romatzyh, in which different spellings of a word are used to indicate the correct tone. Casual, learn-as-you-go students who are chiefly interested in basic conversation are likely to use their own personal system to jot down new words or phrases rather than trying to use one of the established phonetic systems. While the country's official phonetic system is Pinyin, Chinese characters continue in use as the country's "authentic" written language. There is an ongoing program to simplify characters. But they still have a long way to go before it gets much easier for the foreign language student.

Foreigners who talk about planning to "study a little Chinese"—as they might take a few evening classes in flower arranging—shouldn't expect to get much beyond counting to ten and saying "Good morning" and "Nice day" in a way that they can be understood. Chinese doesn't lend itself to a little casual study. Aside from the word and its tone, there is the sequence and meter of a particular phrase of sentence. As with a musical score, if you drop or scramble some notes it's just wrong. While an idea can be conveyed with a few jumbled words in many other languages, Chinese doesn't work that way.

Unlike the French who seem rather pained if I try to speak their language, the pragmatic Chinese really don't expect you to speak Chinese well and they rather relish the confidentiality it affords them. Interpreters and local staff at international hotels can ease otherwise incommunicado transients through the day. Few foreigners ever learn the language well enough to actually negotiate, and you can quickly find yourself on very thin ice thinking otherwise.

One of the biggest problems a beginner encounters is in not grasping the distinction between the many regional dialects and the national language. China has some 600 spoken dialects, some of which differ so much they are virtually separate languages. The national language, long known as Mandarin and now called Putonghua in the PRC, is sometimes known as *han yu, chun guo hua,* or *guo yu.* Beijingers sometimes call it *Beijing hua,* the language of Beijing. If you're not familiar with these synonyms when someone says, "You understand Chinese very well," you can be put in a very embarrassing position. Foreigners can expect to have some trouble being understood, or will find their pronunciation being corrected, simply because they often are talking with someone whose *accent* is different. Even Chinese from different regions have this problem. You often see these people diagramming Chinese characters with a fingertip over an open palm as they talk, to get the meaning across. One important thing to learn is to be able to recognize when a problem is the result of the other person's accent rather than your own pronunciation. Until then, the hapless foreigner is inclined to keep changing their pronunciation around until they finally realize they had it right in the first place.

Another common problem is the inclination to presume that if a foreigner says something, it will be in a foreign language. Particularly in a rural area, if you are going to say something in Chinese, start with *Ni hao,* which means "Hello." That tips them off that you speak Chinese and the next thing you are going to say is going to be Chinese too. Otherwise they often tune you out on the presumption that whatever it is you are saying is in a language they don't understand.

*   *   *

It's easier to learn Chinese if you have a sense of humor. Fortunately, Chinese maintain the most gracious unflappability and indulgence toward foreigners who have the audacity to try to take on their language. Dining with my old friend Donald Anderson and his wife on his assignment to Hong Kong as American Consul General, we were into the soup course when I offhandedly tuned in on a chat across the table, between a visiting official from Beijing and an American businessman who lived just across the border from Hong Kong. The American, after a full year of intensive language study in the US, had spent nearly a year in China.

"Your Chinese is very good," the Beijing official told him.

The American properly deflected the compliment.

"Really," the official insisted. "Few foreigners speak Cantonese as well as you."

"But I'm speaking Mandarin," the American replied somewhat pained.

With his spoon stalled in mid-trajectory, the gentleman from Beijing contemplated that for an instant, looked up and said graciously, "Your Mandarin is very good."

A dozen years ago at a hotel coffee shop in Washington, DC, two Chinese came in, took seats next to me at the counter and began chatting with each other. Eventually, one of them mentioned an afternoon appointment and commented on the time without realizing his watch was fifteen minutes slow.

"Actually," I volunteered in Chinese, pointing to my watch, "It's now 1:05." He turned, casually thanked me in Chinese, reset his watch and resumed his conversation with his friend. At 1:06 he paused in mid-sentence, turned slowly with his eyes remarkably rounded and said in English, "How did you do that?"

Perhaps you're familiar with the riddle—If a bilingual person speaks two languages and a trilingual person speaks three, what do you call a person who speaks only one language? The answer, an American. I find that awful truth a little embarrassing.

If someone speaks your language and you don't understand theirs, you are at a distinct disadvantage. An example of this involves the true story of Chief Sitting Bull who, in his later years, was invited to speak at a railroad last-spike ceremony. He received a standing ovation from the American crowd after saying he hated all white people and called them "thieves and liars." The ovation, of course, was due to the fact the audience had no idea they'd been insulted because of the interpreter's having taken liberties with what the old chief really said.

In recent years English lessons have become a regular and popular feature on prime-time Chinese television and radio, in addition to being taught in the schools. On a visit to the northeast I turned on the television in my hotel room one evening after dinner and found two channels carrying English lessons while another had someone teaching Japanese. (There wasn't a single soap opera, game show or situation-comedy to be found on the dial.) The English-language *China Daily* reported: "English fever has become so widespread in Anhui Province" that the parrot in a city circus which formerly entertained audiences with Chinese expressions now is saying "hello" and "bye-bye" instead.

That cultural footnote surprises me less than an experience I had about a decade ago in Beijing. Looking for a particular shop, I asked a woman, coming out of an alley on a bicycle, if she knew the place. I put the question to her in Chinese and was shocked when she pointed and answered haltingly, in English, "Straight . . . not far . . . right side." Can you imagine how long you might stand around in Cedar Rapids until some Iowan came by on a bike who could say that in Chinese?

The Chinese are admittedly having trouble moving along as rapidly as they would like with their English language training programs. But they *are* making headway. We shouldn't be surprised to see English become China's second language before long, providing them a window to the world unlike anything they have ever had.

It has to do with what they call:

Stand taller—see farther

Old China Hands Won't Admit It

Why There Are No "China Experts"

IT OCCURRED IN THE GREAT HALL OF THE PEOPLE during a visit by US Secretary of Agriculture John Block. At the traditional pre-banquet tea, I was among the American guests who were introduced. I said a few words and was sitting down when Minister Song Jiwen, of China's (then) Ministry of Light Industry, said something I didn't quite hear. The interpreter, looking toward me, repeated in English, "The Minister is impressed with your command of Chinese." As an awkward silence enveloped the large room, I bounced up and loudly delivered a disclaimer to the effect my Chinese was only so-so. Heads turned and a bilingual murmur and titter rippled through the crowd. My old friend Charlie Liu of Washington, DC tugged at my coat choking with laughter and gasped between giggles, "The Minister is talking to the *Ambassador.*" Whoops.

"Oh! Yes!" I acknowledged, "Your Chinese *is* very good Mr. Ambassador." Being a good sport as well as a diplomat—and an Old China Hand to boot—the Ambassador shared in the gaggle of giggles which my inadvertent pirating of his compliment aroused. As the story was retold and embellished it became known (particularly among my detractors) as "The great ha-ha of the people." As unnerving as it was, I took comfort in the knowledge that it's best never to take yourself, or things, too seriously in China. Anyone who's been around long understands compliments are *always* deflected. It becomes such an instinctive reaction that if someone were to say on a steamy summer day, "My but you're sweating a lot," the response just might be, "Not so much. I just sweat kind of ... average." The reflexive sidestepping of compliments is but one of the cultural adjustments which the foreigner makes in the ongoing process of learning to do things differently than he or she might at home.

American Humorist Will Rogers, after a brief visit to China, wrote in his widely-syndicated newspaper column, "Trouble with me is I been in China too long. If I had stayed only a couple of days, I would have had a better idea of China . . . the more you see, the less you know." Rogers concluded it was best to avoid altogether anyone who had been around long enough to have the audacity to try to explain what was going on.

Rogers regaled his readers with that witticism a half-century ago. Today, the philosophy enjoys a following among newcomers who (unfamiliar with the terrain) seem disinclined to believe the counsel of those who've trudged the road. The only advantage in that is the thrill of making your own personal discovery of the difference between what *seems* to be going on and what *is* going on. Those who indulge in scant preparation, muddling along in feeble fashion, quickly fall in with our walking wounded. Typically, they're often unaware they are in need of a tourniquet, a stitch or salve, much less having the foggiest notion of where such should be applied. It's difficult for the neophyte to correctly read his or her progress chart in the flickering light of smiling pleasantries and platitudes from Chinese counterparts. Overcoming our initial ignorance comes slowly because our heads are so clouded with the dust and cobwebs of our accumulated misconceptions.

When a newcomer does start to get the hang of things, it's not uncommon for the folks back in the home offices to begin wondering whether their China guy really knows what's going on or whether he's just gone wacko. In trying to explain the local rationale of something which seems odd to the outsider, it's difficult to do so without sounding a bit odd yourself. I shared with a Cantonese businessman my views on how best to deal with certain situations in China:

"But you surely don't lay it out in quite those terms to the home office?," he asked.

"Of course I do."

"They must think you're nuts."

"Sure, but not as much as they did before they finally started getting the hang of it."

One evening at dinner at the home of Burton Levin, Director of the Asia Society in Hong Kong and formerly US Ambassador to Burma, someone suggested, "The single most important skill anyone needs in China is the ability to communicate back to headquarters what is going on . . . in a way which, if they don't fully understand, they will at least go along with."

Leonard Woodcock, former US Ambassador to China, was more blunt than Will Rogers. He called Americans' lack of understanding "an appalling ignorance." He knew little about China before he was chosen in 1977 to head the new US Liaison Office in Beijing, but, before arriving he read every authoritative book and document on China he could find. And he talked at length with people who had something substantive to share. Woodcock did it right.

There are advantages in acquiring an advanced degree in Asian Studies (hopefully from an institution with properly credentialed faculty). But there's a contradiction which the scholar must face. Knowledge of Chinese history, economics, geography or language helps, but, on arriving in China you soon discover the real learning experience has just begun. That holds true for everyone. It's not like learning to be a carpenter or a policeman and then going out and doing it. With China, the new arrival is quickly caught up in an *unlearning* experience, a sifting, discarding and restructuring of earlier orientations. I've never known anyone doing well in China who wasn't still actively involved in this process. It's like the medical field. There is a lot to learn and to remember and you have to work at keeping up.

While Asian Studies and China Seminars provide helpful background, these programs often deal more with "learning" about China, with little emphasis on "unlearning" about it. Business Seminars lean toward such subjects as the problems encountered in a joint venture in Shanghai. While this may have little bearing on what one might encounter in building a factory in Tianjin, there's hardly anything you can learn about China which won't come in handy sometime. But the key to the whole thing, of course, relates to how Chinese think about things and this critical subject area is generally touched upon only lightly at these sessions, if at all. That's like studying surgery without learning how make an incision.

A word about so-called "China experts." I've never met one. There are experts on Chinese history, cuisine, politics or whatever but not on *China*. That's too big a subject for anyone to master.

Sinologists are something else and the ones I've known are careful never to refer to themselves as experts. As scholars, they study various aspects of the country's literature, art, history or politics. But one who could tell you the names of the first emperors of the last five dynasties, (with the correct tonal inflections) probably wouldn't have a clue how long to steam a crispy duck before frying it.

A number of Sinologists develop into China Watchers, people who study the country and observe its gyrations from afar, hopefully coming up with reasonable conclusions about what's going on. It's a heady business, described by the noted Belgian Sinologist Simon Leys as the art of interpreting non-existent inscriptions written in invisible ink on a blank page.

At the other end of the spectrum are those who arrive in China in an unreal bubbly euphoria, barely able to contain themselves (after years of salivating hopefully for just such an assignment). The fizz soon fades after a series of surprise encounters with the system, which the textbooks somehow failed to mention. I would not hire someone for a China assignment who, during the job interview, babbles, "I think it would be terribly exciting." The person to hire is the one who says, "I know it will be challenging but I'm confident I can handle it." Being an Equal Opportunity employer doesn't mean you have to hire a giddy euphoric for China duty. While tourists find the Yangtze and the Temple of Heaven exciting, six months into a two-year assignment, foreigners invariably find their job more frustrating than exciting. Falling in a manhole in Urumuqi is exciting.

A fact not generally recognized is that while a China assignment is widely perceived as an opportunity for career advancement, it's not unusual for careers to sputter or founder there. It isn't easy for the capable foreigner to do well or to look well. As a friend in the diplomatic corps put it, "Working with Chinese can be quite pleasant but getting your people to understand how you go about doing that here—with the problems and frustrations of the unique system—is not pleasant." He continued, "Home office visitors and others cannot understand why something cannot be done or why it is this way or that. They presume you don't have the right connections or don't know how to do it."

It would be easier if China's system were less singular, or if every Chinese were somewhat less an individual. Just as fried rice appears in different forms around the country—or from one Beijing restaurant to another—cormorant fishermen in Guilin don't necessarily see things the same as Chongqing taxi drivers. And drivers disagree among themselves.

Each new unexpected development in China is potentially an important opportunity for enlightenment. However, people low on empathy or impaired by cultural dyslexia can spend three or four years in China and understand little more about the place than they did a month before they arrived.

As a general rule, newcomers can be sure they have attained a reasonable level of understanding when they begin to find the Chinese less frustrating than their own people back at headquarters.

*   *   *

It's a good sign when you begin to suspect that, in China, there might be another side to reality. This begins to set in when things you'd had every reason to expect somehow fail to materialize. Often, something which might click neatly into place back home may not even vaguely resemble a remote possibility in China.

Recently-arrived foreigners, victims of their own enthusiasm and perhaps pressed by the home office, easily fall under the spell of the old Newcomer's Waltz. Played to the accompaniment of Chinese congeniality, smiles, nods, and banquets, the uninitiated see opiate visions of imminent potentials, projects, progress, or programs which aren't going to happen. Unfamiliar with both the steps and the music, the fired-up foreigner presses for answers and action, without realizing that *no* answer from the Chinese generally is, in fact, *an answer.* Such foreigners become examples of the basic truth that you can't get anywhere in China by being a pest.

There have been a number of articles in the American press, written by reporters who have never been to China, which deal with the "great progress" some local businessperson is making with the Chinese by "charging ahead" with "total disregard" for the "traditional and accepted entrepreneurial approach." While it makes fascinating reading for those who don't know the ropes, I've occasionally followed up on these and I've never found a single instance where the touted approach ever resulted in anything of consequence. Further, I don't ever expect to find one. Such stories are pure fiction, resulting directly from the foreigner's inability to recognize the difference between polite and real interest.

How can you tell the difference? It's a key point newcomers miss. The scenario for the newcomer is perhaps only slightly different from how you might pursue a business deal in your own hometown, except now you are an outsider, unfamiliar with the terrain, misreading the signs, with the possible further disadvantage of being just a bit too euphoric. To strengthen your position in exploring a business opportunity in China, try to establish whether you are in fact talking to those who have authority (and funding) to initiate action. (Ask who else they've worked with, and check with experienced foreigners such as the embassy's commercial people.) In China, real interest is generated in direct proportion to the advantage it affords the Chinese. If, on the other hand, it is something of particular advantage only to *you* (a major sales contract for example) they quite likely will graciously give you face by saying the things you want to hear. But what's *really* in it for them? What reason do they *really* have for going along with you? In China virtually any organization is anxious to hear any proposition in order to discover what might be in it for them. Even if they then conclude they are not interested they can be counted on to continue to be polite and show polite interest.

Then, there's personal interest—the pursuit of opportunities which best serve the selfish motives of a particular individual rather than the organization, the community, China, or you. That is, an official who has merely *polite* interest in joint venturing with someone from California, might have a keen *personal* interest in being flown to California on an expenses-paid "inspection trip." Sometimes something affirmative might come of that. But be careful of personal interest as it can be the least affirmative of the three.

Chinese are well aware of the foreigner's befuddlement. Liu Zongren commented on it in his book, *Two Years in the Melting Pot* which deals with his sometimes bewildering experiences as an exchange scholar in the United States. Criticizing an American who'd written unfavorably about China after a year's residence, Liu cited the old saying about how foreigners are able to write a book after a stay of several months in China, but only a long article if they stay more than a year, and nothing at all if they stayed any longer. It's the Chinese way of saying what Will Rogers was joking about. Liu and I discussed that over lunch in Beijing and he concurred that the business of getting things straight in China is such a long process for foreigners that it only *seems* we are getting more confused as we go along because we keep discovering more misconceptions to clear out of our heads.

*   *   *

My favorite Chinese puzzle is that enigma which is known as an "Old China Hand." Although a common expression, going back to the early 1900s, there is an element of uncertainty as to what exactly an Old China Hand is. It's highly unlikely you'll find the term in your dictionary. Perhaps sensing this lack of definition, the authoritative US-China Business Council has suggested China Hands "understand how the Chinese view the world, how things do and don't get done . . . and how to behave in accordance with protocol and expectations." That would seem pretty much on target, in terms of how Old China Hands are generally perceived. There's a certain leprechaun quality about them in that they are pretty much whatever you imagine them to be. The West has no cultural counterpart to the Old China Hand. Like the panda, they remain a Chinese phenomenon. Perhaps it's a reflection of our own provincialism. We seem to see nothing unusual in a foreigner who can follow our conversation as it drifts from a creamy chocolate mousse, to a hair styling mousse, to a wild moose. When a foreigner has that kind of grasp of English I suspect most native English-speakers would find nothing particularly unusual in that, as if it were, after all, how things should be. The Chinese, however, have a distinct appreciation for foreigners who have worked at being at ease with their cultural subtleties.

It is difficult to establish exactly who the Old China Hands are due to their excruciating disinclination to own up to it. Some companies, consultancies or other commercial endeavors invoke that phrasing in their letterhead or literature but that's simply marketing and not quite the same thing. Only once did I ever hear anyone suggest he was "a China Hand." This occurred at a consular reception in Hong Kong. It involved someone from the State Department who hadn't been in Asia long enough to affect the prefix "Old" or to be aware that such people don't describe themselves that way. While this brief encounter in Hong Kong did establish that it is possible to occasionally come across a Young

China Hand, curiously, these people don't evolve into old ones, just as we don't have old tadpoles and old caterpillars. The disinclination of Old China Hands to come out of the closet surely has a lot to do with their appreciation for the Chinese view that modesty is one of the principal virtues. It is what compelled Wang Lung, the humble farmer of Pearl S. Buck's *The Good Earth* to protest when guests praised the food at the simple wedding dinner in his house. "It is poor stuff—it is badly prepared," he demurred. But he was inwardly proud of his bride's cooking and had never tasted such dishes when visiting friends. An equally compelling concept is that there is wisdom in realizing how much you have yet to learn. Understanding this Chinese balance of modesty and wisdom can become so ingrained in the outlook of those who have spent years there that they develop a knee-jerk reaction to any suggestion they are "China experts." If Chinese comment on a foreigner's expertise, a foreigner who understands how the Chinese see things is conditioned to deflect the suggestion with vigor, not from modesty, but because to do otherwise would simply make the foreigner appear foolish. The Chinese know there are no China experts. Don't be misled by the fact they may sometimes use the English or Chinese words for "expert" in referring to your knowledge of things Chinese or to your command of your particular specialty. There are few things you can do which make you appear more foolish than to have the word "expert" on your business card or to give anyone the idea that you think you are quite something. While Chinese develop a special regard for foreigners who work at trying to learn China's ways, they appreciate a foreigner being cultured enough to be modest about it. I often suspect that in sizing up a new foreign acquaintance, Chinese occasionally are inclined to toss out that "China expert" line simply to see if the foreigner is savvy enough to know how to handle it.

I've noticed on American television, when an interviewer introduces someone on camera as a "China expert," the interviewees react to that introduction with one of two totally different smiles. The one smile, rather on the puffy side, seems to say, "Yes, that's indeed what I am." Switch this guy off. Watch for the smile which is delivered with a slight twinkle in the eye of the "expert" which seems to convey, "I'm not sure why I agreed to do this because there are no 'China experts' but we don't have time to go into that, so what's your question?" When you see someone on TV with that smile, the individual possibly has something worthwhile to say.

Even the Chinese, including the country's top leaders, have found that throughout history China has its own way of unexpectedly and suddenly darting this way or that to confound those who get too comfortable in their planning.

In a typical example, a few months before the opening of the Asian Games in Beijing, program planners were shocked when hundreds of carrier pigeons, being trained to take part in the opening ceremony, were shot dead by hunters who laid in wait for them as they made a practice approach into the city.

For the foreigner, a common bad scenario involves the neophyte who returns from an initial incursion into China and enthusiastically tells the boss or the board or the local paper how swell things are progressing. After a few followup trips or phone calls, however, comments become more cautious. They begin to say things like, "The situation isn't quite what we had perceived in the beginning." Or, "This will require more time and discussion than it first appeared." It's the dawn of realization that the Chinese do things their way. And it's a wonderful thing to come up against because until you've barked your shins on it you aren't likely to get very far. Accept it for what it is: progress. Chinese say when you begin to understand that you don't understand, it is the beginning of understanding.

China Hands polish this to a point at which they know pretty much what will or will not result from a particular strategy, action or inaction. But you rarely find them making outright predictions, because China doesn't lend itself to that. About as far as an Old China Hand is inclined to go out on a limb is "I-wouldn't-be-surprised-if. . . ." But they are usually pretty much on target. And they aren't surprised.

Everything considered, I've concluded that being an Old China Hand is largely a figment of someone else's imagination. If people think you are one, that's about all the accreditation you're going to get. And it's probably the best. Old China Hands have no problem with people thinking that way. It's just that they don't like to let on to anyone that they are one. Over the years I've never been able to get one to admit it or to catch anyone acting like they believed it.

However, years ago walking with someone along the old river front in Singapore, we passed a scantily-pelted alley cat snoozing on a skunky stack of fly-specked shark fin drying on a dirty curb. My companion sniffed and said, "I know a great shark fin restaurant near here." And that's where we had lunch. I'm almost certain he's an Old China Hand.

Aside from occasionally blowing their cover that way, their one common denominator—which tends to give the China Hand in them away—lies in their hearty endorsement of the philosophy:

You can't learn it all

Scattering Bones Along
the Banquet Trail

Eating is the First Happiness

THE ANCIENT RITUAL of the Chinese banquet, an essential ingredient of business, social and diplomatic life in China, is more casual and unstructured than it appears at first glance.

Consider the place setting. Chopsticks, a small plate, a bowl, a spoon, a tea cup and a glass or two. That's it. Compare that to the protocol of formal Western functions with guests taking up, in prescribed sequence, various sterling silver instruments, with a used teaspoon or butter knife to be placed this way or that on a particular plate or saucer. Chopsticks may be set down in virtually any manner. Some dishes, such as steamed shrimp, Peking duck and minced pigeon in lettuce, are eaten with the fingers. (Hand towels are brought around during the course of the meal, to tidy chins and fingers—and there's no rule whether you take the one on your left or your right. In out-of-the-way eateries, a shirttail, handkerchief or tablecloth edge serves equally well.)

While a dab of gravy or a splash of red wine on the tablecloth at a Western dinner may unnerve the most composed guest and perhaps unsettle the hostess as well, to the Chinese, eating is simply too pleasurable to be encumbered unduly with such distractions. It simply doesn't matter and it's to be expected, given the inherent hazards of lofting drippy bits of duck from the serving tray to your plate. If something small is dropped, let it lay. Something more obtrusive can be chopsticked to the side of your plate. To the Chinese, the enjoyment of food is the First Happiness, and even after some 5,000 years of formalizing their culture they've somehow never got around to imposing heavy social constraints on it.

"Have you eaten?" is the most common phrase in the Chinese language. This is followed by, "I invite you to eat." These are among the first phrases a foreigner picks up, often acquired socially before the first language lesson.

In Taipei, shortly after I'd started studying Chinese, I was hurrying to lunch and was behind schedule. Scurrying into the elevator, I wasn't sure which floor the restaurant was on. In my haste, I jumbled my inquiry to the gentleman riding up with me. Instead of saying, "May I please inquire . . ." I blurted out, "May I please invite you . . ." As I recomposed the phrasing in my head, the stranger replied in Chinese, "Thank you. I have an invitation for lunch." His casual response revealed he wasn't particularly surprised to have a befuddled stranger suggest, "Join me for lunch?"

Banquets have a more fancy setting and a greater selection of special dishes, but aside from that the ground rules are about the same whether it involves a formal affair, a regular dinner or a small lunch, breakfast or snack. At a banquet the host will chat briefly with guests over tea before inviting them to the banquet table, where a few words of welcome will be spoken. Other than that, a state banquet in the Great Hall of the People doesn't call for much more structure than a small breakfast among friends in a railway station café.

Upon arrival in China, VIP's are given a welcome banquet. The feasting continues as they travel around the country. The foreigner thus indulged should give a return banquet in honor of the local people a day or so before leaving the community. You're at somewhat of an advantage as you need simply observe what the host does at the welcome banquet and then do essentially the same thing in hosting your return function. (Remember to make provision for the drivers' meals also. They generally eat by themselves unless you happen to be traveling together.)

The choreography of the welcome banquet generally runs along the following lines:

- Hosts gather in the dining room before guests arrive. Foreigners usually will be picked up and escorted to the function.

- The first three or four guests are expected to enter in protocol order, the company president first, senior vice president second, and so on.
- Before proceeding to the table there will be five minutes for tea and small talk. This serves to set a relaxed mood and affords time for any rearrangement of place cards which may seem prudent because of the sequence of the guests' entry, or to adjust for someone who didn't show up. (Don't infer anything from where you happen to be seated from one occasion to the next. This relates more to how they perceive you in the pecking order of the moment, rather than how they feel about you personally. Of more consequence is that they chose to invite you.) The host indicates when it's time to move to the table.
- Protocol aside, it's well to have the foreign company's China Hand at the same table with important visitors who are not on close terms with China. This helps to keep the conversation within the realm of reality, and the China Hand can thus listen for innuendoes and later clear up any misconceptions on either side. ("What he meant when he said that was. . . .")
- The first course is almost always cold appetizers. The host serves the No. 1 and No. 2 guests while the secondary host mirrors the action on the opposite side of the round table. The guests should mildly protest this courtesy and after one or two more courses, and further mild protests, the host will settle back and let the guests help themselves. The host will signal when it is time to begin eating. However, as new dishes appear, guests are expected to dig in. Don't hold back waiting for others who are, in fact, waiting for you to proceed. The exception to that is on the occasions when—as at a more fancy restaurant—a waiter or waitress serves everyone individually.
- Early in the meal the host says a few words of welcome and, either standing or sitting, proposes a toast to the visitors. The usual practice is for the No. 1 guest to wait until the arrival of the next course before returning the toast. The toast should be brief and generally along the theme of "new, growing and lasting relationships." If the host toasts your newly-established

friendship, you propose a toast to the *future* of the friendship. If it's more than a one-table affair, at some point the host usually goes to the other tables to toast those guests. It's appropriate for the No. 1 guest, and sometimes others from the host's table, to tag along. There will be more glasses hoisted throughout the function and guests may initiate some of this. (Regional variation—on my first visit to Inner Mongolia, when I stood to present a toast at the start of the banquet, I was resoundingly shouted down by my gregarious guests who explained, "Here, the little speech means it's time to go home!" In Mongolia you drink. Then you talk.)

- After a dozen or more courses, a dessert of fruit or some other sweet will be served. People generally do not linger over conversation when the meal is finished, unless it's a gathering of close friends or if they are aware foreigners are inclined to do this. With the Chinese, the meal is the thing.

- Following dessert it's the guest's option to conclude the dinner by thanking the host and rising. If the host rises first, it may be assumed that the guest has lingered a bit too long.

- If the hosts know you tend to chat after dinner, while you know they're likely to want to be on their way, it can get a little awkward if both parties try to defer to the other. The way to break this standoff, and unequivocally conclude the function, is to down your glass with the toast *Men qian qing,* meaning "Sweep your front door clean." Either host or guest can invoke this, and it always draws a relieved chuckle from the group.

- Paying a restaurant bill should be done in the most unobtrusive manner possible. Studying it in front of guests is to be avoided. If it's a large function, this is best attended to after the guests depart. Don't show concern for how much the meal cost or insist on an itemized receipt. Table-top jousting for the bill is best not done unless you're with a very close friend or a person with a very international outlook. While Chinese may do this among themselves, if you've been invited, let them pick up the bill.

In hosting a return banquet, a newcomer had best rely on the counsel of local staff or Chinese associates in working out the guest list, seating arrangement, menu and other details. The invitation is generally extended a day or so after, rather than during, the welcome banquet. Standard procedure, if you don't have local staff, is to enlist the aid of the host organization's interpreter. A typical approach would be along the lines of, "I would like to host a banquet. About the same group as we had the evening I arrived, unless there are some others we should include. I'd appreciate it if you can find out for me which date is best and if you'd assist me with the menu and the seating." This avoids the question of exactly when and where it will be, and is vague on the point of who is to attend. The indirectness keeps things flexible and relaxed.

When unfamiliar with the community the best bet is to use the same restaurant for the return banquet, or ask the interpreter where the group likes to eat. People tend to gravitate to particular places for such functions, so they are familiar with the menu and the price. Thus, ordering the No. 1 or the No. 2 menu will make a more positive impression than the No. 3 menu. (Face. Theirs and yours.) A safe practice is to ask their interpreter to choose the menu, stipulating that the dishes "be about the same" as at the earlier function. Rather than an imposition, this gives the interpreter face, as ordering food is important business.

Unlike the US, where you might invite Rotarians and Jaycees, don't cross organizational lines unless you are very sure of your ground. The selection of guests for a dinner is so critical I never presume to indulge in this, beyond the top one or two invitees and possibly proposing a few others.

As you get on closer terms with the people involved, the traditional seating arrangement becomes less of a factor for most mealtime get-togethers. You simply invite your "old friends" to sit where they please and "not stand on formality." Ease yourself into position so the No. 1 guest just happens to end up on your right.

The more relaxed the meal, the better. That isn't always easy, given the limitations of language and the fact you often may be with people you've just met, who may be sizing you up. Chinese who haven't spent much time around foreigners are usually a bit reserved also. To remedy this, ages ago the Chinese deduced that a tipsy guest is a happy guest, and they liberally load up guests with libations. The beverages are most often beer, sweet wine and—too often—a crystal clear, throat-and-mind-searing liquid steamroller known as "Moutai." Made from sorghum, and usually at around fifty percent alcohol, it is served throughout China. (Though the label has the old form "Kweichow Moutai," the name of the province is now written "Guizhou," and the city "Maotai." Similarly, Qingdao's beer is still Tsingtao.) There's said to be a variety in Hebei Province which averages seventy-five percent, in case you've been looking for something to take the varnish off an old desk. On occasion they'll serve a somewhat less jolting type, a "Moutai Lite," which hosts claim is "only thirty-eight." (This is not to be confused with a handgun made by Smith and Wesson.) According to the New China News Agency, real Moutai, made from sorghum, "can only be brewed at the Moutai winery in Guizhou" as "a unique mix of some 100 species of micro-organisms which directly affect the taste of Moutai has formed in the air over a limited area around the winery."

Through a couple of thousand banquets, I have never seen a foreigner take Moutai by choice. Conversely, Chinese think our cocktails and premier "sippin' whiskey" taste like drain cleaner that's gone bad. Throughout China, people relate that President Nixon said he liked Moutai very much on his first visit to Beijing. I think he may have misspoken. President Nixon has also been quoted as saying the Chinese will not push the drink on a foreign visitor. That's perhaps true if the visitor happens to be President of the United States.

An invitation to join in a toast cannot graciously be declined. Your host will be pleased if you do it with gusto. Ladies need only sip if they choose. Non-drinkers can just touch the glass to their lips or toast with a soft drink or tea. This fulfills the social obligation. The magic words are, "I'll just sip a little." (In Chinese *sui bian,* literally "as one pleases.") Hosts and all the others at the table vigorously strive to subvert your efforts but generally acquiesce if you can stand the pressure. If all else fails, say you've just had a liver bypass and have to take it easy.

The late Premier Zhou Enlai only touched his glass to his lips when toasting. If you respond to their invitation to drink with, "I'll just sip like Zhou Enlai," they usually don't argue further.

When hosting, and proposing toasts, you must invite guests to *gan bei,* that is, "dry the glass." For a host to say, "just a sip" comes across sounding miserly. In any event, gan bei often carries less suggestion of an actual "bottoms up" than visitors infer.

While a gan bei or two may help create a relaxed atmosphere, the uninitiated foreigner is hereby forewarned that accomplished banquet-goers develop a remarkable sleight-of-hand whereby they consume far less alcohol than it appears. As you begin to get the hang of it, you appreciate that it is less a deception than a traditional art form, in which friends try to outdo one another in good-natured hoodwinkery.

When someone proposes a toast with fingers covering the glass the odds are it's empty. And the odds against your surviving unscathed are ten-to-one. A variation involves simply toasting with a glass that's not quite full. This can sometimes be affected by employing the tremulous, spill-as-much-as-you-can toast, which, properly and quickly executed as the other person's eyes are diverted, can result in half the drink being splattered over the rim of the glass. When toasts are proposed with little porcelain cups there is a distinct likelihood that the other person's cup is empty. A skilled practitioner may cork the cup with his tongue and only pretend to drink. It is perfectly acceptable to ask, "Would you mind letting me see whether you have something in there?" I wouldn't suggest doing that on your first toast with the mayor, but it's common among friends. (Asking the mayor to give you a peek after the third or fourth toast is perfectly acceptable.)

Tiny bubbles in someone's glass means you're being sandbagged with soda pop. Someone having a glass of dark tea beside a glass of brandy bears particularly close scrutiny. The same applies to someone with a glass of coke or orange juice alongside a little glass of crystal clear Moutai. After a toast, watch to see if this individual takes a sip from the soft drink glass before taking a bite of food. If the soft drink glass becomes slightly more full with each "sip," you're dealing with the old spit-back gambit. Put a question to them before they can get their hands on their soft drink. If they gulp and their eyes pop before they speak, you've scored. One of the most dangerous devices is when others at the table begin toasting you individually, one-on-one. To get this under control, simply broaden the invitation to include everyone at the table each time you are invited to a one-on-one toast. That will slow them down. Archimedes' principle of liquid displacement works equally well in China so if you notice ice in someone's glass, be sure you get a piece too. Moist hand towels are usually provided at dinner. If someone is raising the towel to their lips after toasting, you can be sure the towel's alcohol content is running higher than the individual's. While standing for a toast, with a little flair you can empty a small glass into your towel without anyone noticing. On occasion, with everyone's head tipped back, I've seen someone shoot the drink past their ear, missing the mouth altogether. If you try this, be sure there isn't a waitress standing directly behind you. These young ladies tend to shriek and drop plates when splattered. There are other techniques, but it would take the thrill of discovery out of it for you if I revealed all of them.

What do you do when you apprehend Chinese in minor Moutai infractions? Invite the culprit to a replay with a full glass in full view. They'll find you much more fun to be around if you're not a complete pushover.

Never have a cocktail before going to a Chinese banquet and once into the food and drink it's wise to take on a few fatty morsels of pork or duck to help line the stomach and slow the progress of the Moutai into your system. A snack of cheese in your room before dinner accomplishes the same purpose.

If Chinese tell you they "haven't learned to" drink they likely aren't bluffing. Stories to the effect that some are unable to drink are true. Medically stated, it has to do with enzymes within the liver that are involved in the metabolizing of ethyl alcohol. Some Chinese have a great increase in the amount of the isoenzyme in the liver, producing excessive acetaldehyde. The result is, their faces redden and they become weak and light-headed. Doctors call it "Oriental flush." After only a little indulgence, I've seen these individuals pass out colder than a moose snout in February.

With cunning and perseverance, it is sometimes possible to circumvent Moutai altogether by mentioning during your pre-banquet chat that you've heard "great things" about the wines being produced through China's joint-venture endeavors with European winemakers. The dry white table wine industry, which got underway in the 1980s, produces some excellent products—considerably more user-friendly than Moutai.

Providing a memorable meal and libations for a guest is one of the highest forms of hospitality and it reflects the intensity which Chinese feel about food. It always has been a pivotal part of their holidays, ceremonies and customs.

My Grandfather Schneiter used to tell a story about mourners bringing food to a Chinese cemetery in America. A town wag taunted, "When are your folks coming back to eat that food?" One of the Chinese replied, "Same day yours come back to smell the flowers."

Chinese have evolved strong traditional beliefs for just about everything that appears on the table. The underlying concept is, "The shape helps the shape." If the food in its natural state resembles a part of the body, it's said the food benefits that particular piece of anatomy. The walnut's wrinkled bi-lobed shape suggests it's "good for the brain." Eating with old friends, someone plopped a sautéed duck foot onto my plate and with the hint of a grin suggested, "Eat that and you'll be a good dancer." Other beliefs seem devoid of any rationale, suggesting—for example—that giraffe tail is good for the kidneys. While these may strike a Westerner as quaint or curious superstitions, if you are convinced something is good for you, it could well have a beneficial effect.

Foreigners who know a little about China understand that you don't generally discuss business at dinner. This is felt to be particularly true with people they don't know well or if it involves a sensitive subject or negotiation. However, among friends or any time they bring up something of a business nature, feel free to get into it.

When traveling on your own, or with a tour group, overblown gourmandising is not generally much of a problem. It's the official mission and higher-level business trip which spawn full-scale, industrial-strength banqueting. This is the realm of Falstaffian encounters which rarely run to fewer than a dozen courses. That doesn't count the curtain-raising selection of assorted cold appetizers. When you're involved in a week-long Olympiad of luncheon and dinner banquets, the challenge is formidable. It's a good idea to pace yourself and take it easy on the early courses. Take just single helpings and leave a little on your plate from each serving. Empty plates signal the host to pile more food on.

The Chinese classify certain foods as having warming, cooling, restorative or neutral qualities. Thus, as winter approaches they will suggest snake or red ginseng for the reputed warming attributes. This isn't just to warm you up, as a Westerner might take a bowl of hot soup on a cold day. It's for the *season*, like antifreeze in your car. Bitter melon, green bean soup, and herb soup are considered cooling foods, which are to be avoided by pregnant women. Oranges and Chinese broccoli are neutral. Yellow turtle, mutton and the curious black-skinned chicken are noted for their recuperative powers. The thin dried peel of an orange found in South China is brewed into a tea to relieve a sore throat. They say the older the dried orange peel is, the better. I was told it was common up until recent generations to have 200-year-old orange peels in the family medicine chest. Today, they use fresher ones, probably no more than forty years old.

Along with the belief in ancient traditional medicines, the Chinese are inclined to see their diet as being so healthy that it surpasses anything that anyone else eats. Nutritionally, there is much to be said for chicken soup, steamed fish and boiled dumplings. But as one soon discovers, banqueting runs alarmingly high in fried foods, fatty batters, sodium, saturated fats, skin and organs, spices, and the occasional mystery preservative your body hasn't previously tried to metabolize. A luncheon and dinner banquet circuit of more than a few days begins to tell, and two weeks is devastating.

Beijing residents, according to the *China Daily*, consume up to three times the recommended daily intake of salt and about twice as much fat as is considered healthy.

Heavy usage of the flavor-enhancer monosodium glutamate is said to result in the reaction in some people known as the Chinese Restaurant Syndrome. Headaches, burning sensations, numbness, pressure in the chest, facial tightness and insomnia are among the common symptoms. A Thai friend related that his ears turn red and he itches all over. While eating less of it is perhaps the best solution for those bothered by MSG, it's been suggested that some may find relief by taking a couple of aspirin or other anti-inflammatory medication before eating.

* * *

A change I've watched with bemused interest is the incursion of the Western-style reception into China. The Chinese have been good sports about this curious social phenomenon which, with its stand-up sipping with a smattering of finger foods, is the antithesis of their way of entertaining. (Even at a proper multi-course sit-down Western meal, Chinese invariably come away hungry.) Chinese efforts at hosting receptions in China, so far, tend to be combinations of their classic banquet with a little cocktail session preceding it. One of these, in the Beijing Hotel a few years ago, featured a thirteen-course, sit-down "snack" with everything from roast duck to sandwiches.

An American friend in Beijing said he was partial to holding receptions when entertaining because "you can see a lot more people in less time." Looking at it from the Chinese perspective, that's what's not quite right about it. This will change. Receptions have long been accepted in international, upbeat Hong Kong and other major Asian cities. Foreigners who host a reception should not think that they can pull it off with the same easy formula which works at the country club back home. A Beijing duck and shark fin soup banquet gives face to both the guests and the host. Peanuts-chips-and-dips don't. A banquet is an opportunity for the guests and the host to share a relaxed evening together. It says, "You're important to me and I have time for you." A reception doesn't. But if a reception is your choice, maintain a constant effort toward enhancing its success by observing the following.

- Don't let Western guests cluster into little foreign enclaves reminiscent of Shanghai in the 1930s.
- Invite enough interpreters and other bilingual guests to ensure unclogged communication channels.
- Pay close attention to properly welcoming and seeing off Chinese guests; make sure they are getting along and that strangers to the system are not shy about approaching the buffet table.
- Have a good selection and a good volume of good food.
- Unlike a banquet which should conclude with your feeling relaxed, at the end of a reception in China the host should be well wrung out (having done such a masterful and attentive job of seeing that everything has gone all right).

* * *

When it comes to ordering Chinese food, the key is to have things in balance, with a pleasing variety of courses in a logical sequence so each dish is different in content, preparation and appearance from the previous one. The rule is, at least one dish per person for larger groups; a higher ratio of dishes for just a few people. (For two people four smaller servings should suffice while affording a good variety.) The size of servings varies in different restaurants so the host should ask the waiter if the order provides enough food for the group. Rice may be too basic a food for special guests and the amount of rice "required" depends on how much fancier food you provide. When ordering, ask if anyone would care to have a bowl of rice to accompany their meal.

* * *

A quarter century ago, an international hotel food and beverage executive was quoted in the Hong Kong press as saying French cooking came via Russia, Greece and Rome from China. I wrote my longtime friend, Phil Paxton, to get his reaction. Born in China and an authority on the cuisine, he created *The Magic Wok* television show in Australia and following-up on that wrote *The Magic Wok Cookbook*. His response was, "I have to say that I would be more comfortable in believing that French, Greek and Russian food are derivatives of the Mongol kitchen or the Tartars."

The hordes of Attila the Hun, a multiracial and multilingual patchwork of tribes, roamed and ravaged much of Europe, including the northern part of the Roman Empire, for nearly two decades from AD 435. And, whether their origin was west or east of the Urals, many were described as having the skin coloring, slanted eyes and other characteristics of the Mongols. That suggests chopsticks in the saddle bag.

Phil further notes "over the eons, creative people dressed up their recipes to what we know today." He credits the French with being the pioneers of European cuisine, and adds, "The Italians have managed to keep their culinary ties to the Chinese much closer than the others have."

Regardless, my Italian friends are loath to concede that Marco Polo brought back the idea for spaghetti from China. Italian legend has it that the first pasta in Italy originated in Naples, at the other end of the country from Polo's home town. Then there's Italian ravioli, which is only a twist of the wrist away from Chinese *jiao zi* dumplings. In Shanghai's stately old Jin Jiang Hotel I ordered ravioli soup, and was startled when it turned out to be that old Chinatown standard, won ton soup. Pizza has an almost direct counterpart in the wheat flour wrapper used for Peking Duck and other dishes. One thing is certain, if you want to liven up dinner conversation with Chinese friends, tell them that you heard that Marco Polo taught the Chinese how to make dumplings.

*   *   *

A discussion on Chinese food would not be complete without a few words about, ah ... exotic dishes. Neophytes on the banquet circuit are immediately identifiable by the plaintive call, "What is this I'm eating?" Somehow, it's virtually impossible to say that without it sounding like, "What on earth is this?" The Chinese realize they eat a number of things Westerners wouldn't touch with a ten-foot chopstick. Unless you're an Old China Hand or writing a cookbook of Asian specialties, your host may infer from such questions that you're a little uncomfortable with the cuisine. As any good trial lawyer knows, if there's any doubt about your being able to handle the answer, don't ask the question.

When eating something which appears to be an unusual rendition of beef, just let it go at that and enjoy it without asking about it. It most likely *is* beef. But it could be any number of things, none of which is likely to hurt you. How you feel about any food depends on what you're accustomed to. If you'd never eaten eggs before you might be inclined to fret about where they came from. A particularly tasty Chinese dish is ham served with a thick substance they get from insects. Sounds awful? It's honey.

Snake, fish head, shark fin, and bird nest are among the most outstanding and flavorful soups I've encountered anywhere. Even the most picky eaters would agree, providing they didn't know what went into the pot. If the flavor suits you, the idea is to enjoy it, not to preoccupy yourself with what it is. In the event you suspect it's something which rates particularly low on your scale of acceptability, or for that matter, the evolutionary scale, try not to think about what it looks like in its natural state, how it slithers about, or how you might go about cleaning it. Develop the attitude, if-they-can-stand-to-clean-it-I-can-eat-it. If treated to duck feet, it's a matter of thinking of something other than what they've waddled through. It's food, remember, and the folks who came up with that particular recipe harbor a distinct respect for longevity.

By trying not to think about it, I've managed to eat a few hundred feet of snake over the years. Actually, the sweet white meat could pass as chicken. Not something a Westerner might order if dining alone, when delicately julienned in its savory broth and garnished with fragrant sprigs of coriander, it beats turkey noodle soup. In southern jungled areas, where snakes are plentiful, the soup is more of a thick stew and the meat is served chunk style. Sea snakes are delicacies in southern coastal areas. They apparently can't be skinned and are served in a manner which makes it appear as if they'd lost a territorial dispute with a lawn mower.

Marco Polo noted that snake meat was popular and commanded a good price. He chronicled the reputed medicinal merit of serpent gall and this belief enjoys a strong following today. As a further historical footnote, snake also was a part of the diet of the Peking Man.

Going back further, it's been suggested if Adam and Eve had been Chinese we'd still be in the Garden of Eden as they'd have eaten the snake.

With their orientation toward food, I was surprised to hear a Chinese remark, "I'll eat anything, except turkey."

Seizing upon that as something which would surely afford me a new insight into the Chinese character, I asked why he wouldn't eat turkey.

"I don't like turkey," he replied.

On that note, we started on our fish head soup. Despite the disinclination of Americans toward this delicacy, it's a widely held view in Asia that the head is the most tasty and nutritious part. They think it's silly to cut it off and throw it away. It's said, in the old days when Chinese bandits kidnapped someone, they would give the person a fish to eat. If the person didn't eat the head, the bandits took that as a sign the individual was too low-brow to be worth much ransom. However, if the person ate the head, the bandits figured they had someone of class who'd fetch a good price. If you are served fish head soup be appropriately flattered.

One's esteem for shark fin soup may be enhanced simply by reading what's involved in its preparation. It's boiled twice for a total of two hours and then usually cooked four more times with chicken meat and stock, mushrooms, ham, green onions, ginger, parsley, wine, soy sauce, peanut oil and so on. One of the most expensive and prestigious of all soups, guests seldom decline a second serving.

Apprehensive initiates into the delights of exotic Chinese cooking are sometimes hoodwinked into believing bird nest soup is actually made with translucent noodles. The fact is, the high-protein, clean little nests are fashioned from solidified saliva of cuddly cave-nesting Collocalia swifts. This is the only type of nest used for this purpose and the harvesting at nesting sites has raised ecological concerns. Believing it to be noodle soup, newcomers invariably are delighted with its subtle flavor and texture. For the record, it isn't the simmering of twigs, feathers and other funny stuff Westerners imagine it to be. Though available in a fairly wide price range, top quality, sparkling-white, cookie-sized nests sell for about US$100. That would make enough soup for four people.

Rather than being apprehensive, foreigners would be better advised to hope they are deemed worthy of the less pedestrian local specialties. The appearance of an unusual and/or exotic dish may suggest you're on the way toward acceptance.

If you can graciously handle something like a dollop of fresh snake bile in your drink and relate to their appreciation of it, you've made a good start toward developing a better understanding of the culture. It's an important part of becoming an insider.

Perseverance makes all things easy

Chop Suey Facts and Fables

Beyond Chop, Mix and Fix

CANTONESE FRIENDS, returning to Hong Kong from a trip to the US enthused, "In America now you can get fresh exotic produce and other foods for proper Chinese dishes. And you can get all the right spices and herbs." A happy turn of events but unlikely to dampen America's enthusiasm for our old familiar favorite, chop suey. Like fortune cookies and Chinese-American food in general, chop suey has become a staple of the Great-American-Melting-Pot menu. It has become common knowledge in America that this dish is "not really" Chinese. But, as with so many things we think we know about China, it's time we unlearned that also. The Chinese invented chop suey in the first place and then reinvented it in the United States when they got here and found we didn't have it.

According to one popular account, chop suey was created by a Chinese diplomat and his aide as a bland, somewhat familiar dish to relieve an overdose of American banqueting during a visit to the United States in the 1880s. There's another version which credits its creation to a Chinese houseboy in early San Francisco. When his employer returned home late with friends and asked for Chinese food, the houseboy whipped up something which delighted everyone. Asked what it was, the houseboy replied, *"Chop suey."* And what was the translation of that? "Leftovers," he replied. A Chinese version of this late-snack scenario casts a Ching dynasty official and his cook as the principal players.

The least plausible but most engaging version I've heard so far was related by someone from the American Midwest who was taught in high school that chop suey was created by Chinese cooks as a mock Irish stew for laborers on the transcontinental railway. The stories are as fanciful and varied as the dish itself.

While it can convey the idea of leftovers, the name chop suey is an approximation of the Chinese words for "chopped mixed." Although the pronunciation varies in different regions, it comes-out essentially as *za hui.*

In Cantonese, the dialect of the early immigrants, the phrase is *tsaap ooi.* The dish has a number of hash-house variations which are popular around China. They go by different names, depending on the region, and provide students and laborers with an inexpensive fast food.

Chop suey can be almost any dish which is chopped and mixed. Fried rice is a type of *za hui.* The same goes for chow mein, which they call *chao mian,* meaning fried noodles. Some American cookbooks have the same basic recipe for both dishes, with the choice of rice or noodles determining whether it ends up as chop suey or chow mein. In recent years, the genius of American marketing has given us a chow mein "*without* noodles." With that concept established in our creative merchandising system, we have since seen the introduction of chow mein "*with* noodles."

A Cantonese friend, returning from a trip to Los Angeles, told of ordering chow mein at a Chinese restaurant and being served a sort of summer-camp hash in a sauce with neither noodles nor rice.

"Hey!" she said to the waiter in their mutual South China dialect, "You call this chow mein?"

"No," the waiter responded innocently. "*Americans* call it chow mein."

Her father, who operates a restaurant in Honolulu, confided, "Chop suey is the one dish no customer can complain about because nobody knows what it is supposed to be."

Chinese-Canadian friends tell me when they order chop suey in Vancouver they specify that it be "Chinese-style." In the mid-1980s, the dish began appearing on menus in a few international restaurants in Hong Kong. A Chinese here, before ordering that, would be inclined to ask, "What kind of 'chop?'" For the adventuresome international gourmet, Hong Kong now has come up with chop suey soup and chop suey noodle soup.

The *English-Chinese Dictionary of Food Industry*, published by China's Ministry of Light Industry, defines chop suey simply as: "fried, mixed chopped," and notes it's "a famous dish in American-Chinese restaurants with the name being a direct translation from the Chinese."

Its naturalization process began in the gold fields and railroad construction camps of the early American West, as Chinese laborers—not chefs—tried to imitate home cooking with the limited materials at hand. They were creative. A few years ago in the mountains of Idaho, an abandoned rice terrace was discovered, a leftover from the days Chinese miners combed the back country. Anyone who has attempted Chinese cooking without such essentials as ginger, sesame oil or coriander can appreciate the problems these pioneers faced. That's like preparing an egg sauce and not having any eggs. So you fake it with cream, a little oil and food coloring or whatever is handy. But you can tell it isn't really Hollandaise.

While gold fields played out and the work gangs disbanded, little out-of-the-way chop suey joints survived, eventually to become an integral part of the American scene. Ethnic restaurateurs have introduced the dish around the world. In South America you're apt to encounter it on the menu in such form as *carne de vaca en chop suey*, with the rice served separately.

Etymologists note that the first recorded appearance of "chop suey" in America occurred in 1888, roughly two decades after work was completed on America's first transcontinental rail line.

American chop suey is a curiosity to visiting Chinese partly because it is not typical of their better cuisine to sauce-up a rice dish. As it's prepared in the Orient, *za hui* is generally a vegetable and meat or poultry dish, without rice as part of the mix. Of the thousands of Chinese meals I've had in Asia, I don't recall any rice dish served in this manner, except for the spicy shrimp which is poured sizzling hot over crisp chunks of fried rice.

It is something of a taboo to spoon the wonderful sauces which remain on a serving dish after the food is consumed onto your rice. Savoring leftovers this way is not generally done when eating out, although it's common when eating with friends or family in relaxed circumstances. This might suggest that the servings are inadequate or that you don't get enough to eat at home.

Unless eating in fairly formal circumstances, I usually spoon the sauces over my rice anyway, whether I'm hosting or a guest. Always, the Chinese (who have been politely holding back) do the same, just as they do in the privacy of their home. Thus garnished, the rice becomes a do-it-yourself chop suey in the best tradition of the cardboard-container-carrying-Chinese-chow-crowd in the United States.

What the heck. Regardless of its form or presentation, properly prepared carry-out Chinese-American food is fast, convenient, versatile, nutritious, economical, portable and flavorful. About the only way to enhance it would be to change the packaging to an edible container, like a spring roll or a Peking duck wrapper. While American takeaway Chinese chow isn't quite what you'd find in China, it's a successful blend of East and West that still retains some national identity.

Chinese who have not spent much time abroad truly believe their cuisine is simply the best in the world and the rest of us eat what we do because we have no choice.

Delegations I've taken to the United States from the PRC prefer to go to Chinese restaurants, even if it's a matter of eating our chop suey. Sightseeing with a group in New York City one weekend, I lured them to a sidewalk hot dog stand with: "Let's try one of these."

"What is it?" one asked, as the others suddenly took an intense interest in the architecture at the higher levels of the tallest buildings.

"It's an American fast food that might be good in China."

They weren't hungry. I bought a kraut dog, munched away, and egged them on.

"See, it's a little loaf of bread like in China. There's mustard, sauerkraut and processed meat. You invented all that stuff. And these are onions, like yours."

One of them agreed to give it a try. On his first bite he nodded and asked, "What do you call it?"

"Hot dog," I said.

"Dog?"

"We just call it that. It's made from beef or pork. Sometimes chicken or even turkey."

He thought that over and between bites muttered, "Americans are strange . . . you don't eat dog . . . but you call this 'hot dog' and it's maybe turkey."

At that, overwhelmed with curiosity, everyone decided to try one. Having endured that American ritual, we headed off to Chinatown for more civilized fare. That evening, the subject drifted to food preferences and someone mentioned that in the north, live baby mice are sometimes eaten as a tonic. They shook their heads and wrinkled their noses. I pointed out that they relish snakes, owls, sparrows and lizards. Their response was, that's all good stuff. But eating a live baby mouse is . . . "really strange."

After the first four or five yards of snake and eel I haven't really come across a lot of edible exotica which I would rate as strange, much less *really* strange. That classification I would reserve for an item I found in an American recipe book, which seems the most unlikely marriage of Chinese-American cookery imaginable. This was a ground round steak concoction known as hamburger chop suey. Holy smoke. Even Ronald McDonald would probably agree that's carrying things too far.

I recall with some bemusement what I considered Chinese cuisine in San Francisco in the early 1940s. In those heady days before Pearl Harbor the city basked in a cozy rainbow glow all its own. I knew hardly anyone who had been to New York. The trip, after all, took nearly a week by train. That was about the same amount of time it took Pan Am's China Clipper to island hop to Hong Kong. Street cars from an earlier era clanged and swaggered casually down to the end of Market Street where a fleet of ferries bobbed patiently, waiting to ease unhurried travelers to distant points across the bay. The Powell Street cable car was then a vital part of the city's public transit system, rather than the amusement ride it is today for tourists headed for Fisherman's Wharf. Cabs went anywhere in the city for a dollar. San Francisco was smaller then. Dollars were bigger.

In those days one the city's more popular Chinese restaurants was not in Chinatown. It was situated a few blocks south. Gaudy and crimson and with an all-Chinese staff, the place seemed to ooze authenticity.

Drinks were topped with colorful little paper parasols. I was sure this was exactly how it was done in China. Later I would find this wasn't how it was done at all. It wasn't until the mid-1980s, shortly after the entry of new Western-managed international hotels into China, that I began to see these little party-favor parasols on drinks and fancy ice cream dishes. These new hotels are spiffy images of their comfy counterparts in the outside world, with the little umbrellas serving as token reminders to tourists that they are having an international experience.

"Honey, are we in the Paris Hilton?"

"No dear, see the little Chinese umbrella stuck in your maraschino cherry? This is the Shanghai Hilton."

My chagrin was further compounded in later years on discovering there were no fortune cookies in China. A meal is concluded with fruit, a sweet soup or perhaps pastries. While their origin is unclear, it seems they appeared first in America. One account has them springing from the imagination of a Japanese entrepreneur. Another suggests Cantonese laborers in the early West baked encouraging little notes inside cakes in hopes of enhancing their luck in this strange land far from their native fortune tellers. Whatever their genealogy, fortune cookies' tap roots are snugly seated in Chinese history. In overthrowing the Yuan dynasty, Ming revolutionaries communicated with messages hidden in moon cakes.

In my early encounters with what I took to be Chinese cuisine I invariably ordered a somewhat Cantonesque almond chicken. This was chopped chicken breast and celery, awash in a light sauce, laced with almonds, bean sprouts and various unidentified floating objects. While it looked authentic enough, nowhere in China have I ever come across anything quite like this Chinese-American dish. It appears in some American cookbooks, but it isn't in any of my dozen-plus Chinese recipe books. A major ingredient was celery. But unlike the bulky "Western" celery, Chinese celery is spindly, pungent, and used sparingly. Suspecting China doesn't have almonds either, I starting asking around and after accumulating conflicting responses was finally able to establish that China produces large edible apricot pits which pass for almonds. Finally, in Singapore's Dragon Palace Restaurant, with friends from Beijing, Anhui, Shandong and Hubei, almond chicken caught my eye on the menu. None of the Chinese had ever heard of it before, even in the menu's Chinese-language version "apricot kernel chicken." Ordering it out of curiosity, it turned out to be rather dry deep-fried chunks of chicken. Nothing at all like the old San Francisco standby.

It isn't surprising that Chinese visiting the United States are invariably surprised in their early encounters with local "Chinese" food. The typical lament is, "I rarely saw anything on a menu I recognized." Indeed. The gummy pork noodles in Chinatown during my teens were (literally) oceans apart from such authentic delights as duck going to see the Emperor, Buddha jumps over the wall, ants up the tree, make money fungus, happy family stew, or nine jewels. In the northern city of Harbin, local favorites are moose snout and bear paw. Comfortable with that sort of thing, imagine the dismay of Chinese visitors when they see on an American menu—scrod, battered mushrooms, fish fingers or frogmore stew. And what might one tell them if they ask, "What are 'bacon scritchings'?"

Jovial Wang Shu Wei, Director of the Shanghai Food Bureau, told me, "The trouble with Chinese food in America is the same thing that's wrong with American food in China." Anywhere outside China, the authenticity of cuisine in a Chinese restaurant can be judged by the number of dishes on the menu you've never heard of. If you come across something called "strange flavored chicken," you've likely stumbled onto a place you'll want to tell your friends about.

True Chinese cuisine is so varied, on the banquet circuit in China at every meal you'll have at least one thing prepared in a way you've never seen before. At these functions an announcement often accompanies each dish to explain what it is.

One of the major differences between Chinese and Chinese-American food is with the latter you *do* seem to be hungry again an hour after eating. That's not the case with authentic dishes, which rely less on water and sauce. Although real Chinese cuisine sticks to your ribs, the Chinese do consume an inordinate amount of food at a single sitting.

With the immigration of Chinese just prior to, and during, World War II, some American cities experienced a more authentic Chinese restaurant fare. But the difference between Chinese and Chinese-American cooking did not become obvious until the influx of outstanding chefs born and trained in China following the thaw in relations between Beijing and Washington.

Without doubt, the best place for Chinese food in the United States is the Embassy of the People's Republic of China in Washington, DC. If they opened a carry-out counter in the lobby and sold dumplings, onion cakes, and steamed barbecued pork buns, they'd have one of the hottest takeout businesses east or west of Beijing.

Along with the fortunate upswing in authentic eateries in recent years, our supermarkets, even in small towns, began stocking a variety of fresh and processed Chinese foods, as Americans began to unravel the mysteries of this classic cuisine at home. Additionally, with the ongoing influx of Asians into America, small well-stocked Oriental provisions stores have mushroomed across the country, stocking such previously unknown delights as fresh lemon grass.

For the uninitiated, true international culinary excursions may sometimes prove more shocking than delightful, so it's well to be prepared to try to be a good sport about it if that happens. At a fancy "do" with PRC Embassy people in Washington, DC, halfway through a course, an American lady at our table asked, "What's in this wonderful soup?"

"Fish lips," the host replied.

She blanched, blinked and put her spoon down. I figured she probably wouldn't much care for fish bladder soup either. . . .

Then there's the sweet dessert which I ordered for lunch with an American associate who was visiting Hong Kong.

"Ah! Thousand fish-eye soup!" I exclaimed as the greenish concoction, thick with tiny, bobbing, translucent spheres, was placed before us.

Walking back to the office he ventured, "I really don't know how you could do that."

"Do what?"

"Eat fish-eyes."

"It's just gastronomic license. That was chilled honey dew melon and tapioca. It's ambrosia in a bowl." In my enthusiastic assault on it I'd failed to notice he hadn't touched his.

Confucius had it right:

Don't take eating too seriously

How to Read Chopsticks

Chinese Do . . . So Should You

CHOPSTICKS ARE ONE OF THE OLDEST, most functional and widely-used creations of the human race. A model of simplicity, they are at the same time the ultimate in functionality. Whether fashioned from silver, ivory, wood or plastic, they're just a pair of sticks of equal length. They're one of the most simple, practical and enduring of all creations of the human mind. Chopsticks have been traced back to the Western Han dynasty, about 200 BC, and they remain the same today.

Because of their shape, as a gift they symbolize straightforwardness. Presented to a bride they carry the wish for the early arrival of a son. The words for "chopsticks" and "soon son" are pronounced the same.

In addition to being used at the table, they are deftly employed in the kitchen for mixing and stirring. Laid across the top of a pot they hold up the lid to prevent it from boiling over. A pair can also be used to pry tops off bottles. At the family table they serve as teaching aids, inflicting a rap on youngsters' heads when discipline is required. According to legends of imperial intrigue, a silver chopstick will change color in poisoned food.

Serving food bite-sized enhances the practicality of chopsticks, with the additional advantage that smaller pieces can accommodate more of the flavorful marinade. When fish or fowl are served whole, the food is cooked until easily broken up by the diners' chopsticks. Either way, the versatile chopsticks prevail.

Rudimentary as they are, chopsticks readily flabbergast visiting heads of state who politely give them a try on official visits to China. Photos of encounters between world leaders and chopsticks clearly reveal the chopsticks having the upper hand. High-level dignitaries are exempt from any expectation of proficiency. For the rest of us, it's a different matter.

The Chinese feel that using chopsticks is the correct way for cultured people to eat. Our wielding of a knife and fork approximates the way they butcher pigs. In China, food preparation is an ancient and subjective art form, classed by gourmets as one of the world's great cuisines. And, of course, the Chinese see it as simply the best (if not the only "real") food in the world.

Foreigners are probably unaware of what they reveal in the way they handle chopsticks. These implements become flashing little semaphore flags to others at the table. Proficiency and ease with them will give the Chinese cause to believe that you really do enjoy their food, and that perhaps you aren't just another Treaty Port Carpetbagger intent on making a fast buck who is just going through the social motions. In moving around China, the first meeting foreign visitors have with a new group is often at a lunch or dinner. In these initial get-togethers, long-lasting impressions are formed which can ease or impede the newcomer's progress—somewhat like those which attended the 1976 campaign visit of President Gerald Ford to Texas where, at a key function, he reportedly ate a tamale without removing the corn husk in which it was wrapped. William Broyes, Jr., writing in *U.S. News & World Report* on the "Tamales Principle of Politics," suggested Ford might have won Texas, and the Presidency, had he known how Texans eat tamales.

In somewhat the same spirit Chinese take note whether new-comers handle chopsticks skillfully, so-so, or in a stumblebum style. Someone at the table will invariably comment on the stranger's adeptness. Competence merits, "You handle chopsticks very well." Lesser dexterity will elicit, "You've learned to eat with chopsticks." Others never look up to see how the person is doing. They took note of that the moment the chopsticks were picked up.

If the host suspects a visitor's clumsiness might prove an embar-rassment or a threat to survival, he or she will offer silverware. It's common for an attendant to scurry over with a knife and fork for a Western guest when the meal begins, particularly in less-traveled places where locals are inclined to assume Westerners are unable to use proper utensils. It will warm up an encounter and draw chuckles if you smile and feigning ignorance ask, "What are these things used for?"

While the Chinese automatically draw inferences about a stranger from his or her handling of chopsticks, this isn't shown by anticipatory gawking and gaping. It's something which people who use chopsticks simply are aware of. And, in the case of a guest—particularly a foreign one—hosts pay close attention to how things are going.

Tapping out a little tune with chopsticks on a cup or bowl signals that, as well as having a musical bent, the visitor hasn't spent much time around Orientals. From that, the Chinese might infer that the stranger wouldn't be doing it now if it weren't strictly business or a social obligation.

On the question of whether it's proper to wipe your chopsticks when you're taken to a restaurant, the rule is, if it makes you feel better, do it. Chinese do it frequently and carry it further by wiping plates and glasses as well. Feel free to follow suit, after taking note whether it's a Five Star or a Falling Star restaurant. Never do it in the Great Hall of the People or in someone's home . . . unless *they* do.

If a chopstick falls on the floor, some Chinese let it lie and ask for another. Folklore suggests a dropped chopstick forebodes separation, prompting the superstitious to throw down the other stick to cancel the hex.

Bowing deeply to meet your chopsticks halfway over the plate with each bite—for fear of dropping food—reveals your inexperience. On the other hand, if you use chopsticks more or less as the Chinese do and don't stir food idly about your plate or peck tentatively at something you can't quite identify, your upbringing will be deemed not totally devoid of cultural considerations. It's one of the best possible ways to get a good start.

For a subtle *coup de theatre,* try to learn to pick up chopsticks the Chinese way. I've seen only a couple of Westerners do this. People who eat with chopsticks three times a day develop the knack of picking them up in one smooth sweeping motion, with the sticks in the proper position. Westerners fumble about, bring the other hand into play, then tap on the table or plate to improve their grip and align the tips.

The difference in style is due in part to the grip the Chinese use. We are taught to place one stick snugly into the crook between the thumb and first finger with the other stick teetering on the top of the thumb. That's why Westerners have to use the other hand, to secure this adjustment each time the chopsticks are picked up. Chinese who eat with chopsticks every day don't do it quite that way. That is, the bottom stick is sometimes an inch or more above the crook of the thumb. The top stick is generally held somewhat down from the tip of the thumb.

Chopsticks should be held with a gentle grip, like a fencing foil, and they can be set down just about any way you wish. They can be placed on the plate or you can lean them on the rim. They can be set down directly on the tablecloth or placed across the top of a bowl. Watch what the others do. A little porcelain rest may be provided alongside the plate, in which case use that.

For those who have never used chopsticks, but want to give it a try, basic lessons are included with the price of a meal in every Chinese restaurant in the world so we'll move along to some more advanced techniques.

Using chopsticks for soup probably wouldn't cross the mind of many who are unaccustomed to this gentle alien art. But it's common in the Orient, particularly in casual, informal gatherings. You hold your bowl with your thumb and any two fingers. This is the proper way to hold rice bowls, soup bowls and tea cups, rather than clenching them in your fist. Pick out the chicken, shrimp or other chunks with your chopsticks. If you prefer to leave the bowl on the table rather than lift it, that's fine. The soup is finished off with a small porcelain spoon or sipped from the bowl like tea.

Another useful application of chopsticks is as tearing implements. This is necessary when confronted by a beyond-bite-sized chunk of, say, chicken or pork. And it's much classier than holding one stick in each hand and sawing away in knife and fork fashion as foreigners sometimes do. Step One is to locate a part of the piece less sturdy than the rest. Step Two, press the tips firmly into the weak point and carefully exert pressure to separate the ends of the sticks, breaking the piece in two. Practice at home by breaking up a slice of bread on a flat plate. When that gets easy, try it with a piece of dry toast to hone your touch.

Develop a good command of this before attempting it in public. Improperly applied, you can loft chicken fat an amazing distance. Until you get the hang of it, a less hazardous method is to pin the food down with the chopsticks and work it apart with your little porcelain spoon. The basic idea, though, is to enjoy your meal so no one will mind if you simply pick up an oversized piece with your chopsticks and chomp away. To develop a comfortable utilitarian command of chopsticks, you can practice with virtually any food which is fairly firm and manageable. To mention a few—scalloped potatoes, green beans, macaroni, stew, fries, salad, bouillabaisse . . . whatever. It's a mistake to restrict practice sessions to Chinese restaurants.

To fine-tune your dexterity, put some shelled peanuts on a flat dish and see how fast you can move them one at a time to another dish. Our youngsters learned to use chopsticks by competing in these "peanut races." Shelled peanuts are quite often on the table before the food arrives. You can take some from the serving dish with your spoon, put them on your plate and eat them individually with chopsticks. You have to be fairly good with the sticks to do this, and the Chinese, noting that, will occasionally challenge you to a little competition. That is, laying two peanuts side-by-side and trying to pick them up together. It's not as difficult as it sounds. If you can lift three, the reactions are well worth the time spent practicing it.

One of the more difficult aspects of the field of chopstickology is how to get over the embarrassment of dropping something. We all occasionally return from a banquet with a lapel that could serve as a Rorschach test. Of course, proper concern should be expressed if you happen to squirt a gravied sea slug into your neighbor's lap. Ungainly slippery things such as sautéed hard-boiled quail eggs or button mushrooms require extra practice. Rather than foregoing the mushrooms altogether, get gravity on your side by slipping the sticks under them, held parallel and close together. Then lift slowly. This creates a cradle for the object you hope to get into your mouth before it launches into free flight. For practice try this with an unshelled walnut in a cereal bowl.

The porcelain spoon can be used as a safety net by positioning it under these slippery things as you move them onto your plate or into your mouth. Or, taking a more pedestrian approach, dispense with the sticks altogether and lift the item with the spoon.

Never just dip casually into a communal plate taking whatever fortune turns up at the end of your chopsticks. Casually reconnoiter your target before you go after it. It's not a question of finding the biggest or best piece. It's simply a matter of going for an item you can feel comfortable with. Probing and poking around in the bowl isn't done. Chinese youngsters who try to get away with that are likely to be asked if their next move will be to jump in and kick the food around until they find the piece they want.

Any time you can hear the clatter of chopsticks on plates at your table you've got a problem. It signals that things are dragging, and it's time for an injection of conversation or perhaps a toast. Almost any question about their culture is good for a spirited exchange of ten or fifteen minutes. The appearance at the table of the ubiquitous banquet dish of scallops affords an opportunity for a toast by asking how to say "scallops" in Chinese. Someone will respond with "*gan bei*"—which is pronounced the same as the phrase for "bottoms up"—and at that you lift your glass and say, "Excellent suggestion! *Gan bei!*" That's always good for a chuckle and helps to get the conversation underway again. Laughter is an essential ingredient at meals. Chinese say, "Before you talk seriously, you should first laugh together."

You'll be a hit if you learn to balance spinning crockery on chopsticks like the Shanghai Acrobatic Troupe. But if you don't have time for that, at least develop your dexterity to the point where you can feed yourself without leaving the table hungry, feeling awkward or poking yourself in the nose. It's guaranteed to bolster your all-important first impression.

As I was once admonished by a saucy fortune cookie:

Don't stick your chopstick through your own paper lantern

Chinese Mice Don't Eat Cheese

Learning Something New Every Day

IN THE EARLY DAYS of our wheat food promotion in Asia, the story was the same virtually everywhere. People didn't eat bread because it was terrible. The best that could be said for it was that it kept your hands clean when you ate a sandwich.

Except for what passable fare you might encounter at one of the few new international hotels, hamburgers throughout the Orient defied digestion. The common practice was to prepare them early in the morning (using ingredients of questionable parentage) and then let them stew through the day in a sunny display case until they took on a hard, oily inedibility, with the lettuce acquiring the texture of wet tissue. Asians quickly decided they didn't like hamburgers. They said they preferred rice, and I had to confess that in Asia, I'd rather eat rice too. Before long our industry was working closely with McDonald's to establish a beachhead in South Asia. Properly prepared and presented, hamburgers *had* to be a hit there. After all, a mix of relish, mustard and ketchup is about as close as you can get to sweet and sour sauce without using a Chinese recipe.

I wasn't surprised when Taiwan's *China Post* reported later, "When the first Big Mac was served in Taipei on January 28, 1984 few would have imagined that in less than three years, Taiwan would be transformed into a veritable fast-food jungle with over forty-two fast-food chains vying for the public's food dollar." Not only was it affording a more balanced diet to people who'd been eating as much as 300 pounds of rice a year, the new merchandising system (the article noted) introduced "quality control and sanitation procedures." Seven years later, I journeyed by train just across the border from Hong Kong to Shenzhen to participate in the opening of the first McDonald's outlet in the People's Republic of China. Marketing experts were awed to find the entire week's inventory sold out in less than three hours. Within weeks that McDonald's had become one of Shenzhen's top tourist attractions.

The acceptance of properly prepared and correctly marketed hamburgers illustrates how—by identifying a circumventible consumer attitude and working aggressively toward improved quality, wheat foods have become a staple in Asia's more developed countries. In urban centers like Hong Kong and Singapore, in stores and shops where food is prohibited, it is now common to see a sign with a line-drawing of a hamburger with a diagonal red slash across it. A decade ago people would have had trouble working out what the picture was supposed to represent.

In the early days of our marketing efforts, we ran a consumer study in Singapore and found Chinese there had only a vague idea of what foods are made with wheat. In Manila, I asked the five-year-old son of a Chinese friend if he knew what noodles were made from. "Worms!" he giggled. And that was the best guess he and his seven-year-old brother could come up with. (Today I find that less surprising than I did back in the 1960s, since a recent survey revealed that half of adult Americans don't know that white bread is made from wheat.)

In our early Asian efforts, by looking beyond what consumers thought they thought, it was possible to develop a multi-billion dollar annual market among an Asian clientele which, at the outset, wasn't at all interested in the product. In China for example, a decade after the opening of our market development program, wheat consumption doubled as better quality, more convenient and more varied wheat foods became available and purchases of US wheat were reaching a billion dollars a year.

If you work at it, it's possible to discover something new about China and the Chinese virtually every day. And this may come from the most unlikely quarter. Years ago in Taiwan I learned something from a mouse which had taken up residence in our home during one of the cold winters which the island experiences, despite its straddling the Tropic of Cancer.

As soon as we became aware of the furry intruder I bought a little wire mesh cage, which traps the mouse alive, and baited it with a piece of cheese. Several days later, with the Cheddar still untouched, a deliveryman noticed the arrangement and said sagely with the waggle of a finger, "Chinese mice not eat cheese."

While it's widely "understood" *Chinese* don't like cheese, it hadn't occurred to me the same might hold true for the mice. But the idea did have a ring of truth. If there was no cheese in the home, even a reasonably intelligent mouse might have trouble figuring out it was supposed to go into the cage to eat something it had never before encountered. There had to be a reason why our beady-eyed little boarder hadn't been enticed so far. Rather than having baited a trap it appeared all I was really doing was airing some cheese. I asked the deliveryman what a Chinese mouse might prefer. "Fish," he said confidently, "with soy sauce." I'd somehow never thought of a mouse eating fish or that one might prefer it with a dash of soy sauce. In fact, that's about the last thing I'd have thought of using. As he went out the door he added, "Mouse like little ginger on fish."

I replaced the cheese with a little leftover fish laced with a touch of soy and, of course, shredded ginger. Finding this more to his liking, our uninvited little freeloader was soon apprehended. It was an endorsement of the universal wisdom, "When in Rome do as the Romans do," which in its Chinese version is, "When visiting a village ask how the villagers do things."

There's another Taiwan mouse story which illustrates the importance of not taking anything for granted in Asia. My wife Charlene, who was vice-principal of the Taipei American Elementary School at the time, mentioned that a number of mice were being caught around her office. I asked if they were being caught alive and she confirmed they were. I suggested that might account for the good hunting, noting that followers of some Asian religions, on capturing a cobra in the house, for example, would be inclined to release it alive in the garden. Might the school possibly be dealing with only a couple of mice, which, following their capture, are liberated in the playground to return for another fish-and-ginger treat? "That has crossed my mind," she said. "I'm checking the mouse 'disposal squad' in the morning." She returned home the following day with a grand grin and a fresh story of enlightenment. The mice were, in fact, being effectively dispatched. The dispatcher was an alligator.

"A what?"

"An alligator," she replied. "They feed the mice to an alligator."

"Where?"

"In the motor pool."

"The school has an alligator in the *motor* pool?"

"My reaction exactly," my wife said firmly. "When I heard that, I marched right over there and said, 'I want to see the alligator.'"

"That's a great opening line. I bet it got their attention."

"Actually," she replied, "they were pretty casual. They asked, 'What alligator?' I described the function of the one I had in mind and they said, 'Oh! You mean *that* alligator.'" With that point cleared up, the motor pool crew showed her the large metal tank where the knobby creature was kept and explained it was only a temporary arrangement, as the alligator was actually collateral for a debt someone owed one of the crew. She advised them to find a new depository for the collateral and to come up with a less innovative but equally effective system for dispatching the mice. (It's imperative in Asia to have an inquiring mind and to ask questions . . . or you may discover too late that someone nearby is raising an alligator.)

*   *   *

The belief that Chinese don't care for cheese has been embraced by Chinese and Westerners alike, but it's not quite true. It's another one of those things where a little unlearning will get you nearer the truth. If you ask someone in China whether they "like cheese" you're virtually assured of a negative answer. Except for ice cream, dairy products have not been widely available or particularly popular in the past. In reality, Chinese aren't much inclined toward a "whiffy" Western cheese. But that shouldn't be surprising. After all, supermarkets in America carry relatively little of the smelly stuff in comparison to the mild varieties. But while Chinese seem confounded by those of us who relish a chunk of stuff which smells like a Ming dynasty camel saddle, a sniff of their own "stinky *doufu*" bean curd delivers an uppercut that would jolt the senses of a rhinoceros.

An example of their low tolerance for our smelly cheese involved a friend, who on arriving at his hotel in Beijing, discovered he'd picked up the wrong bag at the airport. His bag contained some particularly sniffy cheese which he was bringing to European friends, and when he phoned the airport to inquire about it he learned the bag was there in the customs office. He said he'd pick it up the next day, but the official response to that was, "No! You come pick it up *right now*." He did and he didn't have to open it for customs inspection.

But it doesn't necessarily follow that someone doesn't like cheese simply because they don't care for the smell of a particularly lusty one. In fact, the Chinese produce their own varieties. In Kunming, I purchased a white, very mild sheep cheese from a curbside vendor from the hill country. Just north of Macau I discovered a cheese-like fermented bean curd which, pressed into flat paper-thin wafers, is popular as a topping for rice porridge. Its refreshing zippy tang is on par with Europe's best. In a Mongolian yurt I've eaten a heavily sugared hard white cheese, and in the high country near the Russian border nomads provided a midday snack of local bread with chunks of hard sour-milk cheese. Anywhere in China that you find goats, yak or sheep you'll find cheese.

It was this question of Chinese and cheese which provided the unlikely catalyst for one of South Asia's recent outstanding business success stories. Up until the early 1970s, pizzas were available in only a few international hotels, and a couple of Italian restaurants scattered between Manila and Singapore. The patrons were mostly local or visiting foreign *aficionados*.

Pizza's lack of pizazz suggested either South Asians just didn't care for the product or there was a good market potential ready to be pursued. Suspecting the latter, Shakey's agreed to test the product in Taiwan in cooperation with our organization. The market study was to hinge largely on the reaction of passersby in downtown Taipei, who would be invited to sample pizza and evaluate it. If the test was a success, a vigorous marketing thrust would introduce pizza throughout the region.

One of the key questions in the initial draft of the survey asked people's reaction to the cheese topping. I warned that if respondents knew that the topping was melted cheese, they would say they didn't like it, which would "confirm" that South Asia lacked a market potential for pizza.

The question was rephrased, "How do you like the *sauce?*" The Chinese loved it and the first franchised pizza outlet opened in Taipei soon after. Pizza Hut estimated in 1991 that in Hong Kong alone, the pizza industry sold a total of 3.4 million pizzas annually, which adds up to more than 100 tons of cheese consumed with gusto.

By taking a closer look at what everyone had always said was true about the Chinese and cheese we found that it really wasn't correct after all. The new perspective launched a major food industry in Asia, creating thousands of jobs and bringing consumers pleasure, a new convenience, and a more balanced diet. The *South China Morning Post* noted sales of Western-style fast foods in Hong Kong are among the highest per-capita in the world today. Where a dozen years ago you had to know your way around to find a decent hamburger, consumption of them by Hong Kong's six million souls now is estimated to be in excess of 1.5 million per week.

In China never take anything at face value. As with the "fact" of Chinese not liking bread or cheese, remember, appearances can be deceptive.

That's why the Chinese say:

Don't adjust your shoes in a neighbor's melon patch

Where Luck Arrives Upside Down

Superstition Can Be Serious Business

F EW WESTERNERS DELVE very deeply into *feng shui,* the Chinese
pseudo-science which harbors some of the world's oldest and
most elusive superstitions. It has influenced Chinese thinking for
at least 3,000 years and was perhaps being practiced a millennium
or two before that.

From the earliest days, palaces and government residences were
aligned and built on its principles. The words translate literally as
"wind and water" which, in keeping with its ancient mystique,
reveals nothing whatsoever about its nature. Its mystery is enhanced
by the few, select masters of this supernatural fraternity who guard
its inner secrets well. Involving the misty business of geomancy and
iconography, it harbors the world's longest-held trade secrets.

While not a science, it touches upon aspects of architecture,
geology and astronomy. Basically, it is a steeped-in-superstition art
form, involving talismans, the earth and its elements, ancestors,
good fortune, ghosts, and warding off evil.

Feng shui was a dominant force in the countryside, villages, cities
and palaces of Old China. But it fell from favor in the land of its
origin at the mid-point of this century. With the establishment of
the People's Republic, officials denounced *feng shui* as primitive
superstition. It has continued to flourish, but Chinese government
policy rejects the idea that cutting a tunnel or a mine shaft through
a mountain might unleash evil forces on the neighborhood. A
peasant song of the 1950s serves notice on the supernatural with the
lyrical challenge, "Make way for me you hills and mountains, I'm
coming."

Despite official pronouncements, a poll by *The Peasants' Daily* in 1989 found that nine out of ten rural people are superstitious and sixty percent engage in "feudal" superstitious practices. (That suggests something more formidable than pulling the covers over your head to demobilize the Closet Monster, a ritual commonly invoked by our youngsters on dark stormy nights in our jungled neighborhood above Taipei.) Pollsters found superstitious practices are common among young and old alike, and most villagers routinely seek counsel from a medium on important matters. Keeping current on what's going on in the countryside, the government followed up the survey with a campaign to rid the country of "six sins," which included hocus-pocus practices related to astrology, palm reading and *feng shui*. If this sounds a bit exotic to Western readers, surveys in the US have found that forty-three percent of Americans believe in lucky numbers, twelve percent believe in lucky charms and one in four believes in ghosts.

Feng shui thrives as a fact of daily life just across the border in sophisticated Hong Kong. A typical news report read, "Disgruntled Yuen Long Ha Tsuen villagers will continue their bid to stop their *feng shui* being disturbed by land excavation work ... if their demands are not met." Villagers cited two sudden deaths, hospitalization of eighty-six wedding guests with food poisoning, and a serious traffic accident as part of a chain of incidents they attributed to the disruption of their previously placid *feng shui*.

The idea is, if a place has good *feng shui* the people there will have good luck. People don't have *feng shui*. Places have *feng shui*.

The power of *feng shui* is a major force in community matters. Residents of a Hong Kong satellite city won government approval for a project to preserve as parkland an area known for centuries as "Dragon's Heart" which is said to enjoy particularly favorable forces. The price tag was US$2 million.

*   *   *

The grip of superstition, historically, has been stronger in the south of China. Marco Polo noted its following when he visited the coastal area below the Yangtze. A city square, he recorded, would be filled with astrologers, which he called "magicians." Over the centuries, illusion has been employed by mystics, psychics, healers and other practitioners of what, to the unwary or uninitiated, may seem magical arts.

This is acknowledged by the practice of Chinese magicians who, early in their show, expose one of their tricks to the audience. That is, after doing a simple sleight-of-hand effect, a magician will repeat it slowly from a different angle so everyone can see how it's done. At that point, the reaction of the audience is more entertaining than the entertainer. They point and poke one another in their excitement in seeing that it was, after all, just a trick. Such audiences often are made up largely of unsophisticated country folk. On occasion, the Chinese press carries stories about some back-country "witch" who's been involved in hoodwinking and exploiting the local people with smoke-and-mirror "miracles." In showing audiences how one simple trick is performed, magicians demonstrate they are not involved in the old, out-of-favor, dark side of the occult.

Only on one occasion have I visited a fortune teller and that occurred in Bangkok in the early 1970s. Over my protests, an American diplomat—of all things—dragged me along with him to see this highly-reputed and allegedly mystic individual whose modest little home was in a bright green bamboo grove just outside the sprawling steamy city. That's what bothers me about fortune tellers. Why do they live in such seedy surroundings if they can foretell the future? I responded reluctantly to a few questions and the Enchanted One proceeded to thumb through dusty old books of prophecy. Finally looking up from the brittle, amber-hued volumes, he intoned in wide-eyed wonder that on such-and-such, not-too-distant date something would occur that would drastically alter the course of my life, forever. That got my attention. Would the change be for the good? He shuffled through more lore with much contemplation and cross-referencing and finally concluded it would be. As it turned out, he was absolutely right on both counts—that was the day I met Charlene. I haven't had the nerve to go back to a fortune teller since and I have been particularly firm in declining Chinese friends' offers to take me to see the Tell-You-When-You're-Going-To-Die man.

Fortune tellers can be found throughout China today. But the country's leaders no longer turn to *feng shui* masters for counsel on matters of state, as the old emperors did as a matter of course. If you know the neighborhood, it's possible in China today to find an unobtrusive, inexpensive fortune teller. But business isn't what it used to be.

Pu Yi, the Last Emperor of China, consulted oracles. In his autobiography, he writes of wondering "what place, what garment, or what food was propitious and what was unlucky." If he encountered a brick on the path, he'd pass it on the left if he felt that was luckier than passing it on the right. Of course, there's nothing new or unusual in leaders consulting soothsayers. In early 1988, American newspapers which daily offer their own horoscopes reported that Mrs. Reagan was consulting an astrologer and subsequently influencing the President's schedule.

*   *   *

The *China Daily* reported the arrest of four men in Shanghai who, accused of defrauding passersby, were summarily packed off to the provinces from which they came. They had been using little trained birds which select a tiny scroll bearing a prophecy for the customer. It's a sort of feathered fortune cookie, a cute entertainment, long practiced at market places, festivals and fairs in the old days. In the case of the four bird handlers in Shanghai, their entrepreneurship likely would have been viewed more favorably, had they not chosen to charge nearly three days' wages for a "prediction." If they'd asked only a few coins, their effort might have evolved into a lucrative and acceptable pursuit. With a little imagination, instead of being sent home, they could have developed a brisk trade, playing to foreign tourists in the lobbies of China's posh new international hotels. It wouldn't surprise me to see them there one of these days, after officials see the economic advantage of letting birds swap tiny slips of paper for tourists' dollar bills.

Fortune-telling birds are not really what *feng shui* is about. But the idea of seeking good omens for the future, is. In this sense, *feng shui* is somewhat similar to our brand of astrology. Both emerged out of the early mists of superstition, with overtones of the occult. They both deal with the idea that celestial forces influence individuals and it has been argued there's no hard scientific basis for either of them.

The Chinese zodiac operates somewhat on the same principles as the Western one. The creatures and some of the applications vary but the systems are essentially first cousins. Instead of a twelve-month cycle, theirs is twelve years. The signs, in sequence, are: the Rat, Ox, Tiger, Rabbit, Dragon, Snake, Horse, Sheep, Monkey, Rooster, Dog and Pig. While some of these creatures are held in low esteem in the West, all display positive characteristics in the Chinese view.

The Dragon and Tiger are generally considered the two most auspicious years to be born in, with other factors such as the date and time of birth and the configuration of one's facial features also being taken into account. Those born under the sign of the Snake are seen as wise and intense, while a Rat person is said to have charm and ambition. People in China today take notice of the sign under which a child is born but they no longer take the astrological implications seriously. So they say.

With the approach of the Year of the Dragon in 1988, newspapers reported a national effort to dissuade couples from trying to have a "Dragon baby," with the admonition "It does not necessarily bring extra intelligence to the child." The old belief is that those born under the Dragon sign will be blessed with good luck and power, as with Deng Xiaoping who was born in the Dragon year 1904.

While the Western Gregorian calendar is used throughout China, many people are not sure when their birthday falls under this system. Someone born on the 27th day of the seventh moon in the Rooster year 1945, would have to do some calculation to determine that this date corresponded to September second that year. With that established, the individual's birthday might thenceforth be observed on that date. On the other hand, someone who observes the lunar birthday, must check our calendar each year to see when the 27th day of the seventh moon occurs. As a matter of fact, it isn't uncommon for Chinese to celebrate on the Gregorian date, with the family perhaps having a gathering on the lunar date. Coupled with this is the old practice of observing the seventh day of the new year as Everybody's Birthday. People don't chalk up another year on their age with this one, but friends and family might get together for a little dinner.

Typically, Chinese don't dwell on this and we needn't either, but it is part of the cultural package. And it's good to know such things if you spend much time around them. You can miss an important Chinese birthday party by forgetting to take the calendar variation into account. By going on last year's date you could miss the party by weeks.

While it appears that virtually every adult Chinese in Hong Kong has a serious grasp of the basics of *feng shui*, many turn to the professional counsel of the *feng shui* man when things get complicated, or for important matters, such as a wedding or investment.

One of Hong Kong's leading practitioners currently charges US$500 to upgrade the *feng shui* of an office. The consultation requires from two hours to half-a-day. It's not uncommon for Western businesspeople to avail themselves of the service. While skeptics say that *feng shui* holds no power, no one doubts the influence of the *feng shui* man. In strengthening the forces of good in a home or office, he may suggest rearranging furniture, moving a wall or door, or simply bringing in a bowl of fish. It's not essential that the Western client comprehend what this is all about, or have any faith in it. But heeding the advice serves to strengthen employee morale and work attitudes, which bear directly on business success. It illustrates how some elements of the mystic system are fully compatible with Western logic. When someone noted it's bad *feng shui* to build a house at the bottom of the hill, I asked why. He explained, "A boulder might roll down on it."

A Cantonese friend told me of an associate who was plagued by colds during the summer. The family doctor and traditional herb remedies had provided no relief so a *feng shui* man was called in. After looking over the office it was suggested that a "bad dragon line" ran from the air conditioner to the nearby sufferer's desk. By moving the desk away from the air conditioner the problem was resolved.

A Westerner might use a different logic to make the same prescription.

*   *   *

Even long-time Western residents in the Orient, unless they've devoted some study to it, are apt to miss the many implications and applications of this murky mix of superstition and common sense. It's likely that nearly every building of consequence in Hong Kong has been situated and built with the principles of *feng shui* in mind. A major contemporary example is the Hongkong and Shanghai Banking Corporation, one of the community's most powerful institutions. The company made architectural history with the opening of its forty-five-story high-tech building in Hong Kong's central business district. The structure has been acclaimed by architects as "one of the most bold and innovative buildings ever seen;" the architectural "achievement of the 20th Century." (Never mind that its detractors say it looks like the back of a refrigerator.) With a project cost of some one billion US dollars, it is quite a building. In terms of *feng shui* vibrations, the site on which it stands is considered one of the best in all of Hong Kong.

Architect Norman Foster of London, in the initial planning of this remarkable structure, made a visit to *feng shui* expert Koo Pak-ling in the New Territories north of Hong Kong. According to the newspapers, Foster said Koo "did, in actual fact, produce the first sketch on the scheme."

Feng shui also entered into the final phases of the project when a geomancer was called upon to help direct the placement of two massive bronze lions which had originally been installed at the entrance of the old bank building in 1935. Propitious siting of the lions was considered vital to ensure the company's future success.

An aesthetic touch which is difficult to miss is the spacious open atrium where the first four floors of this building should be. Less apparent to the foreigner is the fact that forlorn "four" is considered the most unlucky of all numbers as it sounds like the word for "death." Although this sort of superstition has fallen from favor on the mainland, in predominantly Chinese areas elsewhere in Asia, buildings and hotels often have floors numbered in the sequence of one, two, three, five. It's similar to the Western attitude toward the number thirteen. Although I've seen no evidence of it in continental China itself, it would be an audacious hospital in Hong Kong or Taipei which would presume to have a "death" floor between the third and fifth story.

Not long after the opening of the Hongkong and Shanghai Bank, work began nearby on the seventy-story Bank of China. The bank's opening was targeted for August 8, 1988. The numerical sequence 8/8/88, occurring only once a century, symbolizes money/money/money-money to the Cantonese because the word for "8" also implies "to generate wealth." The building caused a *feng shui* clamor, with *feng shui* experts saying, "the sharp angles of the tower are like dangerous daggers pointed at businesses and homes in the area." The press further reported, "a willow tree was planted in the garden of the official residence of the Governor of Hong Kong to counteract the bank's alleged evil influence."

*　*　*

Since the 1960s, license plates in Hong Kong which are considered to bear fortuitous numbers have been auctioned for charity at the beginning of the new year. In a recent auction, the most coveted plate of all, number eight, commanded a record price of US$640,000. The lucky bidder was firm in the conviction, "Whatever it cost, I would have paid." He said he wasn't sure which of his eight cars would get the lucky plate.

Singapore exemplifies Asian state-of-the-art sophistication, yet, behind the beaded curtains and wisps of joss stick smoke, cauldrons of *feng shui* simmer briskly. Singapore's Hyatt Hotel is a classic modern example of the influence of superstition on architecture. On the advice of a geomancer, the fountain in front of the hotel was relocated and, it's said, if the water spout is maintained at a certain height, it will ensure prosperity. On entering the hotel, foreigners are likely to be only vaguely aware that the front doors are set at a slight angle from the front of the building. The hotel lobby was originally designed with the cashier's desk directly in line with the front of the building, violating a basic rule of *feng shui*. It's believed that such placement would cause the firm's money to "go out," which is the reason the doors were set askew.

While Westerners tend to have a desk facing the door in order to be better positioned to greet visitors, Chinese who court good fortune are disinclined to do this, simply because of *feng shui*. I saw this demonstrated some years ago in Taiwan. With the departure of an American executive, the position was filled by a local staff member. The first thing the new man did was move the desk so it faced away from the door. Coincidentally, this change positioned his chair in such a way that it afforded a view of the entire outer office. From the perspective of Western management, this appears a sound move, enabling the executive to monitor at a glance what's going on. But I knew the local replacement and I knew that moving his desk was purely a matter of *feng shui*. The happy fact that it just happened to be good administration was a bonus. It wasn't supervision. It was superstition. And it illustrates how easy it is for foreigners to misinterpret what's going on, even when it comes to moving a desk across a room.

A visitor to Taiwan may carry home fascinating stories and photos of a visit to a "Chinese temple" without being aware of the curious and complex hodgepodge of faith, ancestor worship and superstition it represents. Daoism, the only religion to originate in China, is heavy in mysticism and secret ritual. Buddhism is an import from India, and Confucianism is a moral philosophy rather than a religion. All three are quite often jumbled together within a single temple. Indeed, the simple, brassy or gilded statue above the altar may be Buddha or the town deity. And while the inconspicuous little old woman in the shadows—vigorously shaking out semi-circular fortune-telling tiles—may appear to be a simple villager, she is perhaps seeking an auspicious date for her son to fly to London to preside over a board meeting.

*   *   *

To the Western eye, the most obvious piece of good-fortune paraphernalia is the *feng shui* mirror, a small round or hexagonal object which hangs over windows and doorways to deflect malevolent influences from the home or business.

There are a number of neighborhoods in Hong Kong where windows across from cemeteries or hospitals literally sparkle with these little warders-off-of-evil.

If someone puts one above an outside window, neighbors directly across the street often will respond with a mirror of their own, or perhaps a wok, establishing a sort of armed neutrality, in the *feng shui* sense. Mirror talismans have been used in other countries. The

Metropolitan Museum of Art catalog has offered reproductions of a Judaic "Talisman Plaque" from the Fifth Century AD which was the representation of the wall of a synagogue "with mirrors set in circular niches" which "were believed to distract and ward off the evil eye." It was a Middle Eastern version of the *feng shui* mirror, suggesting a Silk Road link. Dennis Leventhal, in his book, *Sino-Judaic Studies: Whence and Whither* states, "It is inconceivable that Jewish merchants did not join the endless line of camel caravans."

*   *   *

Nothing seems too small a consideration in the historic Chinese quest for good luck. Accustomed to cosmopolitan Hong Kong, I was mildly surprised to discover the lease on our apartment specifically prohibits our keeping "any insect" (whose chirping) "may or does cause annoyance to the landlord or the tenants or occupiers of the said building." Keeping a cricket in the home in a special cage, cared for as a pet, has long been considered good luck, although its dreaded cousin, the locust, has for centuries wreaked havoc upon China's crops. Wagering on cricket fights is no longer condoned but cricket-keeping today retains its popularity in many parts of the country. In spring and summer, cricket vendors ply their trade in the markets and byways. Crickets are sold on Hong Kong's Bird Street and Shanghai has a veritable Cricket Market not far from the riverfront. China's black field cricket, along with the larger green tree cricket, and the tiny "golden bell" cricket (smaller than a grain of rice) are undoubtedly the most popular pets in the country today.

At the Red Pepper, my favorite Sichuan restaurant in Hong Kong's flashy Causeway Bay district, they keep a tank of large goldfish just outside the rest rooms. On a counter near the kitchen door is a smaller bowl with little black mollies. I asked the waiter about it. He confirmed the *feng shui* man had prescribed the color, number and placement of the fish. The fish are a part of the company staffing pattern, doing their bit to help things along. On one occasion I noticed that the tank near the rest rooms was empty. It had been cleaned a few days before as the fish had contracted a fungus. That evening, without the fish on duty, one of the rest room doors somehow automatically locked and remained tightly closed through much of the evening while a waiter tried to find a key.

Pet fish figure heavily in both attracting good luck and warding off misfortune. The death of a *feng shui* fish is taken as a good omen. The idea is, in dying, the fish absorbs bad luck which otherwise would have befallen the owner. The popularity of fish tanks in shops and restaurants might cause foreigners to get the idea Chinese are the world's foremost fish fanciers. Maybe they are, but there's more to it than that. The undulations of the fish suggest the movements of the dragon, the most powerful and favorable of all *feng shui* figures. This symbolism, continuing day and night in the movement of the fish, is believed to bring particularly good luck. Schools of little black fish, particularly mollies, or larger colorful ones, are favored. The *feng shui* rule is, at least one fish for every member of the household—or the business staff—so everyone is covered. Often, there will be nine fish, symbolizing, "long time good fortune." You will see these good luck nine-fish tanks in hospitals run by Christian orders. Why not, if it sets the patient's mind at ease?

A Cantonese friend in Hong Kong suddenly acquired a bowl with nine fish for his office. When I asked, he said it was there to counteract the bad forces emanating from a high-rise under construction a few blocks away. Parting his drapes he pointed out how the design of the building created three sharp corners aimed at his window, an effect he described as a negative "cutting" influence. "The more distant that sort of thing is, the less problem. That building is too close for comfort," he explained. Also, just across the narrow street, he pointed out two recently-installed air conditioners jutting out like "clenched fists." He didn't much care for that either. They did appear ugly and angular on the smooth face of the building. Any significant alteration to the surroundings will most likely prompt local people to ponder the possible *feng shui* implications of the change. I asked if his keeping the drapes closed was a further consideration. No, he explained, that was done simply to counteract the disruptive influence caused by a young lady across the street who left her drapes open while dressing in the morning.

* * *

Toward the end of our eight-year stay in Taipei we witnessed an environmental change which had notable *feng shui* implications. The American School had experienced devastating floods every year during the typhoon season. This had not been a problem before, and it was generally conceded by school officials and the foreign community that it resulted from urbanization of the area. Before, the typhoon runoff—occasionally whipped along by winds of well over 100 miles an hour—had spread across the broad Tamshui flood plain. But now, thanks to the march of progress, slowly rising water could funnel straight through the school, twelve feet deep, leaving mud, debris and venomous snakes in its wake. However, if the subject came up in conversation with locals, they would note that the trouble started shortly after an old temple bell (salvaged from the ignominy of a junk heap) was installed in the school ground. Believers maintained that the old bell disturbed the spiritual equilibrium of the area. Temples have been associated with good *feng shui* since the earliest days, but some objects which were once in them—antique carvings for example—are said to bring bad luck if removed.

The reason red is the most popular color with Chinese is because it is considered the most beneficent of all colors. At Chinese New Year, red paper renditions of the character for "good fortune" are hung on, over, or alongside virtually every door. Particularly in the south, the signs are quite often hung upside down in the hope luck will run down into the home or business. The practice stems from the fact that the Chinese phrase "good luck arrives" is pronounced the same as "upside down good luck." I wear a jade ring with the character for "good luck" inscribed in the gold setting. At the insistence of Cantonese friends, I wear it so the top of the character points to my wrist. That is, it appears upside down to my view.

Positioning the character this way, they say, causes the good luck to flow toward me. Wearing it the other way, they say, would cause good luck to flow outward.

The concept isn't far removed from the Western practice of hanging a horseshoe over a cabin or barn door, with the points of the horseshoe aimed skyward, so the good luck "doesn't run out." Some Chinese do the same in Hong Kong with a horseshoe mounted, points up, on the grill of a car. Horse racing is Hong Kong's most popular sport and it's a safe bet that these car-mounted shoes are from a winning horse.

Officials in China today show little outward concern over any free, folksy, harmless traces of the old school of spooky stuff. Likely, in casual form, it always will be part of the diversity of this country, particularly in rural areas, where eighty percent of the people live. In the south today you still occasionally see a mirror over a window, or a floor god "altar" beside a doorway with joss sticks sending blue curls of smoke skyward. In Hong Kong, just across the border, countless windows and doorways are thus embellished.

After decades of official disfavor, the way fish are boned at the table in South China's coastal areas affords perhaps the most revealing vestige of the old ways. Fishermen the world over are a superstitious lot and among Chinese fisherfolk it's said that turning over a fish at the table foretells bad fortune, specifically the over-turning of a boat at sea. Dining with Chinese in the south, I have rarely seen a waiter turn a fish while de-boning it.

Despite all the hocus-pocus and preoccupation with good luck, it was one of their own sages who long ago observed:

Good luck befalls those who work hard

Getting the Great Wall Straight

History's Longest Political Statement

THE GREAT WALL IS THE LONGEST political statement in the history of the world. Estimates vary from something over 1,500 miles to just over 30,000 miles. As with many other things in China, a lot depends on how you look at it or who you ask. It isn't simply a reflection of the Chinese disinclination toward exactness. Nor does it fall into the category of being a state secret, as is the case with so many things here. No one is sure just how long the Great Wall really is.

The Great Wall is actually many walls, not the continuous, serpentine, stone presence it's generally presumed to be. A jumble of tangent sections and watchtowers run tributary to it. In some strategic places there are rows of walls. Many sections have been almost worn away by time and weather and some are so remote and ancient they are known only to a few experts.

Viewing the Great Wall simply as an engineering marvel, a Wonder of the World, or a Herculean defense system misses the point. It was, and is, much more. Had the Great Wall not been built, China and the Chinese today would be different. And, world history surely would have been played out along different lines.

The wall provided China an essential long-term cohesion, allowing them to follow their own course in relative peace, while keeping the barbarians at bay.

Set apart from the world on three sides by seas, jungles, deserts, steppes, and soaring snow-capped rock, the Great Wall brought down the lid on their geographic isolation. Thus ensconced, they got down to the business of peopling China's south, east and west. The north could be left to the barbarians, rather than to risk strengthening them through access to Chinese industry, skill and livestock. And, after all, the best farm land, weather, rainfall, and growing conditions lay south of the wall.

Had China's isolation been less thorough and had the Chinese been aware of what was going on in Egypt, Rome and Athens, it might have caused them to see the overall scheme of things somewhat differently. Had they been less complacent and more properly aware of political, technical and military developments in the West in the early 1800s it would have afforded them a more objective view of the world. Their introversion led them directly into the damaging decades which were to follow. The isolation mentality which the Great Wall nurtured contributed directly to the humiliating Treaty of Nanking of 1842 which, by Chinese definition, turned China into a foreign-dominated, semi-colonial and semi-feudal country. People throughout China, including those involved in negotiations with foreigners, know well the ramifications of the Treaty of Nanking and they harbor strong feelings about it. It is perhaps one of the reasons foreigners in China today tend to find things to fret about during and following contract negotiations.

The beginnings of what we know as the Great Wall go back to around 400 BC when a number of independent state walls of considerable length defined the political structure of northeast China. About half were located south of Beijing and were far from where the Great Wall stands today.

In unifying China, Emperor Qin launched a nine-year project in 217 BC to join and lengthen some of the walls into a more extensive single system. Although there had been earlier Great Walls, the Qin project is considered the first Great Wall of China.

About 100 years later, in the Han dynasty, the wall was thrust westward into Xinjiang Province, some 400 miles beyond where it ends today at Jiayuguan. At its westernmost point it penetrated the searing fringe of the deadly 600-mile-long Taklimakan desert. One of the most inhospitable places on earth, it is known as "The place no bird can fly across." Travelers, venturing west from here were advised: "Bid farewell to your friends here. Beyond are only a few strangers." Squinting into the afternoon sun across this gritty moonscape, early Chinese easily concluded the world ended some-where out there.

The magnitude of the Han project caused it to become known as the Second Great Wall. A Third Great Wall was undertaken during the Jin dynasty. This sixty-year project of restructuring and relocating was completed in 1198. The Mings undertook another refurbishing and relocating between 1368 and 1644. It is this—the fourth wall of its kind—which we know today.

The extension of the structure into the arid West during the Han era made it possible for that distant frontier to develop. This led to the establishment of overland trade routes, a network of trails which became known as the Silk Road. In remote Xinjiang Province, the Silk Road skirted north and south of the Taklimakan's deadly and seemingly endless sea of scorched sand. Today China's road system through the area still follows this ancient and circuitous detour, although with recent oil exploration, some service roads are prob-ing the bleak interior.

For centuries the Silk Road was the only link between East and West. It was the Silk Road, tucked snugly in the shadow of the wall, which made possible Marco Polo's journey to the court of the Great Khan at Shangdu, the fabled Xanadu of Coleridge's poem. Polo's account of his travels would later help inspire Columbus to try to reach China by sailing west.

Today, with modern military hardware suffering obsolescence almost before it is off the production line, it is difficult to imagine the wall serving for centuries as the most impregnable and extensive defense system in the world. It also represented the most advanced communications network.

Within hours its beacon towers could transmit messages hundreds of miles by relays of cannon fire or the light and smoke of wolf dung bonfires. (That innovative fuel was favored for its reputed thicker columns of smoke.) Outposts could alert headquarters, and even report the strength of approaching marauders or armies.

The wall also functioned as one of the earliest and most effective applications of the art of psychological warfare.

Imagine a scraggly troupe of sweaty bandits, astride hairy little ponies, pillaging happily across the countryside and suddenly reining up in awe in front of this King Kong of a wall. Drooling over the loot which surely lay on the other side, they follow it for weeks, seeking a point at which it might be breached. Instead, they are unable even to find a piece of high ground from which they might be able to see what is on the other side. Idle talk around the evening campfire finally and inevitably turns to the proposition: "Let's just go home and forget about this."

Though one of the most famous structures on earth, much of its history is hazy and we know less about it than we presume. The greatest inaccuracy is the goofy idea that it is visible from the moon. This was a shaky proposition even before American astronauts went up there and found the earth appears as "a big blue marble" with no detail at all. Different sections of the wall vary somewhat in size, but it is roughly about as wide as your average country road. Even the broad avenues of New York City are barely discernible in satellite photos from only 300 miles above the earth. Nevertheless, it *is* the largest single structure on earth and it can be seen from *space*. And though it isn't visible from the moon, it has been clearly established that it is possible to see the moon from the Great Wall. That should be good enough for anyone.

Another widely-held and erroneous presumption suggests the wall marked the country's northern boundary in the early days. Chinese historians scoff at the suggestion. China's influence had for centuries extended well beyond the wall, which simply follows terrain selected by strategists and engineers as the most suitable. Rather than serving as a national boundary, it was simply a demarcation between order and the wilderness. Another inaccuracy is the popular postcard image of a massive, gray, stone façade. Much of the wall, particularly in the western desert, was built of pounded earth, sand, reeds, straw mats and willows and much of this has simply weathered away. That's not surprising. Two hundred years ago an imperial edict declared there was no longer any military reason to keep the wall in repair. Most of the wall is in ruins today. The Chinese press reported "less than twenty percent" of the wall retains its original appearance in the Beijing area.

Long sections of the Great Wall have simply been torn down for building material for homes, pig pens and even toilets. While this dismays the government, it is difficult to protect a historical site which stretches clear across the country, often in seldom-seen places. Not long ago, six farmers were fined and ordered to return stone slates from the wall which they had appropriated to build courtyards. If that seems senseless vandalism, recall it's the sort of thing that's been going on around the world from earliest history, with Greco-Roman antiquities being converted to roads or shelter and Mayan icons being melted into gold ingots. Hong Kong's Kai Tak airport was extended by the Japanese during World War II with stone from the ancient wall around nearby Kowloon City.

In recent years the Chinese government has pursued an aggressive ongoing restoration program on the wall. Despite the lapse in maintenance over the past two centuries—a blink of the eye to the Chinese—there have been few periods in recorded history when they were not engaged in work on this or similar walls, a testimony to their tenacity and singleness of purpose, coupled with today's concerns for protecting historical sites and attracting tourist dollars.

The imposing stretch of the restored Great Wall near Beijing is perhaps the one thing in China which is exactly what the visitor expects it to be. As the world's premier tourist attraction, it annually lures millions of foreigners into the country, the very thing its builders wanted to discourage. To compound the irony, foreigners are now solicited for funds to help further restore and maintain it.

Visiting this wonder of the ancient world one may be too caught up with its majesty to give much thought to the miserable circumstances of the unfortunates who labored on it. These public works were not undertaken on balmy afternoons as community projects of the Lions Club or the local Jaycees. Conscripts, prisoners and garrison troops made-up construction gangs. Working on the wall was a duty, so harsh, in fact, it's said the Great Wall is the longest cemetery in the world. Many of those who died on the job were interred in the wall. Seventh Century records dealing with the building of one 300-mile section reveal there was one death for every three feet the wall advanced.

More than a notable and historic curiosity, the Great Wall stands as testimony to what you can if accomplish if you take things one step or one stone at a time. As intimidating as the thing seems, the fact that it's there (and there, and there, and there) impresses me less than the monumental audacity that was involved in getting the idea to build it in the first place.

It took equal audacity for Deng Xiaoping to declare in the 1980s that "Closed door isolationism . . . doesn't work." On that cue, the country hastened its modernization program, structuring and restructuring and introducing reforms faster than ever before. Foreigners who were regularly traveling in and out of the country began to find things a little different each time they returned. That was true even for those making the trip every few weeks. You'd begin to become aware of the longer hair and fewer high-heeled sandals on the young men. The young ladies began wearing frocks and lipstick and were doing something with their hair besides shearing it straight across the forehead and at lobe-length the rest of the way around. Youngsters started sporting bright colored clothes and, slowly, so did the grown-ups. Foreigners used to arrive in Beijing with no idea where they would be staying. It was not unusual to have to change hotels in mid-stay, or to double up in rooms. With the advent of the international hotels it is possible to direct dial around the world in a matter of seconds. In the early 1980s, getting such calls through often required a wait of six hours or more. And when you finally reached your party you usually had to shout to be heard.

In those pre-Internet days, sending a cable from one of the leading hotels required a substantial block of free time and a sense of humor. Typing skill helped also as even in the Beijing hotel you had to type your own telexes, which were sometimes sent to the wrong country. One evening after my telex had been dispatched I found I didn't have enough local currency to pay for it. They wouldn't accept credit cards and it wasn't permissible to have the bill charged to my hotel room. It was agreed I would go to the money exchange office in the lobby and convert Hong Kong dollars. One of the clerks was assigned to tag along to keep an eye on me while my companion, an Embassy official, was required to stay behind to serve as collateral.

The ensuing years have seen the country propelled headlong into the jowls of what Charlie Chaplin caricatured in *Modern Times*.

Those not closely and directly involved in it are likely to be aware of only its more obvious aspects, such as new buildings and traffic congestion. And yet, the Great Wall seduces strangers into the delusion of "the unchanging timelessness of China." Quaint conical straw hats and weathered old junks bob along here and there just as they always have. Across the country, vistas from the top of the Great Wall are still much the same as they appeared to garrison troops in ancient times. But a postcard view of the Great Wall, splashed with the reds of autumn, tends to obscure the fact that in the span of this century—particularly in the last half of it—China has endured more lunges and lurches of change than any other country in the history of the world.

But as new things appear, bringing change to China, they—in turn—are changed *by* China. Procedures, schedules, ideologies or whatever, all are subjected to this sinification. Nothing seems to escape. A subtle example which caught my eye involved the plastic hard hat which is worn at construction sites. When these first appeared here they met with some resistance from those who preferred the local version, fashioned from wicker. However, I recently saw a worker in Guangzhou wearing a modern hard hat, which he'd modified by snipping the crown out of his old straw work hat and draping the wide floppy brim over the top. It looked odd but it satisfied the new safety rules while retaining the comforting shade of the old hat. Chinese have long been masters of this art of dealing with (and shaping) change. And through the millennia, the wall has stood over them as a reminder of the immortality of the race and the individual's contribution to that. I don't know of anyone who looks at times past in quite the same light as the Chinese.

Lunching in Hong Kong with Chinese associates, the subject of Macau came up and I said something about its having been under Portuguese administration some 400 years. "Yes," they replied in unison in a tone which led me to suspect this might be a theme worth pursuing. Although 400 years seems a long time to me (about twice as long as my country has been in existence) I suggested that 400 years wasn't really a very long time. Their response was predictable. They agreed, 400 years isn't very long.

One day my assistant asked me about an elegant American-made lady's watch. "This has been in the family," she said. I noted she didn't add "a long time." She asked how old it might be. I guessed it to be perhaps sixty to eighty years old. "Oh, not so old," she said in much the same way a shop clerk will say, "This bowl is Qing dynasty. Not very old. Maybe 150 years only." It's this way of looking at things which enables Chinese leaders to set national goals which they hope will be attained perhaps twenty years from now. While they are projecting perfectly reasonable and realistic targets, it is not the sort of thing you are likely to hear from a Western incumbent who wishes to remain incumbent. Typically, a Chinese mother enrolling her youngster in kindergarten in an English-language school in Hong Kong is likely to have Harvard, rather than crayons, on her mind.

*   *   *

In trying to get a better understanding of China, it's important to remember, things are changing but the country will remain for some time a place of paradox, wavering somewhere between the China that is and the China that isn't. The most notable example of this is the Great Wall, which, designed to repel outsiders, now serves to attract them. Or more personally, trained to inflict upon the Chinese a variety of lethal infantry skills during the Korean War, I later worked for years throughout China on programs designed to modernize their food industry which is one of the most strategic elements in their arsenal of national interest. The transition isn't difficult if you have a little faith in the future.

It's well to try not to be surprised by anything that happens in China, but a few years ago I was a bit startled when someone at a welcoming banquet on Hainan Island inquired with a warm smile, "Didn't we meet in Korea?" That was the first time anyone in China had made any reference whatsoever to that business. We had a cordial chat on the subject and agreed it would have been nice for everyone concerned if General MacArthur had understood that

Chinese will always cross their borders to meet an oncoming army just as Americans are compelled to cross oceans to do it.

As our world grows smaller there is some indication we are starting to take history a bit more seriously and actually try to learn something from previous unpleasantness. The Chinese have always done that. If we can get better at doing it together we can perhaps— together—do a better job with whatever lies ahead.

It follows the old wisdom:

We sit in the shade of trees our parents planted

Anyone for Polo?

Marco's Neighbors Thought He Was Nuts

Marco Polo suffered a fate which commonly befalls Westerners who acquire a fair grasp of goings-on in China. That is, he was not taken altogether seriously back home. There is no trace of his grave in Venice. Professor Yang Zhijiu of Nanjing University has noted that there are no records of Marco Polo in Chinese historical books. But that is more likely a reflection of local attitudes toward transient foreigners than a question of whether Polo really did go to China. Scholars note his descriptions of the country and conditions have been "precisely confirmed."

Had he not been imprisoned by the Genoese, he might never have gotten around to writing about China, producing a work which eventually was accepted as a wonder of the literary world. While there are some 300 versions and translations of this record of his travels, the Chinese version didn't appear until 1913.

Shortly before his death when friends urged him to tone down some of his stories about China he grumbled, "I have not told the half of what I saw." Among the things Marco Polo didn't mention (which surely would have set the neighbors to twittering) include the Great Wall, tea, matches, Chinese ladies' bound feet, the wonders of Chinese art and the compass. He didn't mention the Silk Road either but that's because that term wasn't coined until a German geographer came up with it in the 19th Century.

The young Venetian was one of the most traveled people of his time but he was hardly a trail blazer. China's bleak and arid northwest frontier was known to foreign travelers fourteen centuries before Marco Polo learned the air is better if you stand upwind from a camel. Arab middlemen had established trade routes on China's south coast eight centuries before he passed that way on his trip home. Happily, Western historians have never suggested Polo "discovered" China (as they have done in the case of every other Westerner who stumbled into some out-of-the-way place which the locals had known about all along). Polo was shown the way to China by his father and uncle who had been there years before. While the journey was no small undertaking, involving some three years of travel each way, its significance lay in the fact that Polo was an observant storyteller whose experiences were enhanced through his tolerance for the unusual. (Tolerance for the unusual works equally well for the traveler in China today.)

The first merchant-adventurers who challenged these shores, steppes and deserts often had little more to go on than greed, favorable winds and perhaps a sketchy map which gave only a rough idea of what lay ahead. The fabled Silk Road was actually many roads and detours, much like the meandering Oregon Trail of the early American West. Historians still aren't sure of the location of all the Silk Road's byways. Scraps of old fabric and other trade goods are occasionally found in remote and barren spots, and reveal that there too was a forgotten stretch of the ancient route.

In addition to these lesser and lost byways, there was a little-known Southwest Silk Road, dating from about 100 BC, which ran from Chengdu south to Vietnam and then west through Burma and India. Another was a sea route to East Africa, opened by the navigator Zheng He in the Ming dynasty. He established this trade route nearly a century before Vasco de Gama found his way around the southern tip of Africa from Europe. Although Xian is generally considered the eastern terminus of the Silk Road, it ran all over the place, even south and east from Xian down into the area of present-day Hong Kong.

A clearer picture of East-West trade routes through better maps came slowly. Until some 300 years after Polo's travels, maps of the world still were based largely on the writings of the Greek geographer-astronomer Ptolemy who lived about AD 150. (Ptolemy's underestimation of the size of the oceans was what caused Columbus to think he'd reached the fringe of Asia.)

Two centuries before Polo's travels the Chinese etched a detailed stone map of their country outlining the coastline and major rivers in startling accuracy. It's been called the "most remarkable cartographic work of its age." Not until the early 18th Century did European maps of Asia finally begin to resemble today's maps of the Orient.

Polo was an uncommon individual but he had one thing in common with almost everyone who has ever come to China: a spirit of adventure. In many ways, the country today offers as many challenges and adventures as Marco Polo found. Its western plains, hills, mountains and dunes look as they did when Polo passed and he would recognize many of the tastes, sounds and smells which travelers today encounter along the more remote reaches of the old route.

Despite the challenges, travelers who take on China today find the going much easier than it was just a few years ago. Then, rooms in the better Beijing hotels looked like Chicago's low-rent district in the Roaring Twenties with rusted bathroom fittings and a single light bulb dangling from the center of a high, chipped plaster ceiling. Coming down in the morning to a spacious old hardwood-floored dining room to which clung an aura of pooped-out pride, you might find one or two other people among the dusty potted palms working silently through a breakfast which the menu asserted was toast and two fried eggs. (Except for the buffets at newer international ventures, hotels in China insist in providing *two* fried eggs no matter how firmly you insist you want only one. Hard boiled eggs—often duck—can be acquired singly, but not fried. A soft boiled egg, judiciously timed to three-minute tenderness, seems to be out of the question. The reason for this is quite simple. It's because that's the way it is.) Aside from the eggs, China's hotel industry has made impressive strides since the early 1980s. In the cities hardly anyone looks out the window anymore to see if the sun is shining before telling you when your laundry will be returned. The spiffy coffee shops are jammed with spiffy, scrubbed people who have just jetted in from some distant developed land where the coffee shops, outwardly, aren't all that different from what China now has to offer. It's becoming more international and comfortable all the time, to the consternation of old traditionalists who fear it makes China "less Chinese."

Anyone with the means and moxie should visit China, at least once. There are any number of ways to go about that.

There's that old *Slow Boat to China,* the ballad which was popular in America back in the days when couples snuggled on the dance floor and actually danced the same steps together. The mellow old refrain is more than just a romantic notion. With a spectacular coastline of over 14,000 miles, an approach by sea is ideal for an unhurried visitor.

With a full briefcase and some snacks, I've found coastal steamers a productive and relaxing way to travel. The really adventurous have found their way through icy Himalayan passes or along orchid-flecked jungle byways. Or, by camel through massive mounds of sand. From Hong Kong, you can approach up the Pearl River by hovercraft, hydrofoil, ferry or steamer. Then, there's the Trans-Siberian train from Europe. Travelers enthuse over that route. For most, the speedy, mundane comfort of a jet plane is the preferred and perhaps only practical choice.

China's borders touch Mongolia, Russia, Korea, Vietnam, Laos, Burma, India, Bhutan, Nepal, Pakistan, Afghanistan, Tajikistan, Kyrgyzstan and Kazakhstan. Then there's tiny Macau and China's Special Administrative Region of Hong Kong. The coastlines are washed by the tides of the South China Sea, East China Sea, and the Yellow Sea. Without even trying for variety I've entered China's mainland from ten directions by eight different modes of locomotion, including walking in from Hong Kong. That simply involves a train ride to the border and a short stroll across the bridge into Shenzhen.

Coming into China by way of Honolulu helps first-timers to realize they're a long way from home in more ways than one. Honolulu's palmed and plumeria-scented blend of East and West is ideal to ease the transition. Caucasians represent twenty-three percent of Hawaii's population. Japanese make up another twenty-three percent. Other Asians, Hawaiians and other Pacific island people make up just over eighteen percent, and about thirty percent are of mixed parentage. That Honolulu causes visitors to forget where they are is revealed by the question, "How much postage for a letter to America?" As evidence that the Japanese are not coming, but have in fact arrived, announcements at the airport for international westbound flights are generally made first in Japanese.

Today Hong Kong is my choice for the first-timer's next stop because it is the most internationally upbeat Chinese community in the world. The product of a Western system, tempered by its international exposure and the Chinese way of doing things, Hong Kong hurtled into the 1990s as a monument to the best that East and West can bring together. It's been called the most efficient city on the planet and the nucleus of Asia. The city has its own special brand of salve to help ease the transition of Westerners into the real world of the Orient. English is widely spoken and if you find your system needs a quick croissant, pizza or Swiss chocolate fix, they're within easy reach. Hong Kong is a lot like San Francisco, only zippier. And it's a little like several other great places around the world, only more frenzied. Craig Clayborne, America's premier gastronome, says Hong Kong is the greatest city in the world for food. Just a few days with the cuisine and routine of this former colonial base camp should condition the traveler nicely for the journey north.

For the first-timer, I recommend the air conditioned "soft seat" express train from Hong Kong to Guangzhou. ("Hard seat" trains are best avoided altogether.) To get to the train at Hong Kong's Hung Hom Station you must enter a corridor over which there is a large "No Entry" sign in both English and Chinese. It's a gentle reminder that where you're headed, things are not quite the same. This historic Hong Kong/Canton line is one of the more comfortable and interesting introductions to the country. From Hong Kong you also have the option of going up the Pearl on that slow boat, if you have the time for the overnight cruise to Guangzhou. The ferry is faster and equally comfortable.

Probably the least inspired visit on record involved a tourist who, some years ago, took the twenty-minute morning flight from Hong Kong to Guangzhou, rode a cab from the airport to a hotel for a sandwich and then took a cab to catch the mid-day train for the three-hour ride back to Hong Kong. He found China "absolutely fascinating" and couldn't wait to get home to share with his friends the thrill of his adventure. It's a style the Chinese call, "Looking at the flowers from a galloping horse."

Traveling on your own in China can be tricky and requires stamina, resilience, fortitude and cunning. A friend, stranded in the backcountry and unable to get a train ticket back to Hong Kong, wasn't even able to find out how long it might be before he might *get* a ticket. Accustomed to this sort of thing, he returned to his hotel, emptied his vitamin bottle down to two tablets and returned to the station and said that these were heart pills and if he didn't get to Hong Kong in two days he would die. Right there. At the ticket window. He was on the next train. The story illustrates that problems in China can be impossible to resolve unless you actually get someone's attention.

Travel can be made easier if you remember the following rules (which are well to keep in mind during foreign travel almost anywhere).

- If you forgot to leave it at home, be sure to drop off your impatience at the border.
- Daylight, non-stop flights, during seasons of moderate or good weather, are best. At the airport, always check to make sure the airline does not accidentally take the wrong ticket. It's hard to get anyone to fly you from Shanghai to San Francisco on a ticket which reads, "Beijing/Shanghai."

- Never carry anything through customs for a stranger. Never. In some Asian countries (where drugs are particularly frowned upon) the penalty for disregarding this advice can be death by hanging.

- Reconfirm flights two or three days before departure to lessen the likelihood of your reservation being canceled. In phoning the airport to confirm that your flight will depart on time (to save yourself the possibility of a several-hour wait in the departure lounge) remember that the answer you usually get will be the *scheduled* departure time. Always ask where the plane is *now*. If they can't tell you that, they have no idea when the plane will actually leave.

- If provided with a heated or chilled damp face cloth on boarding (or in a restaurant) do not rub your eyes with it as everyone else does. My doctor advises, "Don't rub it on *any* opening of your body that you can't put your elbow into."

- If possible, dress up, not down, to travel. Flying and foreign travel can be full of surprises and it's easier to get people to take an interest in your problem if you're dressed like you might possibly play golf with the head of the airline. As China's most noted modern writer, the late Lu Xun, wrote, "If your clothes are old, bus conductors may not stop when you ask them." A man with a tie is rarely much hassled by customs or immigration people and he virtually always will get a sympathetic ear from ticket agents and the like. A neat dimple in the material just below the knot tends to strengthen the illusion that here is a guy who did not just fall off a freight train. Ladies should dress in a manner appropriate for a hasty exit from the aircraft in the event of an emergency.

- Never put your passport, tickets, or anything else of value in the pocket on the back of the airline seat in front of you. Use that only for stuff you don't want to see again. Carry a photo copy of the page from your passport which has your photo, birthdate, passport issue date, etc. This will considerably hasten getting a new passport if the original is lost or stolen.

- Do something to your luggage to lessen the likelihood of its being mistaken for someone else's. Secure a colorful strap around it or tie a ribbon on the handle. Make it distinctive. My luggage went astray only once, and briefly. That was in Jakarta, when my things failed to appear on the carousel and turned up later on a great mountain of stuff which belonged to a touring ballet company. The red ribbon on the handle of my suitcase happened to match the ones on theirs. That's the only time the system failed me. Be wary of the suggestion to just pack a small bag for a side trip, leaving the rest of your luggage behind for a few days until your return. Savvy travelers don't get separated from their luggage.

- Don't discuss politics unless you happen to be the Ambassador or you can do it fluently in the local dialect.
- Put stamps on your post cards and letters yourself at the hotel or post office and drop them in the mail box yourself. Pocketing stamp money is a major international crime, and there is also the risk that the mail might get mislaid. The very first joint venture labor dispute to be arbitrated in Beijing occurred in early 1989 and involved two employees who were fired for failing to mail post cards "promptly" at one of the international hotels.
- Look both ways before crossing a street, and keep looking in each direction with each step while you're crossing. Foreigners are always considered to be at fault in traffic accidents.
- Always glance back in a taxi when you get out in case you've left something behind.
- Never pass by a bathroom unless you have a good idea of when you might pass another one and always carry some tissue or small denomination bills. The small bills will come in handy in small shops and stalls too, as these places always have trouble making change.
- Never sit or lean on a railing above a drop and always watch where you're going so you don't step off, or in, anything. Don't presume that a railing will support your weight. Unrailed drops and holes in streets and sidewalks are commonplace.
- If an elevator malfunctions in any way, take it as its way of saying it is about to do something funny. Get off and take another one. Or walk.

- In summer, keep a folding fan handy. In winter, carry a few sheets of newspaper and if you get stuck in a frosty railway station, spread them under your coat for added insulation. Too often, cold rooms lack heaters. Hot rooms too often lack air conditioning. Throughout much of Asia, if there is air conditioning available it is almost always cranked up to an almost unbearable chill, as if to make sure you notice they do have an air conditioning system.
- The Basic Rule is, when in doubt, don't.

* * *

Few visitors tour China without a stop in Beijing. But most sightsee only along the major thoroughfares and thus miss much. Taking just a few steps off a busy boulevard into one of the city's 3,000 narrow little *hutong* alleys is a magic carpet ride into another world, reflecting an atmosphere of old village tranquility. You hear the universal language of a baby crying, children playing, a wife scolding, old folks laughing. Despite the current swift pace of modernization, in Beijing's back lanes today there are willows, streams, flowers, vegetable patches, byways, vendors, chickens, cottage industries and toddlers. Chinese feel a closeness to the countryside and these inner-city enclaves are usually quite rural in nature. The high rises and busy streets which surround them seem rather like old village walls, setting these places apart from the outside. If you want to explore but have a bad sense of direction, carry along a card or something with your hotel's name on it in Chinese. Anyone will be happy to aim you in the right direction if you get turned around. It's surprising how many people in back lanes speak a little English these days. It would be impossible to remain lost for long. The Chinese simply wouldn't put up with it. Although they may give no hint, everyone takes note of a stranger's presence. Should you even *look* like you might be lost, that will be duly noted and you'll be hastily repatriated to familiar ground by the nearest local functionary . . . or a hastily assembled convoy of neighborhood children.

* * *

Be discreet in taking photographs. While it's gauche elsewhere in the world, it's downright impolite in China to take a picture of someone without first asking permission. Some tourists seem to think that people in foreign countries are employees of Disneyland who have put on costumes and are choreographed to entertain them. Before taking a picture of someone buying a fish, ask yourself if you'd like someone in a conical straw hat, pajamas and sandals to rush up to take a picture of you buying a fish in the supermarket. (Back home that could get you a mackerel across the side of the head.) Parents are usually happy to have you photograph their youngsters. Workers are generally pleased to be photographed at work, unless they're doing something particularly menial. If someone refuses outright, it likely means they are sick and tired of having foreigners take their picture. This is less a problem in rural areas than it is in the cities where the novelty long ago wore off. Never mind. There are a billion other Chinese to photograph.

Applied with discretion, an instant camera still works wonders. But a word of caution. If you take an instant photo of a group of youngsters, be sure to give it to the biggest kid. I made the mistake once of giving the picture to the smallest one and once I turned to leave, the biggest kid had acquired the photo and the little one had acquired a lump on the head. One of the most effective devices I've seen to loosen up the locals was employed by an American tourist of retirement age in Beijing's Forbidden City. While his wife listened intently to the tour guide, he stood to one side delighting Chinese youngsters by giving away penny balloons he blew up as people came by. He was a great hit with adults as well as youngsters and seemed to be getting much more out of the cultural experience of the Forbidden City than his wife was.

Village youngsters might take a little more coaxing to accept a free balloon. Foreigners generally don't get very deep into the backcountry so they are a bit of a curiosity, perhaps best viewed from a distance. Exploring rural byways in Taiwan by bike in the early 1970s, Charlene always caused quite a stir with the children because few had ever seen blond hair, except on witches or ghosts in films. On her approach, they would often high-tail it over the nearest hill in a cloud of dust. On trips to rural China now, if she pauses in a park or store, within moments she is ringed by a large curious crowd wanting a closer look at the yellow-haired lady. At out-of-the-way tourist spots the Chinese visitors seem as intrigued with her as they are with the local scenic or historical attraction, and they often ask if they can have their picture taken with her so they can prove to the folks back home what they saw. Exchanging backcountry stories with a Chinese-speaking Embassy friend recently, he told of being in a remote village market and hearing a child ask, "Mother, is that a man or a woman?" The reply was, "Neither, dear. That's a foreigner."

If you're ever curious about how you're perceived in a foreign situation, simply note how the children act and react around you. They pick up their attitudes from their folks at the dinner table. Some years ago in Beijing I glimpsed a child of about five who, as I passed, turned to a playmate and (with her fingers in a V) pulled her bottom eyelids down and pushed the tip of her nose upward with the first finger of the other hand. It was an eloquent portrayal of a round eyed Big Nose. That was the only time I ever saw this counterpart of Western kids pulling their eyelids sideways into ovals to parody Asian features.

All over China I've found having some command of the language gives a foreigner a Pied Piper appeal with the youngsters. On a recent weekend trip to a famous temple in out-of-the way Jiangxi Province, a few hundred village youngsters were trundling into awaiting buses when I struck up a chat with a couple of stragglers. Within seconds I was surrounded by the entire bouncing, babbling group whose enthusiasm made it clear they'd never seen a big nosed Foreign Devil up so close before. With as much composure as I could muster under the circumstances, and on their spirited squealed assurance that they did indeed know *The Two Tigers* song, I led them through a few vigorous choruses before waving them giddily on their way.

While we recognize that youngsters are pretty much the same everywhere, we tend to lose sight of the fact that grownups are too, once we get to know each other.

The opportunity to finally get to know the Chinese has been better the past few decades than at any time since Marco Polo.

Come to China and see for yourself because:

One look is better than hearing about it 100 times

The Far East Isn't Always

Where the Compass Points South

IMAGINE A SHANGHAI BARTENDER talking to his wife after a busy day at an international hotel.

"A 'martini'?" the wife asks.

"It's a cocktail, with vodka or gin."

"My goodness," she exclaims, "Didn't you say that stuff smells like the paste the herbalist put on your rash?'

"Exactly. And into this you pour sour wine."

"You're joking."

"Really. Then you add a twist of lemon or a green olive. Well, I accidentally used a cherry instead and the customer made a complete fool out of himself over it."

"The cherry must surely make it taste better. He should have been pleased."

There you have it again. The old law of nature—Bird look down. Fish look up. Frog look across.

A Chinese proverb advises how to resolve conflicts arising from such contradictory perspectives: "You can't explain the ocean to a frog." Or, as Americans say, "Don't go there."

Then we have those occasional historic viewpoints which are heavy with the potential for epic consequences. As in the case of Columbus, who was at odds with virtually everyone in his view that one could reach the Far East by sailing west. Ferdinand and Isabella, taken with his audacity, were willing to bankroll him to the tune of $US14,000 so he could go and see.

On his arrival in the Caribbean, Columbus sent men upriver to a native village, thinking it might be Beijing. Nearly fourteen years later—and after three return voyages—he died believing he had been on the fringe of China. Columbus was unaware of how far he was from the Orient because his notions about the size of the world and the Atlantic were badly distorted. He was wrong about where he was and when he got home he didn't understand where he'd been.

This "Columbus Syndrome" is commonly experienced by visitors and newcomers to China today. One example involves an American who spent a week filming a TV documentary in one of China's Special Economic Zones near the Hong Kong border. Developments in the Special Economic Zone were certainly impressive, surpassing what I saw in post-war Europe or Japan, but there's little to be learned about China from a short visit almost within sight of Hong Kong. Travelers who are cautious about drinking water and salads should be equally careful about the endemic Columbus Syndrome. A British businesswoman summed it up: "Just about everyone who comes into China the first few times on business discovers something they find frightfully illuminating which they think no one else knows. It's always something of little consequence which people who work in China knew all along."

While Westerners were "discovering" China, the converse has not been a particularly heavy preoccupation. In 1793, the sparkling and epaulet-ed arrival of the first brief British embassy to the Imperial court in Beijing pleased both the British and the Chinese, but for different reasons. The Chinese saw it as recognition that the most powerful bunch of barbarians on earth accepted the semi-divine status of Emperor Ch'ien-lung. A letter from King George III requesting a permanent envoy to the court, who could handle trade matters, was presented to the Emperor in a large diamond-encrusted gold box. The Emperor responded by taking note of England's "humble desire to partake of the benefits of our civiliza-tion" but brushed aside the proposal for a permanent envoy. The properly polite letter was couched in the same terms the Chinese used in communications with their tribute-bearing neighbors.

Historically, China's attention has been directed more toward the relationship between north and south, as evidenced by the Great Wall itself. Barbarians were in the north and, in more recent centuries, they were tolerated in the south at the water's edge.

Although the foreigners were typically pleased with their foothold and the prospects for trade, this was about as far away from Beijing as they could be sequestered.

Since ancient times, the south has held special significance. The Chinese appreciated the warm regenerative glow of sun and spring which comes from the south. The mausoleum of Mao Zedong stands at the southern end of Tiananmen Square in Beijing along the imperial processional way into the Forbidden City. Marco Polo noted the Great Khan's throne faced south, just as virtually every other throne and processional way I've seen in China. Beijing's imposing Temple of Heaven and its throne are laid out on the same alignment.

*　*　*

Where Americans might think of themselves in terms of the North American continent or the Western Hemisphere, Chinese tend to see things as either being inside or outside China.

The idea of "The Middle Kingdom" is quite literal. That's how *Zhong guo* (China) translates and Chinese maps invariably position China in the center.

On occasion you may hear a foreigner suggest there are negative overtones in the word for "foreigner" or "outside person." However, this "outsider" connotation is found in languages throughout the world, as in the German *der auslander,* which sounds ominous enough to be the title of a Wagnerian opera. Webster defines "foreigner" as "a person from another country, thought of as an outsider," which seems no more or less xenophobic than the Chinese equivalent, *waigwo ren.*

Other ideas, though, can lose much in the translation. After several years of assuming "the Far East" was perfectly clear to everyone, I began to suspect perhaps that wasn't the case. Chinese friends confirmed my suspicions. In China, the Far East is Japan, with Tokyo long having been known as the "Eastern Capital." From that perspective, Japanese are sometimes inclined to refer to

America's Northwestern states of Oregon, Washington and Idaho as "the Northeast."

Years ago at lunch in Taipei I said something about the Kipling quote: "East is East and West is West, and never the twain shall meet." They were unfamiliar with the quote (and Kipling), but I was making the point that a better understanding did seem to be developing between East and West. Despite their sense of exclusivity, there is an old Chinese adage which holds: "Under heaven, all men are brothers."

Kipling's "never the twain shall meet" continues to serve as a popular incantation among foreigners along the byways of the Orient. Even well-traveled, English-speaking Asians sometimes invoke them when a situation gets out of synch. A roll of the eyes and a shrug of the shoulders is sometimes added for emphasis. It's commonly reduced to the short form: "East is East, and West is West." The point foreigners seem to miss is that these encounters can be equally frustrating for the Asians involved, but they are less inclined to lose their composure.

Rudyard Kipling's sound bite from *The Ballad of East and West* has become a handy escape clause for those who want to avoid the effort of trying to understand what Asia and the Asians are all about. Kipling wouldn't have approved. The point of the poem is that East and West *do* come together in the friendship between the border thief, Kamal, and the Colonel's son.

Kipling is easily cloaked by his heavy mantle as the Old Colonial scribe. But, born in Bombay and speaking Hindustani before he spoke English, Kipling had a better grasp of the East than most Westerners, then or now. And, aside from his glorification of the British Empire, he did return from time to time to the theme of conciliation with:

"If you've 'eard the East a-callin', you won't never 'eed naught else. . . ." Or, "Ship me somewheres east of Suez. . . . [where] I've a neater, sweeter maiden in a cleaner, greener land!"

On the question of race, it was the Old Colonial who wrote: "You're a better man than I am, Gunga Din," and: "There are only two kinds of men, sar. The alive and the dead."

Kipling knew there was a great deal to be learned from the East and it is important to take the time to learn it.

The Bridge on the River Kwai was a great literary and film success, but many miss the point. Pierre Boulle, the author, lays it out in the very first sentence of the book: "The insuperable gap between East and West that exists in some eyes is perhaps nothing more than an optical illusion."

That idea still today is worth some serious thought as styles and skylines change. In the early 1980s, Beijing's building boom had not yet gotten underway. It was mostly a one-story city with little gray-tiled houses and shops tipping this way and that along its ancient streets. It looked as it had in photographs of nearly a century earlier. A few years later, the skyline became a forest of towering modern buildings. From my hotel room in the center of the city in the fall of 1988, I counted forty skyscrapers under construction to the north. The Singapore and Hong Kong of the 1960s have virtually disappeared, replaced by modern, gleaming cities.

Lifestyles are changing with the scenery. Skies are crisscrossed by airliners which in minutes traverse what would have been several days' travel for Kipling. Technological advancements find us using the same laptops, wearing the same clothes, watching the same shows on TV and hearing the same music. Like it or not, we are becoming a global village and having some appreciation of how the other villagers see things has always been a basic rule of human relations and understanding and all the good things which go along with it.

So, when someone says: "East is East and West is West" try responding with the Confucian suggestion that one should try to see a question from all sides without bias.

*   *   *

For years before coming to Asia I'd heard that "Chinese compasses are backwards," but it wasn't until arriving here that I discovered what was involved. All compasses align north-south, but the Chinese choose to call the instrument a "point south needle."

In a variation on the theme, there are old compasses which have the character for "noon" at the bottom. Thus when the "point south needle" is in alignment with the sun, it's time for lunch. It's a reverse application of the technique of using a watch as a compass—if you point the hour hand at the sun, midway between that and twelve will be due south (or in the southern hemisphere, this finds north).

A compass position is assigned to each player in the game of *mahjong,* but the east and west positions are reversed from how they appear on a map. Thus, moving counter clockwise, the play begins from the east position and moves to south, to west, to north. In keeping with that orientation, Northwest airlines translates into Chinese as "West-North airlines."

*   *   *

One of the more popular dishes in both East and West is the chicken, and both have a number of ways of preparing it. There's a notable basic difference, however, in the way the bird is cut up. In the West, chicken is usually disjointed into eight anatomically recognizable pieces. A Chinese cook, vigorously wielding a cleaver, within seconds transforms the bird into a poultry jigsaw puzzle of chunks approximately the same size. They are dissected with such reckless abandon I suspect that in all the history of China it's unlikely any two chickens have been cut up exactly the same.

Serving poultry with the head either on the plate, or still on the bird, is another culinary cultural marker. Sometimes, in the case of duck or goose, it's cleaved in two, so it's easier to get to the brain, which is as tasty as a *haute cuisine pâté.* Foreigners usually have a little trouble with it. But probably no more trouble than someone from China would have in an initial attempt to dispatch an eight-ounce steak.

In the bookstore of Guangzhou's Garden hotel I browsed through a cookbook which, in English, was directed toward the

Western market. The recipes were well presented and enticing. But the cover featured a full-color picture of a pale, plucked, steamed pullet. Its head was still on and its pointy little tongue hung mournfully awry as if it had been garroted. I suspect few Westerners would be much inclined to buy that one, although the Chinese publishers thought the photo enticing. Then there's dove and pigeon, delicately flavored birds, but not commonly available in restaurants where I come from. But they are found on many menus in China. Served whole or halved or quartered, or sometimes minced in a rolled lettuce leaf, they are marinated in soy sauce, salt, egg yolk, cornstarch and sugar, and embellished with sauces and seasonings fit for an emperor. And they are served with the head attached, or alongside on the dish.

Whenever I have pigeon it brings to mind an incident which took place just a while ago in the New Territories, north of Hong Kong in Shatin. Now a bustling, modern satellite city of more than 600,000 people, in those days it was little more than a quiet crossroad alongside a tidal mudflat. Snuggled in the shade among the nearby richly-green rolling hills was a little old restaurant which was widely renowned for its pigeon dishes. It's still there but is now so hard to find, the last time I took a group of visitors from China to Shatin we ended up having pizza.

In the old days, I often took American visitors there on Sunday outings. One time, a member of the group who was not much accustomed to international cuisine, confided that while he'd found the pigeon delicious, he'd had some reservations about being able to eat one.

On the next visit with a fresh batch of first-timers, I took the precaution of quietly instructing the waiter to cut off the pigeons' heads. That, I reasoned, would surely enhance the visitors' appreciation for the succulent specialty of the house. However, when the platter of pigeons was brought to the table, the heads were still attached, beaks, brains and all. Apparently my unusual request had been misunderstood or disregarded.

As I speculated on how to salvage the situation, the waiter flourished a great pair of shears which he plunged down, snapping across the platter as if pruning a hedge. Pigeon heads bounded across the table in all directions like little brown ping pong balls. The effect was devastating. That was the last time I tried ordering a pigeon with the head cut off.

The experience enhanced my appreciation for the importance of saying exactly what you mean, in a manner which makes it easy for people to grasp what's on your mind. In this case, simply telling the waiter to have the heads removed in the kitchen, and explaining that visitors often prefer them that way, would have gained the desired result. Maybe.

That evening, on arriving home, the waiter's first words were surely, "Honey, you'll never guess the weird way some American asked me to serve pigeon."

Even a pigeon can illustrate that a more understanding and harmonious international society is still some way off. But if we don't make a serious mutual effort to develop better understanding on this crowded fragile planet, what then of our two-legged species?

Mutuality has been a tribal essential from the earliest times. And it is becoming an increasingly important factor in getting along in China, where they have the saying: "Goals are more easily achieved through concession." Developing a knack for give-and-take requires time and it can't be based on you give and I take.

Good Things Take Time

Mr. Wong is Rarely Wrong

The Care and Feeding of Guests

WHEN I BEGAN ESCORTING Chinese delegations on visits to other countries I noted that foreigners have trouble with the family name Wong when it appears as Wang.

The Wongs are one of the largest Chinese families. In Hong Kong's three residential phone books, Wongs fill 295 pages of tiny type in the phone book, with some 141,180 names. With households averaging nearly four people, that means at the other end of those telephone numbers there are some 560,000 of them. If you add the Wongs who do not have phones or are tourists, transient seamen, illegal immigrants, and others, it means if someone is standing on your foot in the subway in Hong Kong, it's quite possibly a Wong.

The family is big enough that a little understanding of them should help broaden our understanding of Chinese in general. Wong means king or ruler and in its written form, 王, appears as a bold, balanced character of three short horizontal strokes, one above the other, connected at their mid-point by a vertical line. This ideogram illustrates the idea of joining heaven, earth and humankind. If you cap the character with two slanted strokes like a little roof, 全, it suggests a king in his palace and conveys the idea of completeness. Add a little stroke toward the bottom on either side of the ideogram, 金, and it looks something like coins in the king's pockets and it means gold. A little pendant stroke on the right side of the king, 玉, means jade. A little box balanced on the king's head, 呈, means a token gift such as one gives to a superior.

Then there's Wang which we rhyme with "bang." The Hong Kong phone book lists only 1320 Wang families. In written Chinese the Wang family name is the same four-stroke character which the

Wongs use. (The same character but spelled two different ways in English!)

I'd noticed on my Chinese language lesson tapes that when the name Wang appeared in English in the exercise book the Chinese-speaker pronounced it, "Wong." But the English-language speaker on the tape rhymed it with bang.

It illustrates how limply the Chinese language lends itself to Anglicization. Or, it might be more realistic to say English is the culprit, specifically the letter "a." As Professor Henry Higgins was finally able to wring out of Eliza Doolittle, this versatile little letter sounds different in "awe" than it does in "ago," "fat," "ate," "air" and "slang." And that's how Mr. Wong—entering an English language class in Beijing or on his grandfather's arrival at the Angel Island immigration center in San Francisco bay—transmutes to Wang, as in bang. I've asked a number of Wongs about this incongruity and get the impression they haven't given it any thought. Chinese are disinclined to devote much time contemplating our incongruities. Many families simply chose the Wang spelling on their own, upon encountering the broad English "ah."

What difference does it make? Well, people like it if you pronounce their name properly. Visitors coming from China are accustomed to having their name pronounced correctly at home. (To put that in perspective, the next time you meet a Mr. Smith, try calling him "Mr. Smythe" and see if it gets a reaction.) In traveling with Chinese delegations in the United States, we fairly often encounter a Chinese-American Wang, as in bang. But when asked, the usual response is, "Yes, my name's really Wong, but everyone here calls me Wang, so I just let it go at that." It isn't unique to the Chinese. When our daughter Heidi was working in New York City, she used to say it was easy to find her name in the phone book as she was the only Schneiter in the city with a "t." That's a Western variation of the Wong/Wang theme. It's likely that other Schneiters, on arriving in America, changed the spelling to the simpler Snider or Snyder. Or they acquiesced to an immigration official's contention that Schneiter should be spelled with a "d." Had Giuseppe Verdi chosen to come to the United States instead of staying home writing operas, he might well have gone by the name Joe Green. Not long ago, meeting someone in Hong Kong named Lang, I commented that it was an unusual name for a Cantonese. He explained, "I'm here on business from England. When I emigrated, they dropped the 'i' out of Liang and gave me an Irish name."

In encountering a business card with the name Wang in the Orient, if you ask you'll invariably find that Wong is the preferred pronunciation. And the individual always seems to appreciate your understanding that there's a difference. This softer, broad "ah" also applies pretty much across the board for the Liangs, Huangs, Tangs, Yangs, and the like.

What about the Wang (as in "bang") computer empire? Good question. The founder of Wang Laboratories was Shanghai-born Dr. Wang An. His name usually appears in the Western form, An Wang, with the family name last. It means, "peaceful king." Born in Shanghai in 1920, he became an American citizen in 1954 and his family name is written with the three vertical, connected strokes, for "king," and is pronounced, "Wong." A Wang official explained to me that the company is pronounced "Wang" (like bang) because "that's how the surname is spelled in English according to the Mandarin Chinese phonetic translation." That is, the name is mispronounced, even by the Chinese, simply because a foreigner misspelled it in the first place.

This is the type of explanation foreigners must be careful of. It sounds valid, but it isn't. In Beijing, our office formerly was located in the same building as the Wang office and one morning as one of their employees stepped onto the elevator I put my Wong/Wang question to her. She repeated the line about "that's how it's pronounced in English." As she stepped off the elevator I turned to someone who'd overheard our conversation, and traced on my palm, with my finger, the four-stroke "king" character.

"Mr. Wong," he nodded, reaffirming my conviction that Mr. Wong is rarely wrong. In the Chinese written language this word is never rhymed with "bang."

I've asked a number of bang-rhyming Tangs why they choose to use that pronunciation. Their answer—which seems to make sense to them—is, "We use the correct pronunciation among ourselves,

of course, but among foreigners we pronounce it the way they do."
A Chinese family in Malaysia goes by the name Farm because that
is how British officials erroneously Anglicized the name when
Grandfather Fan arrived there half a century ago. With their
Herculean sense of pride in family history, how can they be so casual
about generations of foreigners mispronouncing their names? Perhaps because *they* know who they are and they don't seem inclined
to take foreigners all that seriously.

Whether a family spells their name Li or Lee is essentially a
matter of personal choice, although the ideogram may be different.
Then there are our friends who spell the name as "Lie." This
spelling occurred back when the family moved to Indonesia when
it was a Dutch colony, and in that language "ei" is pronounced as
the letter "I" and "ie" is pronounced as the letter "E."

The family name Lin, in the North, is pronounced Lam in
Cantonese. The Northern name Chen is Chan in Cantonese. And
so it goes.

There's the Cantonese name, Ng. How do they pronounce that?
However it suits them. Without a vowel to hang onto, its variously
pronounced as Ing, Ung, Ong, Oong, Nong, Nung, and some
other ways as well. I know one Ng who calls himself simply, "Mr.
N.G." Another pronounces it something like, "Mmmmm." To be
on the safe side, if you encounter this one always ask how the
individual pronounces it. In North China, it's less of a problem as
the character for Ng is pronounced as the family name, "Wu." But
some families pronounce it, "Hu."

Anyone who does not speak Chinese is virtually certain to
mispronounce the name of the former Chinese leader Chiang
Kai-shek. Although his name has been in common usage in the
outside world for more than half a century, it seems always to be
mispronounced, "Chang," like the sound of a wooden spoon
hitting an iron pot. Chiang, which is the family name, is properly
pronounced as a soft "Jeeong."

Many foreigners are unaware that Chinese family names appear
first, rather than at the end of the name, as in our system. At a
school conference in Texas, someone glanced at my wife's name tag
and, seeing Hong Kong in bold letters, addressed her as, "Mrs.

Hong." Charlene was pleased that the lady had learned enough about China that she knew the name wasn't "Mrs. Kong."

This is a common problem when traveling in the United States with a Chinese delegation. Airline and hotel people quite regularly fail to show reservations for, say, Liu Cong Men and the rest of our group because the names have been reversed. In this case, Mr. Liu will be found listed as Mr. Men. The problem sometimes takes other forms. Chinese who work extensively with foreigners or who are on a long assignment in another country may turn their name around so the business card will show the family name last. If you are familiar with Chinese family names, you can usually tell when this is the case. If in doubt, just ask. The simplest solution is for Mr. Liu, on being assigned outside China, to take a foreign first name and carry a card that says something like Paul Liu. Or, he may prefer instead to go by Paul Liu Cong Men or Paul Cong Men Liu. It's flexible. (The selection of a Christian name is often done by the individuals themselves, if they haven't already acquired one from their English teacher. In school, Chinese youngsters are often "assigned" an English first name by a foreign school teacher who has trouble remembering all those Yings, Lings, and Pings.)

In the Orient, I find it easier to make a restaurant reservation or leave a message with someone's secretary in the name of "Mr. Fred," which I am always asked to repeat and spell. Western family names are not always easy for Chinese who have not had a lot of exposure to them and my spelling out S-c-h-n-e-i-t-e-r is easily misunderstood with the Chinese at the other end of the line taking it to be something along the lines of F-z-a-m-c-i-d-c-i.

In addition to getting the names right, if you become involved in hosting visitors from China there are a number of flexibility factors to keep in mind. Chinese visitors from Hong Kong, Taipei or Singapore are generally well-attuned to the international way of doing things. It could be difficult to try to pick one of them out of a group of a half-dozen San Francisco Chinese. However, for most people coming from China, international exposure is a new experience. Delegations I bring out of China are made up largely of individuals who have never been out of the country. Only rarely are there any among them who've had a hamburger and I've yet to see one who has ever had a fortune cookie. On their initial encounter with potato chips, they may try to eat them with a fork.

There are two assumptions a foreign host should resist when entertaining visitors from China. One is that they understand quite a bit about your country. The other is that they don't. It's easy to be wrong on this and it's up to you to try to figure out where on the spectrum they are, so you can help them get as much as possible out of their visit.

One example of how this works involved a delegation of Taiwan businessmen on a tour of the US. One day we happened to share a flight with Senator George McGovern, who, a few years before, had campaigned unsuccessfully for the US Presidency against Richard Nixon. The Senator was a strong supporter of our wheat export programs so I visited with him briefly and introduced him to the delegation. As he returned to his seat I had the feeling our group hadn't grasped who he was.

"That's George McGovern. Senator McGovern," I said.

The nature of their nods, smiles and "Oh's" suggested they had made the connection but I had some doubts.

"He was almost President," I explained. That seemed to clear things up for a moment until one of them asked "what company" he'd almost become president of. Determined to get it across, I tried: "Watergate."

That, they understood. "You mean ... *President*," they muttered, with nods and smiles taking on a firmer tone. It strengthened my appreciation for how easy it is to be misled into thinking you've put your point across with Chinese when you haven't at all. Watch their eyes and their reactions. Listen closely to the responses. Be ready to come at the subject from a couple of different directions if you suspect you're not communicating or they're not comprehending.

An American couple who'd had a Chinese student staying at their home, advised him on his arrival that fresh cake was always available in the kitchen and to "just help yourself when you want a piece." The student thanked them but said he didn't like cake. But the cakes began being decimated at an impressive rate. When my friends said they thought he didn't care for cake the student replied, "Well, in China cakes are different. Dry and very hard." Then he told a Chinese joke about a man on a bicycle in Beijing who was struck by a bus while delivering one of these cakes. The man was injured, the bike was totally destroyed and the cake box was run over. But the cake wasn't damaged at all.

Traveling with a group of Chinese in the United States, one of them said, "Farmers here earn $40,000 a year." I asked where that figure came from. They said they'd asked at a farm we'd visited a few days before and were told that. "No," I said, "*he* earned that much last year. Some farmers earned more. But a lot of farmers went broke last year."

Being on a different socio-economic wavelength makes it extremely difficult for visitors from China to draw clear inferences about things they see or experience on visits outside the country.

On the way to visit a grain terminal we passed a golf course. "Oh yes, golf," the interpreter replied. "We know about it. It's a game rich people play in America." I made a mental note to get back to that. At the grain terminal we were shown around by a husky, tousle-haired employee dressed in faded old jeans, a frayed work shirt and weathered, paint-spattered shoes. As he concluded our tour of their operation he asked if there were any questions. I asked how his golf game was. We learned his long game was pretty fair, that he played once or twice every week and that a game cost no more than the price of a light lunch. While the visitors may never take up the game of golf, they at least have a better understanding of it now.

In these foregoing reminiscences there is a common thread. Until the subject was worked around a little, we and the Chinese were not talking about the same thing. When you're trying to help a visitor better understand something, it's important to first establish what, exactly, you're talking about. We don't always do that and with Chinese visitors it should be a conscious effort on our part every day.

In hosting guests from China on a visit to your community, office, factory, home, or whatever, there are certain niceties which are appreciated. When the guests are settled-in, offer tea, coffee or soft drinks.

Visitors from China aren't generally overly enthusiastic about trying Western foods. It depends on the individual. So, a host may have to probe to establish how they really feel about this. If they've had considerable exposure outside their country, they might relish a steak. If they haven't traveled outside much, they would probably prefer something else. To them, a beef dish at home would most likely involve only a few, small, thin slices of meat sautéed with a variety of vegetables. Although their breakfasts are a grab bag hodgepodge of everything from pickles to boiled peanuts, they seem fairly comfortable with a hearty American breakfast of something they've seen before such as eggs and toast and orange juice. Buffets are the morning meal of choice. They always seem most comfortable with Chinese or Chinese-American lunches and dinners.

However, even the most un-traveled visitor from China should not consider it excessive to have an American-style hamburger or rib barbecue on someone's patio on Monday, a Western buffet lunch on Tuesday, and seafood or pizza on Thursday or Friday. Seafood lends itself well to what they are used to and is always a pretty safe choice. With pizza, don't go out of your way to tell them there's cheese on top. It's good to try to fit in something typical of your country's culture, such as a picnic in the park, a clambake on the beach or a cowboy breakfast at the County Fair. Try to establish their mood by asking, "How do you feel about Western food this evening?" If they say that's fine, you should then ask, "Or would you prefer Chinese?" Given that choice, they often will opt for the latter. Without a choice, they almost always concur in your suggestion.

Chinese generally prefer eating in a somewhat boisterous, well-lit restaurant rather than in a shadowy, quiet, candle-lit place. I suspect it has something to do with their attitude toward food. They maybe don't trust it unless they can see it. A recent study of Chinese restaurants in Hong Kong revealed that the noise levels run so high it can be impossible to understand much more than half of what is said across the table at a normal conversation level. The noise is loud enough to cause hearing damage according to the *South China Morning Post.*

With Chinese guests in your country it's best to make arrangements in advance if you're going to a Chinese restaurant. That way, things flow more smoothly and it shows you have put a little extra effort into it. A phone call to the restaurant can establish how many dishes you need and what courses the restaurant would recommend for the sort of group you are hosting. Chances are, they have a set menu which will suit your purpose. Be sure to mention that your guests are from China and indicate whether it is the northern, central or southern part of the country. Savvy Chinese restaurateurs will be responsive to those inputs. Some fancier dishes must be ordered in advance, due to the longer preparation time and the restaurant people likely can come up with some suggestions for things which they eat themselves but don't have on the menu.

If you defer to one of the guests to do the ordering (because he *is* Chinese) this can be a little awkward with Chinese-American food, as visitors may not recognize anything on the menu. Or, deferring to your pocketbook, they may order more common, less-expensive dishes. You can override this by recommending a couple of house specialties, toward keeping the selection upmarket. It's appropriate to inquire whether anyone would like to have a favorite dish. Then, as Wang Lung, at his wedding feast in *The Good Earth,* be a properly modest host by apologizing that the food and the arrangements probably aren't up to the "high standards" they are accustomed to.

Choosing better restaurants, in keeping with the position of your visitors, is mainly a function of face. I had one group which was terribly impressed because the restaurant we took them to in Manhattan (the one in Kansas) was not only good, they served sea slugs as well. On another occasion, with a delegation headed by a Vice Minister who also happened to be President of the China Cuisine Association, we arrived at a recommended restaurant which—on being taken to a table and seeing a menu—proved to be inadequate for the occasion. This was to be a farewell banquet the evening before the delegation was leaving the US. I'd have lost face if we remained. It would have been a loss of face for the restaurant people if we simply got up and left and that would have been potentially embarrassing for the guests. But, we couldn't stay. I fibbed to the waiter, "We're having a progressive dinner, moving along through Chinatown from restaurant to restaurant so we can try the specialty of each place." With that, we had their Cantonese fried rice, and moved on to a more auspicious setting.

The number of chairs at a meal may carry some superstitious significance, for those who are from places other than the PRC. Some feel thirteen is an unlucky number. Others say fourteen is unlucky as it sounds like "sure death" in Chinese. As for the seating arrangement, unless it is something fairly formal, with place cards, don't try to seat people according to Chinese banquet protocol when they are visiting your country. Simply get them seated by saying, "We're among friends. Just relax and take a chair where you're comfortable."

Asians put a great deal more into attending to guests than Westerners generally do. Americans are inclined to let guests relax with TV, a book or the sundeck and not burden them with a tight schedule. Chinese overwhelm visitors, busying them with early-to-late activities, a couple of banquets a day, and weekend trips and sightseeing. These typically fourteen-hour-days can go on for a week or two. One Sunday in Beijing it took me an hour to convince officials that I really did not want to be taken sightseeing, on their holiday, with the city swirling in a blizzard. Keeping guests on the move is their way of showing visitors they're welcome. Keep this in mind when entertaining Chinese. It isn't so much a question of treating them well as it is one of treating them *very* well.

In the event you are not able to be with guests throughout their visit, simply excuse your absence by saying something like, "I'll see you again tonight at dinner." Resist volunteering details as to what exactly you'll be doing in the meantime. Detailing may suggest to your guests that you consider other things or other people to be more important than they are. If you are absent they can assume it is something you cannot avoid. The explanation of an absence will be evaluated. And, don't excuse an absence by saying you're busy. Refrain from looking at your watch at inopportune times, such as toward the end of a late dinner. If you're compelled to check, glance casually at the watch of someone nearby. Never give cause to suspect you're being kept from important matters. If they suggest it, deny it. Face again. Arrange visits with key people in your company or community whose positions are more-or-less comparable to those held by your guests. This pleases visitors, giving them face. And it gives face to you, demonstrating that you hold them in high esteem and that you have the capacity to call out the artillery for them.

In the past, official visitors from the People's Republic of China were generally not available for press interviews. While it might be said they are perhaps a little more accessible now, there can be some thin ice for your guests—and you—in this arena. They are not accustomed to the free-wheeling, hot-ink journalism we have in some countries. As the Chinese say, "Thin ice is only a problem for those who choose to go skating." Interview questions or answers may be misunderstood. Guests may be misquoted or something may slip out of context. If a question comes up in advance about an interview, ask the Chinese how they feel about it. A prepared press release should suffice in the case of a routine visitor-in-town story. If you have a press conference, advise the news people beforehand of the general subject areas the visitor will or will not be able to discuss . . . and don't allow that to unravel.

One reason for caution is because embassies closely follow press stories about their country, and they subscribe to newspaper clipping services which extend this coverage right down to rural weekly newspapers. It's part of what embassies do. If you're charged with ensuring that a group's visit is a success, part of your job is to protect them. In addition to making sure they look in the right direction when crossing a one-way street, if a TV news crew pounces on them at the airport, be prepared to step in to help keep things on track. Even a good interpreter can have trouble fielding rapid-fire, on-camera questions.

Chinese delegations usually carry modest gifts to distribute to hosts. If you choose to give a return gift, give something simple which reflects a mutual friendship or respect. Traditionally, gifts aren't opened in the presence of the giver, but those who know our customs will usually do so. Firms which have company caps, with their logo on the front, should not give green ones to Chinese. A green hat on a man is taken to mean that his wife has rather less fidelity than an old stereo.

When guests check into a hotel or motel make sure their rooms are comfortable and problem-free. If there is a larger room or one with a better view try to have that assigned in advance to the leader of the group. Generally, it's best to have rooms close together, with the interpreter near the leader's room.

Just as it's best not to cross their organizational lines in our get-togethers in China, use discretion in involving other Chinese in close-knit and relaxed social situations which you've scheduled with your guests. There can be advantages in including Chinese from your firm, Chinese neighbors, friends or the like. But people who are strangers to your group, who may be heading back to China, have the innocent capacity to dampen an otherwise con-vivial evening because traditional formality will prevail.

Traveling on the US West Coast with a delegation, as we arrived at a restaurant for dinner one evening, we were introduced to another Chinese guest (from a different organization in China). Predictably, my gregarious group introverted. There's a Chinese saying, "When with strangers leave seven things unsaid." When the waiter arrived for a cocktail order the stranger asked for orange juice. Predictably, everyone on the delegation asked for orange juice. Chinese have an inclination to refrain from sleeping or drinking in the presence of someone they don't know. Things were not shaping up at all well. I called the waiter aside and told him to bring beers for everyone. When they arrived, before anyone could protest, I stood and invited the stranger to a welcoming gan bei. He drew the members of my delegation into the toast, and suddenly everything was just fine.

Just as potentially devastating as a mystery guest, in taking the edge off a social function, is the deadly anti-social scenario of the guests and hosts drifting into talk among themselves rather than with each other. This is easily avoided by not allowing it to happen.

The physical act of traveling presents its own particular pitfalls. While there haven't been any studies on this, I suspect the average American teenager spends as much time in a private car in one week as many people in the PRC spend over a period of several years, or perhaps a lifetime. What I am leading up to is, you may find some guests on your hands who have a low resistance to car sickness. Watch for symptoms at the start if you'll be putting much mileage on them. Keep the windows open a bit for good air circulation and if there's a choice, a straight superhighway is better than a curvy, old, scenic road. Make a few short stops early in the drive, for photos or something, to see how people are doing. A green Chinese means you've got a problem. In that case, have a doctor prescribe something.

On a junk outing in Hong Kong on a choppy day, one of the guests complained of feeling queasy. He'd previously used those little round anti-motion-sickness plasters which are put behind the ear, but no one had one. However, I had in my wallet a blank adhesive address label so I simply slipped away and snipped it into a little circle with the scissors on my Swiss army knife. Without letting him see it, I told him I'd found some of those plasters below deck and stuck it behind his ear. It worked like a charm.

Chinese share our enjoyment of sightseeing. They like to take pictures and it's a nice gesture to have their snapshots developed for them before they leave town.

Be prepared to be sometimes surprised with what strikes them as impressive. A group which entered the United States through the sprawling and somewhat Orwellian Seattle-Tacoma Airport seemed to take no notice of all its stainless steel, computerization and its efficient automated subway. The spiffy motel and the floating ribbons of freeways were taken equally in stride. The awesome view from Seattle's Space Needle and its shiny monorail elicited polite nods. Then, hurtling smoothly and silently along the monorail into the heart of the city, one of them pointed and shouted, "Wow! Look! A McDonald's."

When it's time for guests to move on to their next stop, they will vigorously protest that they can get to the airport on their own and there's no need to accompany them. "Too much trouble," they will insist. This traditional tableau recalls something said by the late Premier Zhou Enlai. That is, "We Chinese mean what we say." Zhou meant what he said. The catch is, you have to try to work out what it is they are really saying.

If you're in business and they tell you they find your product "very attractive" or "very competitive" it does not necessarily follow that they are going to buy it. If they say the instant rice at the buffet is "very nice" it doesn't mean they prefer it to the flavorful, just-right-to-the-bite, more civilized rice they have at home. On the question of escorting them to the airport, while their protests may be genuine, a good host will persevere and personally escort them, and will remain with them until the plane leaves. It's the way they would do it if you were under their wing in China.

A good host does good things

There's No Business
Like Sino Business

An Invitation to Tea and Symbiosis

BECAUSE CHINA *IS* CHINA, no matter how long you remain there the importance of trying to keep your bearings and paying attention never diminishes. The truth of that transcends anything you're likely to encounter anywhere else in the world. China has more open manholes and other pitfalls than anyplace else.

Some years ago, on the train from then British Hong Kong to Guangzhou, a Western tour guide stood up, turned to her little covey of tourists and solemnly informed them they had just crossed the border into *China*. Her charges stirred in their seats in a subdued state of enchantment which moved the American seated next to me to mutter softly, "And you are about to experience one of life's great illusions." He'd been operating for three years in China on the premise "What you read is not always what you hear, and what you hear is not always what you see." For the foreigner, working in China is something like working in Hollywood's film industry. If you choose to do that you have to learn how to deal with the make-believe and the cosmetology. Success hinges largely on keeping in mind where reality ends.

And that's not all. Murphy's Law—"What Can Go Wrong Will Go Wrong"—has a first cousin in China. I call it the "Asian Equation." It's an extension of Murphy's Law and states, "What Cannot Possibly Go Wrong Will Go Wrong." Some years ago I came to realize there is a Second Asian Equation—"What Goes Wrong Will Go Wrong No Matter What You Do To Avoid It." You've surely had a day where *everything* seemed out of whack, and the more you tried to right it, the more wrong it got. Right? That's Asian Equations 1 & 2. It's endemic there and sometimes—like the Hong Kong flu—a rogue strain somehow squirts out and dishevels some innocent victim in another part of the world. That's why, no matter where you are, you sometimes have a day like that. In Asia it happens a lot. The Asian Equation thrives on cultural quirks, mushy communications and the general nature of things. That's a tough combination to beat. When it strikes, take two aspirin, go to bed and don't even think of answering the phone.

It's disarmingly easy to take things for granted there. Resist that temptation. Play over in your mind trivial details and routine matters which seem firm and clear enough, but often aren't. Developing a knack for thinking the unthinkable gives you an early warning system, alerting you when things begin to slide off-center. As with an optical illusion, something which seemed perfectly clear at first transforms before your eyes into an altogether new design. And sometimes that too begins kaleidoscoping about before settling into a final pattern.

Keep your analysis of a situation and your inflow of information as valid and as current as possible. A minor adjustment of a tour schedule, a phrase in a contract, or even a guest list may suggest a significant change looms just around the bend. You needn't dwell on minor points. But don't disregard them. They often add up to the fact that what seems to be happening, isn't happening at all. Or, as is often the case, something entirely different may be about to happen.

Waiting in line to inquire about some official forms at a government office, as I reached the counter the clerk asked me to take a seat and wait. It's a good idea to get inquisitive if someone suggests you do that. Well-intentioned individuals who suggest it will be only "a few minutes" often have no idea of how long it will take. Anywhere in Asia, the word "wait" should trigger apprehensions.

In this instance, before I could inquire further, the clerk disappeared through the door into a back office. I was alone. It was quiet except for the ticking of an old wall clock, it's hands almost straight up to twelve noon. Might the clerk have slipped out another door to go to lunch, leaving me to cool my heels until his eventual return?

I opened the hallway door and there he was at the elevator with his rice bowl, headed for the canteen. Closing the office door behind me, I approached and said, "I'm sorry, I didn't realize it was lunchtime. Would it be convenient for you if I came back around 3:30 or so? Could you have my papers ready then?" His initial discomfort at being apprehended in his attempted evasion eased into relief. That wasn't at all the barbaric outburst he'd expected to endure in the hallway among his co-workers. Yes, by golly, he could have the papers ready then. That was a bonus. I'd expected it would take at least another couple of days in processing. Had I chosen to make an issue out of his disappearing act it surely would have taken another week or two before my material materialized.

Take a lesson from the way deer move through a forest. At the slightest shift of a distant shadow, a change in the wind or the hint of movement or sound, glistening onyx noses tip into the wind. The animals stand statue-still, blending with their surroundings, and while it may only take an instant, they don't twitch until they have sized up the situation and know what to do about it. They don't crash about blindly like frightened rabbits. The wind constantly plays to their advantage. If a breeze comes up a draw they move down into the valley. If it drifts down, they move uphill, always mindful of what the wind tells them about what's ahead, out of view. Once spooked, they bound smoothly downhill, the easiest and fastest way to get a new perspective on things. That's how deer survive on their own familiar terrain. The technique lends itself equally well to audacious two-legged creatures who range far from home. The alternative to keeping your nose to the wind and being mindful of your bearings is to become a victim of circumstance.

In the event their interpreter makes a seemingly offhanded observation on the way back to your hotel after negotiations, it just might carry the hint of a change of position on their side. Listen closely to casual comments. They might not be as casual as they sound. If, after a meeting or two an older gentleman appears at your next session and sits quietly on the sidelines, that quite likely is the boss who's come personally to size you up.

* * *

China's Winds of Change blow with typhoon force only rarely. They are more likely to be as faint as the rumble in a tadpole's tummy. It's in keeping with the old philosophy which suggests a single falling leaf heralds a change of season. It can be assumed nearly everything said *or* unsaid holds some significance. It's unlike Chinese to say something just in passing without some reason for it.

While missing those signs which do hold significance, newcomers, and people some distance from the action, are inclined to read too much into some development which is really of little or no consequence. Change in China is best perceived if you view it as you would the entire unfolding story line of a motion picture, rather than seeing it as a single snapshot. It's the difference between seeing the film, *Gone With the Wind* in Technicolor or looking at a single faded sepia photo of a Civil War encampment. A single event or development in China is one piece of a jigsaw puzzle, significant only to the degree it really fits and then holds its place as the picture takes shape. In the case of China, quite often when the puzzle is completed, you find that a few of the pieces which had initially seemed to fit are nowhere to be found in the final picture. Those with some grasp of how China operates understand that it's the *trend* that counts; not each isolated event. Scratchings in the morning sand are easily obscured by the evening tide. The uninitiated and the distant observer too often concentrate on the hole, and miss the doughnut altogether. From the outside or as a newcomer or visitor it's easy to seize on something which may be only a transient political or strategic convenience, with little significance or long-term implications. It might have been dragged across the trail simply to make you feel good or to get you thinking along other lines. This is one of the most difficult lessons for foreigners to learn.

Where I come from, a "significant" development usually signals a shift in direction or a change of position. In China, that may not be the case at all. An action or a reaction on the part of the Chinese may well be undertaken for reasons totally different from what the foreigner presumes. The more you can learn, the less likely you will be surprised. In a typical example, China's suddenly buying corn for import into the south doesn't necessarily mean China needs more corn. This may occur because it is easier to import the corn than to ship it from North China by rail. Or, it may be done to correct a trade imbalance with a neighboring corn producing country.

*   *   *

There's an American Indian saying that goes, "Big rain. Little rain. Little rain. Big rain." It means if it pours, it will rain only a short time, while a drizzle can filter down for days.

The philosophy parallels something a Chinese entrepreneur brings up from time to time during chats about opportunity, understanding, and the future. Her admonition is, "Small is big. Big is small." The overblown is easily blown away. The idea of keeping things simple and suited to the occasion is not new. It's pure Confucian philosophy.

It's like the change imposed by the tiny persistent droplets of water imperceptibly lengthening the columns in Guangxi's awesome caverns. Water doesn't always wear away stone. In evaporating, these trickles of liquid lime create stone. The massive formations represent millions of years of nature's patient artistry. The drop-by-drop transformation is barely discernible over the course of a century, but you know change is taking place even though you can't see it. It's much that way with many things we deal with there today and it isn't a new phenomenon.

In 1972, visiting with US Ambassador Walter P. McConaughy at the American Embassy in Taipei, I asked his views on the long term outlook for our doing market development work on the mainland at some point in the future. With China credentials going back to his days as Second Secretary with the Embassy in Beijing in 1941, he said, "President Nixon's visit to Mainland China did open some prospects of eventual major trade with China, but the short term outlook still seems unpromising." The American wheat industry paid attention to developments in the ensuing years. Sniffing the air of opportunity, a few tentative probes were initiated and in August of 1981 I moved to Hong Kong to establish a base to pursue our China market opportunities. Within a few months, China's Ministry of Commerce invited us and two other US commodity groups to establish offices in Beijing, where our bread promotion was compared to Marco Polo's (reputed) introduction of noodles to the West.

In the years since, in cooperation with the Foreign Agricultural Service of the US Department of Agriculture, we have worked with the Chinese on a number of significant and mutually advantageous projects. China's entire wheat food industry has been influenced. Consumers have benefited, through the availability of better, more varied, and more convenient foods which resulted in a consumption increase of 100 percent in the first decade of our market development program. This has contributed directly to the sale of billions of dollars-worth of US agricultural commodities to China, improving the Chinese diet while bolstering America's balance of trade. Our projects with China's Ministries of Commerce, Light Industry and Agriculture, as well as provincial bureaus and agencies, have helped bring about a broad-based modernization of the wheat food industry throughout the entire country—a success story that might be entitled, "East Meets Yeast."

Kentucky Fried Chicken made a highly-heralded entry into China in 1988, the first international fast-food chain to do so. We helped lay the groundwork for this four years earlier with the establishment of China's first Western-style hamburger outlet in Beijing. This was done in cooperation with the same Chinese officials who, a few years later, eased China into the modern, international food sphere by attracting both Nabisco and Kentucky Fried to Beijing. In this process, the point virtually everyone failed to grasp was that China had no potential for fast food.

The country's iron rice bowl, socialist system doesn't lend itself to people wolfing their meals and rushing on to other things. The success of the fast food industry had nothing whatsoever to do with its being fast. The appeal lay in its offering something new and different to millions of people eager to give it a try.

Our activities in China directly and considerably enhanced two-way trade and strengthened relations and understanding between the two countries. American Presidential Advisor Anna Chennault, a Chinese and the widow of World War II Major-General Claire Chennault, said in 1988 that Asia had "finally" come to figure prominently in American thinking largely due to expanded relationships such as this.

Reflecting on these events, and the promise they hold for the future, brings to mind what Bogie said of the Maltese Falcon. "It's the stuff dreams are made of."

Our good fortune didn't require an IQ of 140 or a ton of money. Essentially, it took a little common sense, some understanding of how things are done there, and an appreciation of the importance of nurturing personal relationships.

Despite all the misreading and lack of sensitivity of the round-eyed barbarian in the past, the poor critter finally appears to be making some headway. Through this past decade we've perhaps gained a better understanding than was accomplished in all the previous centuries of blustering, banging and bungling about. A generally more open posture on the part of China, shifting into high gear in the '80s, contributed much toward helping clear the air. In the initial exchanges of delegations, there wasn't much casual conversation. Formality was the rule. Within a few years, discussions and relationships became more personal, with family photos being passed around and things becoming more relaxed and friendly. The roller coaster ride has just begun. A lot of people on both sides of the Pacific (some in high positions) aren't convinced we should try to get along and they haven't yet made up their mind about climbing on board. But a lot of others have and are holding on.

Not long ago, the slightly-informed were regularly presenting seminars to the totally uninformed, dispensing Medicine Show Enlightenments, often gleaned from the experiences of those "who actually" had spent a few days in China. Like going to a marriage clinic run by honeymooners, it was shallow stuff. But there was little else to go on in those days.

Then as now, be judiciously open-minded about anything you believe you've learned. And, like a fine old pocket watch, take a look at it from time to time to make sure it still works OK.

* * *

You've perhaps read somewhere, "If all the Chinese in the world were to march four abreast past a given point they would never stop marching though they marched for ever and ever!"

I believe the first time I came across that was during my early teens. I was impressed. Now I simply accept it as an entertainment, which is probably all "Believe it or Not!" Robert Ripley had in mind when he came up with it. This falls into a broad realm of mystic arithmetic which is based on the idea of some strange or wondrous consequence occurring if all the Chinese were to do something or other, which they've never before been inclined to do. It doesn't take much understanding of the Chinese to appreciate it isn't likely they're ever going to get involved in one of these silly If-All's. You could calculate how much air pollution could be reduced in Shanghai if everyone there took five deep breaths every morning to clear the air. And, it wouldn't change a thing.

As quaint conversation pieces, these awful If-Alls are harmless. However, it's easy for the foreigner to see these as a suggestion of a market opportunity which isn't there at all. In the case of the marching Chinese, or anything that sounds like that, don't try to read things into it, particularly if it has to do with business or investment. At least, not until you've first made a shot at trying to persuade a few dozen Chinese to march past a given point four abreast. If all of China jumped out of bed at the same instant, yes, it might indeed rattle dishes in Los Angeles. But we depart from reality when we begin to think there is anything of social, political or economic substance in these fancies.

While still under construction in Beijing, the World Trade Center there began promoting the idea it would be, "Where one billion people meet the world." That's a slick motto, with a resonant Madison Avenue commercial ring. It could be chiseled in granite over the entryway in a dozen languages. But as catchy as it is, it's simply an extension of the old If-All way we have of looking at China.

Just about anything and everything you've heard about how difficult it is to break into this market is true. It can be tougher than a boiled jogging shoe. The pursuit of business or a career in China is clearly not everyone's cup of tea. It's an endeavor easily dolloped with doses of disenchantment. A point often missed is, China wants to sell more than it wants to buy. That's another way they're like us. This market has had something of the lure of a gold rush. And like a gold rush, it can be rough going, with a few folks hitting it rich while most folks don't. Often, they're ready for China, but China isn't ready for them.

As in sluicing the Sierras or clambering across the Klondike in search of the Yellow Stuff, if you choose to seek your fortune in China, the signs become clear when the time has come to pack up and head home. In the event you have trouble figuring this out, check your balance sheet after a reasonable period of time and you'll find the answer there. However, getting out can prove to be as difficult as it was getting in. If you get the feeling you may be painting yourself into a corner, try to work your way over toward a window. Marco Polo finally left because it was apparent he might not fare too well with whoever followed Kublai Khan to the throne. Hanging on imprudently to imagined opportunities by clinging to If-Alls and wishful thinking has clouded the view of many an entrepreneur and lightened the poke of modern day prospectors who should have known better. While the Chinese will tell you it's important to be patient, it's equally important to be prudent.

When the door to China eased open slightly a few years ago, a tidal wave of euphoria engulfed the world. Otherwise rational business people went loco at the first sniff of one billion bodies. Fortunately, things have settled down a bit. Foreigners are beginning to understand, for example, China isn't going to import a half-billion sets of cuff links. Chinese don't wear French cuffs, which does not necessarily (of itself) suggest an opportunity to sell them long-sleeved shirts. They export those.

Viewing China as a *market* is not the way to go about it. China is, rather, an impressive clutch of individualized markets. Merchandisers who understand that the California market is actually many niche markets of teenagers, young marrieds, retired people, sports enthusiasts, gourmets or whatever, *should* have no trouble understanding it works much the same there. But, because it is China, these same merchandisers have trouble transplanting that understanding west from California.

A first-time visitor to the Orient stopped by the office and remarked with conviction, "Doing business in Asia is certainly different than it is in Arkansas." I'd never been to Arkansas, but I felt somehow he must be right. I pointed out the importance of not seeing this part of the world simply in terms of "the Asian market." Every country is unique and people who approach it as a single package-deal will find the going slow.

In the case of China, there's the modern, aggressive and relatively affluent and highly autonomous southern province of Guangdong, with its TV antennas plucking programs, commercials and ideas from classy Hong Kong just across the border. Population of the province is six times that of Belgium; twice that of California. There's the rapidly urbanizing and industrializing coastal region from Shanghai south to Guanxi Province, with a total population about the size of the United States. Though national capitals worldwide are better stewards of bureaucracy than of business, there's the so-called showcase market of ten million in Beijing, swept by daily tides of tourists from throughout the country. It's largely a question of how foreign entrepreneurs choose to draw the lines to suit their own perceived potentials.

Think of it as a twenty-two-pound holiday turkey. The idea isn't to try to eat the whole thing at a single sitting. Start slowly and consider the options—turkey soup, hot turkey sandwiches, cold turkey sandwiches, turkey salad, turkey croquettes. Turkey chop suey?

Even with the country's birth control efforts, population now stands at more than 1.3 billion, growing by 5.9 million per year with one birth every 2 seconds.

With incomes rising, the baby market has got to be one of the hottest potentials in the country. Particularly with today's smaller families in a society of more indulged offspring. If mamma won't buy it, papa probably will. And if not, every Chinese kid knows grandma and grandpa are sure to come across. Despite outward appearances, people in China have purchasing power. Incomes are low even by Asian standards but the cost of living is low with rent in a standard flat in Beijing running to only a few dollars a month.

One of the problems China has had in trying to attract foreign investment lies in its enthusiasm to develop export markets and protect its foreign exchange rather than to provide foreign business better access to its markets.

There are opportunities there and they should grow as China comes to better understand the international marketplace and to appreciate that world trade does not run down a one way street and that interest will not long be sustained by an Open Door that swings only one way.

Some Americans persist in seeing China in terms of how it was in the late 1940s or early 1950s. Some Chinese continue to see the United States that way. Individuals whose orientation is mired in the early '50s—the Korean War years—feel strong undercurrents of suspicion. We have a sufficient number of these archaics in both China and the US that it's a wonder we've made any progress as all. Their glazed perceptions remind me of a German girl I was dating in the little cobble-stoned town of Kitzingen during the Occupation. She had arrived only recently from the Soviet East Zone so her view of the United States was totally out of whack. One evening we went to see a Western film, with American cowboys speaking dubbed-in German dialogue. Later, we dropped in at a little *gasthaus,* which only a few years before had been a hangout of Luftwaffe fighter pilots. Over a glass of Franken wine and a Camembert and dill pickle sandwich she said something about the film being "the way it is in America." She meant cowboys going into town on dirt roads in horse-drawn wagons. I explained the story was set in the 1800s and that American cities were far more modern than Kitzingen. The *fraulein* insisted, "But in the West in America it is like that today."

There's nothing wrong with seeing the world through your own rose-colored glasses as long as they are relatively new rose-colored glasses.

Not long off the endangered species list in China, "give-and-take" has made reasonable headway from where it was in the 1980s. The trick is to keep the giving and taking somewhat in balance. China has no trouble at all if it works out that you give and they take. Businesspeople have to get accustomed to the idea of being sized up as an opportunity to serve Chinese interests and enhance China's advantage. But don't let it bother you. If it does, just reflect upon how you expect the situation to work to your advantage. If you're a tourist, you'll perhaps simply be seen as something of a novelty and an unwitting source of amusement. That's OK. It's better to leave people in a good mood rather than having them upset about something.

Probably the *worst* mental set is the attitude that you're going to change things, or help to set the Chinese straight. The malady is common among new arrivals. Those with little cultural orientation or preparation are the most vulnerable. The trail is littered with the bones of those who've tried that approach.

Foreigners who live there for an extended period or return frequently, should devote a little time each day to their orientation, particularly as it applies to cultural considerations because these impact directly on—or spin off from—your most routine activities.

Take something as seemingly matter-of-fact as Chinese tea, for example. Offering tea to guests is an important expression of respect. In pouring tea, hold the pot with both hands. The spout should not point directly at the guest when pouring or when the pot is set down. It's a nice touch during an office visit if the boss personally pours tea rather than having some staff person do it. That particularly applies on the refills as the tea cups should not be allowed to become cold or empty. That can be taken as a sign that the host awaits the guests' departure with some enthusiasm. Northerners generally prefer a somewhat stronger and darker tea but a good green Chinese tea, such as Jasmine or *Lung Ching,* is always appropriate. Except in the new international hotels and restaurants, all the tea in China is served without cream, lemon, sugar or ice. You don't have to do it their way. But if you do, they will be pleased that you observe the finer cultural points. It's best to serve guests tea without asking, because if you ask they'll likely say "no" although they mean "yes."

*   *   *

Such historically notable forces as Catholicism, Buddhism, Islam, Marxism, and more recently, capitalism, have all become assimilated in a distinct Chinese fashion. The incursion of anything from the outside always accedes to China's terms and in the process takes on a Chineseness. Buddhism came from India, but did you ever see a Chinese Buddhist statue with Indian features? Any foreigner who harbors the idea of making some personal impact on China— beyond what China wants—might reflect on the fact that, over the centuries, even China's supreme leadership has had trouble from time to time with that. That which is allowed in is more likely to be changed than China is.

Senior leader Deng termed their system "Socialism with Chinese characteristics." In the early 1980s, I noted that even the Marxist goal of "from each according to his abilities, to each according to his needs," was being paraphrased in Beijing as, "to each according to his *work.*"

Author Barbara W. Tuchman summed it up nicely with this post-World War II comment in her epic 623-page study, *Stilwell and the American Experience in China, 1911–45:* "China was a problem for which there was no American solution . . . In the end China went her own way as if the Americans had never come."

The same applies for all the tiny shallow foreign footprints which freckle the face of the Celestial Kingdom. You may sprinkle a few seeds here and there and if it pleases them they may provide some soil, warmth and water. You are free to decide what you want to do there. But China will decide how little, or how much, of that may come to pass. I long ago concluded that what happens to you there is not as important as what you learn from it.

Remembering that serves to minimize frustrations and disappointments. And if you pay very close attention and act with some decorum you can ride the Winds of Change, instead of being bowled over by them. Watch and wait. Look and listen. Don't hurry. Don't worry.

The ripe melon drops of its own accord

Getting Oriented

Variations on Reality

DESPITE REVOLUTIONARY REFINEMENTS and technological advancements over the centuries, one thing about travel remains unchanged. That's the practice of navigators of "orienting" a map by aligning it so its east—in medieval French, *orient*—points to the direction of sunrise. While "getting oriented" now conveys the general idea of simply getting our bearings, "Orient" came to denote that part of the world situated to the east of Europe, and now usually means eastern Asia. Although in some circles it's seen as an antique word, in Asia "Orient" and "Oriental" are very prominent in place and company names.

Getting (and staying) oriented in business or social situations requires your always being sure that you and the Chinese are talking about the same thing. It is alarmingly easy for the situation to be otherwise.

It comes back to my long-held view that most of our problems stem from bad communications. In my own country, for example, when bakers, flour millers and wheat producers discuss wheat "quality" (all using the same word) they are each talking about something different. The farmer sees quality in terms of a high-yielding wheat variety with high germination which is insect and weather resistant, with a high test weight, plus about everything else he can get out of it on the production side. Millers see quality as a wheat which flows easily through the mill with a high extraction rate, low moisture, cleanliness and good protein. When bakers talk of wheat flour quality they refer to its whiteness, taste, granulation, consistency, gluten strength and absorption.

Wheat breeders who develop new varieties of better "quality" wheat must appreciate that the farmer, miller and baker all have a different view of what that is. In the final analysis, it all has to work out to meet consumers' ideas of quality.

It isn't enough simply to be aware that the Chinese see some things differently. It brings to mind a story related to me by an acquaintance who in the early days of testing the waters of rapprochement, explained to local Chinese that the site they were proposing was unsuitable for his planned food industry plant because of their old fertilizer plant next door.

"No problem. We are tearing down that old plant anyway, " they reassured him. Satisfied with that, the entrepreneur went ahead with his food plant, only to find himself later having to point out:

"There's a new fertilizer plant going up next door to my plant and you told me you were going to tear your old plant down!"

"And . . . we did," was the puzzled response.

In my early days in the PRC, promoting US wheat sales, it wasn't a question of "So what do we do now?" The more pressing market development question was, "Where the heck are we in terms of the culture and life style?" My decades of experience growing up among Chinese and working with them in Taiwan, Hong Kong, Singapore and such had little application on that score. A quip going around with the newcomers was, "When we landed in Beijing the pilot announced, 'Set your watch back thirty years'." The cultural and lifestyle advancements in the PRC which I saw in the following decades strikes me as perhaps the most monumental revolution in human history.

Around the world, the concept of "culture" is as subjective as our highly variable orientations toward "quality." Webster's dictionary lists the first definition of culture in the sense of cultivation of the soil. The second relates to the improvement of a plant, animal or commodity and the third relates to the growth of bacteria. We have to get down to the fourth definition before we finally get to the idea that culture reflects refinement of the mind, manners and taste. In that form, culture, like beauty, is strictly in the eye of the beholder. Never mind that we may talk about it a lot. The thing to remember is that when we do talk about it, we may each be talking about something different.

One cozy evening on Cheung Chau Island, Hong Kong, with a fading sunset flickering through the crimson blossoms of a huge old flame tree, Charlene and I chatted in the shade with a few friends. One was a local girl who, in our idle conversation, commented that she couldn't date Westerners because her parents felt "they lack culture." There were surely a number of other reasons why her parents didn't want her dating foreigners. But what made her statement memorable was, in the next microsecond she shattered the still of the sunset with a belch that fluttered Charlene's eyelashes and surely ruffled the composure of nearby birds. It was delivered with such aplomb it seemed as if she were simply punctuating her comment with a verbal exclamation point. In some societies, this would be taken as a signal to the host that the guest enjoyed the meal. In China, it is not an uncommon accompaniment to a banquet. While lunching in Hong Kong, one of these gastrointestinal expulsions of great magnitude ricocheted around the restaurant, causing a traveled-Cantonese friend to refer to it wryly as "Chinese appreciation." However, belching is something young ladies rarely do here in public.

Along with seeing some things differently, the Chinese have the capacity to completely disregard things which a foreigner can't help but notice. For example, aside from the din and clatter, one of the things which fascinated me about Chinese opera in San Francisco's Chinatown during my teens was how the black-clad prop man just strolled casually about during the action with no one taking notice of him. Someone need a cup of tea after a high-pitched oration? The prop man walks on stage with it. The evil general need a hand in getting up after being slain? The prop man returns, helping him up and they walk off stage together. The prop man moves furniture about in full view of the audience and no one is distracted because they learned as youngsters not to notice. One of my early and memorable experiences with these learned blind spots occurred on China's southern tropical island of Hainan, when a huge tree suddenly loomed ahead of us smack-dab in the middle of the road.

As our driver slowed and went around it, I thought it might be interesting to see what I could make of that.

Turning to three friends in the back I said, "I wonder why that tree was in the middle of the road." They asked, "What tree?" I explained and they looked out the back window to confirm we had, indeed, driven around one. Determined not to allow them to retreat into their private contemplations, I said, "Perhaps the villagers enjoy the shade?" Yes, they agreed, that might be it. "Maybe they respect the tree's antiquity?" Yes, that too. "Could be the villagers are superstitious about it?" Yes, that could be the case. I decided against asking if it might be because the village didn't have a chain saw. While the tree caught my attention and demanded an explanation, for the Chinese it was worthy of neither notice nor contemplation. Anyway, trees in the middle of a road, byway or processional walkway are not at all notable. There are other formidable hazards to navigation as well. An occasional utility pole or fire hydrant in the road is not at all unusual. The unspoken reaction to my question was likely, "Why *not* a tree in the middle of the road?" "What difference does it make?" I concluded it was a dumb question.

This business of getting and staying oriented reminds me of the reservations I had in titling the first chapter "Who Do They Think They Are?" In the broader implications of this East-West orientation I toyed for a time with "Who Do They Think *You* Are?" Or for that matter "Who Do *You* Think They Are?" The question which perhaps holds the greatest promise toward starting to clear the air is: "Who Do You Think *You* Are?" *Your* orientation, after all, is critical to clarifying these East-West issues. How can we comfortably call Shanghai "the Paris of the East" but never give a thought toward calling Paris the Shanghai of the West? Quaint, canaled Suzhou is considered the Venice of the East. I'm a bit surprised the Chinese haven't responded by referring to Venice as the Suzhou of the West. Westerners particularly, do sometimes seem a bit presumptuous where China is concerned. A computer ad which I ran across in a US publication is a classic example In inch-high letters the headline read, IN 1455, GUTENBERG BROUGHT THE MIRACLE OF PRINTING TO THE CIVILIZED WORLD. Happily, the ad didn't say Gutenberg invented it. Printing was invented by Pi Sheng in China about AD 1045 and in those days, as every Chinese youngster is taught, China *was* the civilized world.

Ad copy writers in China can be just as culturally disoriented in pitching a product. A case in point was an ad aimed at the Western market which proclaimed, "For a Bright Tomorrow! Guard Your Health. Avoid the Cancer Caused by Smoking!" What's wrong with that pitch? Well, it went on to say you can achieve this by acquiring Anti-Smoking Fragrant Seat Cushions. It's hard to imagine any Westerner going for that, no matter how strong their will to live.

In fairness, up until about the middle of the last century, China hadn't taken particular note of the outside world. But in recent decades, China's leadership recognized that the country's modernization goals can only be met by opening the door to the technology of the modern world. I expect that the number of people traveling in and out of China the past few decades far exceeds the total number who have done so throughout all of China's history.

That's progress, but in China the outsider is perhaps less understood and more closely scrutinized than anywhere else in the world. Until recently most people here had little occasion to give foreigners much thought—in anything other than a negative sense—and outsiders were rarely seen. So always try to act as you would if Mother were watching. Behaving badly in your own country is a privilege of citizenship. Doing it in China is quite something else and the residue of boorish behavior makes things difficult for those who aren't just passing through for a few weeks. Uncivil conduct can, accumulatively, result in severely damaged international relationships for years, or decades.

I keep watching for some sign but I've noted nothing of significance to indicate that any one nationality does a better job than any other when it comes to getting along with the Chinese. A Portuguese diplomat confided that their 400-year relationship has not afforded any particular advantage in terms of today. He lamented that there was little going on between them these days other than an aggressive modernization program in Macau which the Portuguese had fired up. The Japanese like to feel they have some advantage because of their Orientalness, proximity and capital.

British friends have expressed the view that they get along particularly well because, like the Chinese, they are a "punctual, formal lot" and they like to sit around sipping tea. Australian and Canadian friends, with something of a freewheeling frontier style, believe that gives them an inside track. Americans seem to be comfortable in the conviction that things are going to be OK, perhaps on the suspicion that the Westward thrust of Manifest Destiny might not, after all, simply terminate at the end of the Oregon Trail as was originally believed.

They all like to *think* they have an inside track because of one reason or other but that simply illustrates the wonderful skill the Chinese have for helping outsiders to believe what they would like to be the case. The Chinese are as charming with your competition as they are with you. They coddle and charm with egalitarian vigor. Centuries ago they perfected the art of playing one barbarian against the other. It has now become a ubiquitous aspect of international business and diplomatic life.

A Chinese initiative in a relationship here is often likely motivated with the view that the other person can provide some coveted service or assistance. It relates to what they call *guanxi*. It's more than just simple networking. Think of it as the grease which helps slide things along. It can be a one-on-one situation, or a hodgepodge of interrelationships involving a number of people along horizontal or vertical channels of influence, holding oil cans at the ready in a given situation. It can help get almost anything done if your connections are right. In its affirmative form, it does serve to help get things moving. On the negative side, without it things tend to bog down or maybe not get done at all. It's the sort of thing bureaucracy nurtures, much like political "log rolling" in America where one official supports the other in expectation of the favor being returned. But when the Chinese do it, we tend to perceive it as something exotic, and possibly suspect.

It's easy for genuine and mutual friendship to evolve—with or without *guanxi*—and in these relationships, the Chinese can be more fiercely loyal and protective than anyone on earth. Despite their intense ethnic bonds, Chinese friends will even help protect you from one of their own. Other Asians are not inclined to do that.

The more *guanxi* you can accumulate the better. The advantage of having one or two key high-level contacts can quickly lose its luster if someone retires, is replaced, or whatever. The more broad your base of contacts in China the better for your long-term interests.

Fairly early in a relationship, the Chinese may be inclined to begin referring to you as an "old friend." They'll say this on your second meeting but it doesn't begin to take on much substance until a few years have passed and you've laughed together on a number of occasions and wrestled through a few things you didn't entirely agree on. They say, "It takes three years to learn a friend," and "You can't talk well together until you've laughed together." On hurrying things prematurely, they say, "Don't shake the young tree," and, "Don't pull at a seedling to hasten its growth."

It's important to develop your relationships—horizontally and vertically—as much as possible. Don't rely too heavily on a few key contacts as one roll of the dice can turn up an early retirement or something and slip you right back to Square One.

The Chinese will never make light of something of a personal or cultural nature unless they feel very much at ease in your company. Thus, if they chide you about anything—your haircut or the cut of your jacket—that means they consider you part of their crowd. Kidding you about puns they can wring out of your Chinese name or the way you pronounce some phrase is the ultimate signal that—although you can't be Chinese—they don't mind having you underfoot. The same holds true if they joke about themselves around you or share an in-joke. A Cantonese friend confided that "ICAC," the Independent Commission Against Corruption in Hong Kong, is widely taken to mean "I Can Accept Cash." One of the top officials in the Ministry of Commerce, in hosting foreign friends, delights in pointing to a pork or chicken dish which has just been brought to the table and saying, "Dog. You like dog?"

In casual conversation—as opposed to the give-and-take of negotiations—if a Chinese corrects you or suggests you are mistaken, you can infer they feel you are someone worth trying to straighten out. Chinese officials with a slight command of your language are usually disinclined to give it a try. But if they make a stab at speaking it with you it's a good sign.

Strong, affirmative signals which indicate they consider you a cut above the rest can be read in any of the following:

- Their making sure you get the smallest shrimp, which are the tastiest.
- Their offering you the head or the tail of the fish or serving you the part of the fish nearest the head, all of which are considered most flavorful.
- When you no longer hear the generic excuse, "It isn't a convenient time" and they actually reveal what the glitch is.
- Their volunteering information you were unaware of which helps you get your job done.
- Their eventually getting around to asking you, without qualms, for a reasonable personal favor.
- Your frequently being the only foreigner invited to gatherings.
- Their saying, "You understand how Chinese feel about these things."
- When the top officials you want to see are generally readily accessible to you.
- When your chief concerns are taken as their priorities.
- Being invited to their home.

One evening at the airport in Beijing I heard a businessman orienting a new arrival, "Just be yourself here. You're a foreigner and they expect you to act like one." You *are* a foreigner and it's safe to assume you'll act accordingly. But what of the expectation that you might act like a barbarian? They have had those problems, particularly during the last century and a half and that's what people here seem to remember best. When one of us arrives in their midst I sometimes suspect their unspoken perception of that is something along the lines of "Well, here comes another one."

James Clavell phrased it nicely in *Noble House* with Ian Dunross' counsel to American newcomer Casey Tcholok, "You learn the hard way when you're in China that it's best to act a little Chinese."

The best test of how well you're doing equates simply with whether you feel comfortable and enjoy working with the Chinese. If you're at ease and enjoying yourself feel free to assume they are too.

But early or easy attainment of goals or results is not always a good gauge of how well you're getting settled in. It may be that the Chinese are simply fiercely interested in whatever it is at hand and they are determined to accomplish it in spite of your bungling. Or you might have excellent rapport and enjoy a high level of respect but on some key issue your Chinese associates might not be able to deliver because of some glitch in the cultural, personal or bureaucratic structure. There could be any number of outside factors such as a shortage of foreign exchange, a shift in policy or priority or simply mushy *guanxi*.

When this happens, and it *will* happen, fall back on patient perseverance and follow the Chinese Fisherman's Rule:

There is a day to mend your nets and a day to cast your nets

Don't Squeeze Chinese

Nurturing the Knack of Gentle Nudges

O F ALL DELUSIONS, none seems more amusing and enduring than the occasional expression of the intent to "put some pressure on the Chinese." That might work in a laundry or restaurant in Chinatown, but I've never known anyone to succeed with it unless it involved something the Chinese wanted anyway.

Running a close second in the Foggy Notion category is, "It's time the Chinese start doing business our way." While the PRC sees some advantage in learning some aspects of international business style, they prefer to do this on their own terms rather than having it jabbed at them. Force feeding makes no more sense than trying to get their attention by running a gunboat up the Yangtze. This is not to be confused with the question of how far we should bend over backward in business or diplomatic dealings in the PRC. Any of that kind of bending has got to be bilateral in order to be productive.

Any business or diplomatic effort, to succeed in China, must be orchestrated along lines which are compatible with Chinese culture and history and it must clearly serve their interests. Even when those factors are in good balance, success is not always assured. It may be thwarted by unexpected and perhaps unspoken and unseen obstacles, which may be nothing more than the natural result of how things are (or are not) done in China. Obstacles may be concocted by individuals in the organization who don't understand that the manager's success reflects on the entire team. The schemers and saboteurs prefer to see their clandestine orchestration of obstacles as evidence that the manager is really not all that effective. This is a malady foreigners may recognize as it is not unknown in less professional corporate and government structures elsewhere in the world.

Developing and maintaining good working relations at the national political level in China can be somewhat more challenging when Americans are involved, as Americans and Chinese both tend to see *their* country as the center of the world. Perhaps it's the high sugar diet which inclines Americans toward overreacting to things involving China. Or maybe it's our hyper sense of expectation or native impatience. An official in Beijing agreed, "If you push an American's button, they jump straight up in the air." He added that they often land quite some distance from where they took off.

In choosing to inject oneself into the Chinese system, remember that the Chinese may have some interest in hearing how we do things but they aren't particularly interested in hearing that our way is better or that they should mend their ways and start doing things the way we do. Ideas or proposals should always be presented on the basis that, if they feel it might work, they might want to try it. Quite often they do. But as a consultant to the Chinese seafood industry lamented, "They always smile and agree but as soon as I leave they go back to doing it the old way."

Most of China's past encounters-of-consequence with foreigners are not something they look back upon fondly. Going back as far as Marco Polo, foreign aspirations have pretty much been oriented toward seeing China as something to be rung up on a cash register. It's hard for people to concentrate on what you're saying when you're waving your wallet in their face. The Opium Wars, the Boxer Rebellion, Manchukuo, the Marco Polo Bridge incident, a stack of treaties and even Nixon's China visit, which resulted in the highly-affirmative Shanghai Communique all had a commercial ring. Two-way trade can benefit everyone but the long history of coercive trade with China does not ease the effort of those trying to do business there today. The Chinese know their history well. That is, they know their version. Just as we know our version. Chinese schoolchildren can tell you more about the Boxer Rebellion than an American college senior. Despite Beijing's official endorsement of an open door to the West, there are people in China who see the term "lawless foreign businesspeople" as redundant.

On those rare occasions in the past when China's door was opened or set ajar, the enthusiasm of the West was never matched by that of the Chinese. In many instances, these exchanges were pressed on the Chinese by militarily superior powers enforcing unequal treaties which remained in effect until after World War II. That foreigners have been looked upon with suspicion from the beginning isn't surprising. Early exposure was largely limited to foreign pirates ravaging the country's coastline. Of the colonization of Macau by the Portuguese it's been said Christianity arrived riding on cannon balls. Foreign diplomacy in China, up until this century, seemed based on the idea that any problem could be resolved by giving the Chinese an occasional sniff of gunpowder.

The generally barbarous behavior of early foreigners who plied China's coastal waters fueled Chinese doubts about the basic Confucian premise that people are—by nature—good. The not-always-nifty attitudes of today toward foreigners in general rose directly from these early encounters. Sun Yat Sen, who led the overthrow of the Qing dynasty and established the Republic of China in 1912, made it clear his intent was to cooperate with countries willing to work with China . . . on an equal footing.

Despite our unfortunate legacy, the animosities seem finally to be losing ground. But it would be a mistake to presume the Chinese have forgotten their past. Anyone hoping to achieve something of substance in China has an advantage if they know some history, because the Chinese haven't forgotten.

Newsweek has observed that while Westerners look upon contracts as a precise understanding between signatories, in China there is a distinctly casual view toward them. It noted correctly that for the Chinese, "general policies, goodwill and the government's appraisal of its own best interests are more powerful guiding principles" where contracts are concerned. The nature of some of the treaties which China was forced into in the past—the "unequal treaties"—may explain the general indifference toward following the letter of signed agreements. But any contract, treaty or marriage license (anywhere) is only as good as the intent of the signatories to uphold it. In China, as elsewhere, it is often a change in circumstances which contributes to the demise or fraying of the original agreement.

After working more than a year in negotiating Beijing's first modern flour mill project, when it came time to sign the Chinese said an altogether different organization (which I'd never heard of) would sign the agreement. Their efforts to explain didn't ease the confusion. I ventured, "I'm signing with a different organization but as I understand it that means I'm signing with you and I'll be working with you." That was correct. In China people often wear more than one official hat and it can get confusing. That was in the early eighties. Despite its being a pioneering effort, we're still working together very well although a few years ago they unilaterally passed responsibility to an altogether different bureau in the course of a routine organizational shakeup. In another instance involving a major project (a few years after it'd gotten underway) all the Chinese who'd been involved in the contracting had moved on. The project manager changed three times and there was a complete turnover in staff. It taxes your creativity when those you're working with fade away, leaving your network disconnected. Maintaining flexibility, avoiding hasty barbaric overreaction, and showing a willingness to see what they're looking at helps make things work.

Whatever the arrangement is, the odds are it will change.

In most instances in China you're probably better off with goodwill, friendship and a handshake than you are with a signed contract. (This may have something to do with the possibility the Chinese see your contract as providing parameters for future litigation.) Getting across to your board of directors that a handshake is better than a contract is unlikely. But, if a deal begins to clabber, goodwill and friendship will get you further than any piece of paper.

On the other hand, PRC officials are very much inclined toward entering into a memorandum of understanding or working agreement of some sort. This seems more a matter of form than anything else and it's to your advantage if you can work toward keeping things simple and mutually flexible. This could be a bit tricky if the relationship is not well developed and you lack a high level of trust.

With business or marriage, finding the right partner in the first place can do as much as anything to get you started on the right foot and to help keep things moving smoothly. This involves guanxi, the old oil can which helps get things done through a friend's connections. Guanxi also carries obligations. One partner can request a favor of the other and, if it is within the realm of possibility, the other person is expected to deliver. In this form, particularly in newer relationships it can involve the idea "nothing-ventured-nothing-gained" on their part. In some cases, it can take on what I call the Santa's Sack Syndrome, whereby one of your Chinese counterparts keeps upping the ante until they finally establish just how much is actually in the sack. Foreigners have borne gifts for centuries, so what's the harm in asking? There is a thin line between the affirmative concept of doing a favor for a friend or, on the negative side, of using a friendship for a purely selfish purpose. A real friend does not indulge in the latter.

If they get into an area where you can't deliver simply say so and don't try to explain why. They don't respect wishy-washiness any more than they do barbaric behavior. As they get to know you and as mutual respect grows, you're allowed a giant step forward into an area where your frank, gloves-off confidences are welcome and are taken under serious advisement. You'll know when you've reached this point by the nature of the questions and casual comments. Getting there has a lot to do with how you've gone about establishing your credibility. It needn't take a lot of time but don't try to rush it. Once accepted, the word will precede you into other areas you may travel.

The foreigner with the distinct advantage is the one who feels comfortable among Chinese and can relate to them. That's basic human nature but it takes on special significance in China because Chinese prefer to do business with friends. They recognize friends are interested in their welfare and aren't inclined to squeeze or to take advantage. How do you acquire these relationships with the Chinese? About the same way you do with anyone else.

One of the problems foreigners encounter in China fairly early is "the system." Among other things, individuals you deal with perhaps have less authority than you thought and this bogs things down. But when things move slowly it usually means that's the tempo the Chinese feel comfortable with and there's nothing you can do about it. On occasion you may find yourself being pressed because they feel your side should be moving faster. Then there's the element of mystique which the bureaucracy nurtures. This involves things they don't want you to know. When this occurs you'll have only your assumptions to rely on. When they say something must be referred to "the department concerned" they are careful not to indicate which department that is. In China the lines of authority are blurred. It's easy for them to keep you away from key people if they wish. But, as often as not, they'll rush you to them if they know you and it involves a priority of theirs.

A Hong Kong Cantonese suggested, "The system isn't the problem. It's the lack of a system." That may sometimes seem to be the case from the foreign perspective but there *is* a system. The trick is in figuring out enough of it in each situation so you can get it to work for you. You are, after all, dealing with government bureaucracy with all that implies. Top level officials with whom you are working likely have three or four levels of authority above them, which can stifle your best efforts. Everything seems to move through committees, but you can't lobby or network quite as you would elsewhere because you'll have no idea of who's on the committee or where and when they meet. When they're ready they'll update you. Once you get used to it, it works fairly well, and—sometimes—very well. They say, "If you want the tiger's cub, you must enter the den." The guanxi side of that is, "If you want the tiger's cub, ask a friend's help."

Any joint venture potential should be viewed in light of the admonition, "In the beginning the Chinese have a better understanding of how things work and the entrepreneur has the money. In the end the Chinese have the money and the entrepreneur has a better understanding of how things work." That doesn't have to be the case. Those most at risk are those who come with visions of sugar plums dancing in their head. And it is never just the foreigner who gets burned. A joint venture that goes sour doesn't work to anyone's advantage.

Established Chinese businesses, based in places like Hong Kong, generally have enjoyed more success than others in joint ventures in China. But simply being Chinese gives no guarantees—as Michael Bond notes in *Beyond the Chinese Face*, "In Hong Kong, 52,000 firms are incorporated every year, but another 35,000 disappear."

Overseas Chinese come under considerable pressure to give Mother China a particularly sweet deal, so in some ways, it's even harder for them. What few entrepreneurs realize is, PRC national government entities are engaged in the same sort of joint ventures at the local level and they have the same sort of joint venture/contracting problems which Overseas Chinese and foreign businesspeople experience.

We haven't yet spent a lot of time playing marbles in the Great Schoolyard of China, and the disadvantages of limited exposure—thus far—apply equally to both sides. As one another's system becomes less mystical it will ease some of the problems which now plague both sides.

The tide of foreigners which has surged against China in recent years has been somewhat overwhelming for her. As with a ship's shake-down cruise, newness spawns glitches and questions which take time to absorb. In Taiwan the reaction of people to our car's bicycle carrier-rack suggested it was the first one ever seen in the country. They were thunderstruck by it. A person riding a car or a person riding a bike made sense. But a bicycle riding a car? It created a problem with the police. Never having seen anything like it they kept stopping us because they knew the contraption had to be unsafe. As I explained things at roadside, motorcycles roared past, carrying perhaps two adults, an infant, a sheet of plate glass and a gaggle of geese hanging from each side. The police ignored that as it was standard behavior. What I was doing was bizarre.

In a little hotel on the Silk Road I heard a German businessman sputter, "These people have no concept of economics." Well, there are Western economics and Asian economics. I recall a question about someone in the Philippines years ago to the effect, "How can a guy like that get a Letter of Credit approved for a million dollars?" The answer was, he owned the bank. There's an engaging old Chinese saying, "It's false economy to retire early to save candles if the result is twins." They understand *their* economics in the PRC, which until recently related only to the idea of generating a certain level of production or work against a quota and a budget. Profitability, efficiency and dealing with market forces are new to this generation of Chinese managers. But they may come to understand German consumerism faster than that German businessman on the Silk Road learns about Chinese consumers. That would carry interesting economic implications. A number of international businesses, preoccupied with breaking into the China market, could better spend their time strengthening their current markets, making them less vulnerable to future inroads by Chinese exports as China acquires more understanding about Western economics.

The *China Daily* noted that for some time the number of books on economics has increased by more than twenty percent annually. It isn't enough to meet demand. But not long ago the paper carried a cartoon showing a number of tacks scattered on the sidewalk in front of a sign which read, "Bicycle Repair Shop." They're getting the idea.

It wasn't all that long ago that bustling Taipei was a relatively quiet and nice little town with much of its urban area still in rice paddies. Where we lived, in the suburban Tien Mu district, it was so rural an occasional cobra or viper would show up around the house. Our youngsters learned early that if they saw a snake, one of them had to keep an eye on it while the others ran for reinforcements. One afternoon I killed a three-foot cobra which had come to call and instructed our yard boy to carry it down the hill and bury it. Neighborhood boys, heavily into amateur herpetology, later hustled down to exhume it. But it was gone. The yard boy had dug it up and taken it into town to sell the skin and the meat for an amount equal to a couple of weeks' wages.

He understood economics.

The old neighborhood is now a smoggy, concrete, high-rise extension of downtown. In the space of a few years Taipei was flung headlong into the category of international industrial cities. Before, it wasn't unusual to encounter rather exotic orientations toward economics. Visiting a shop in search of a company giveaway gift item, I found something suitable which cost the equivalent of US$5. I asked how much it would be if I took fifty. The unit price remained $5. If I took 100? Still $5. How much if I took, say, 200? At that volume, the price would be $10 each. Why? "Increased demand," was the answer. With that free lesson in exotic economics, I dropped the gift idea. That was twenty years ago and the last time I checked, Taiwan's foreign exchange reserve totaled US$429 billion. There must be a lesson in economics there somewhere.

The basic difference between people who work well with the Chinese and those who don't, seems less a matter of intelligence and chemistry than one of being able to work at seeing the world through their eyes.

For all the talk about how difficult it can be to work with Chinese and for all the deals you hear of which have floundered or fallen through, as often as not the problem stems largely from the poor approach or cultural insensitivity of the foreigners involved.

Almost too much has been said and written about negotiating with the Chinese. But there are some things which are perhaps worth mentioning:

- Always negotiate at the lowest level possible. This will resolve small things before they grow to make negotiation impossible.

- Time is your ally when you're negotiating. It calms tempers and gives rise to less spirited perspectives. Never rush into negotiations.
- Remember, agreement in principle is not agreement in practice. It does, however, serve to save face at that moment.

This doesn't come from a seminar on how to negotiate in the PRC or from some Western Management text. This is lifted directly from Wess Roberts' *Leadership Secrets of Attila the Hun*. Attila learned his leadership skills around AD 400. But this stuff works just as well in the PRC or in the West today. By all means take advantage of every opportunity to attend seminars. But remember, there is nothing particularly mystical about it if you know something about the culture, the system and the history, and have more than just a passing relationship with the people.

The Chinese are somewhat partial to the old negotiating technique (probably invented by them) which is designed to shame the other party into the desired course of action. This is couched in strong terms, criticizing the foreigner's position as selfish or suggesting that the competition's terms are considerably more attractive. (If you are on close terms this will be said in jest.) It's a case where haste should be made slowly as the employment of this device might suggest the foreigner's position is exactly as it should be and the Chinese are simply trying to sweeten the deal. Confrontation is not a good approach because it's negative by nature, it involves face, and they prefer things smooth and orderly. They don't like conflict. A good negotiator should not have to resort to confrontation and should be skilled enough to be able to make the other side feel good about the deal. If that isn't the case, it isn't a good deal, particularly in China.

You may encounter the pain-in-the-neck Chinese. These individuals come in two distinctly different packages. The one you're most likely to encounter is the role player who has been earmarked to deliver an unpleasant commentary or to take a negative position. Two things to keep in mind here. If your responses are restrained and friendly, the "pseudo pain" has the potential of becoming a good friend and confidant. Secondly, he or she might have been selected to play the black hat because they are perhaps perceived as having better rapport with you, putting them in a better position to pull it off.

There is also the pain-in-the-neck Chinese who isn't role-playing or being the devil's advocate. China probably has about as many of these ginks as we have. I rarely encounter one except in dealings with, perhaps, a minor functionary behind a counter or a very rare major functionary who maybe suspects I'm old enough to have helped put down the Boxer Rebellion. They are probably motivated essentially by the inner stirrings of either indigestion or the feeling of inadequacy which early practitioners of psychology used to chat about over chess in Vienna. Alfred Adler, one of the earlier Freudians, put forth the notion of inherent feelings of insecurity and inferiority in the strivings for superiority. You see about as much of this in China as you do anywhere else. Nien Cheng noted in *Life and Death in Shanghai,* that during the excesses of the Cultural Revolution, junior officers "often used the exaggerated gesture of rudeness to cover up their feeling of inferiority." If you ever run up against outright rudeness, it's likely there's an element of shabby self-esteem involved. Rudeness is not a trait commonly found in Chinese.

This brings us to a secret recipe for cooking fish which was shared with me by a Chinese friend during a discussion of business strategy. He said it had been handed down in his family through several generations:

"Never throw fish into pot of hot water. Fish will jump out and cannot be cooked. Instead, put it in cool water so it will be very comfortable and not suspect what you have in mind. Very slowly turn up heat, just a little at a time so fish not notice it's getting hotter. Keep fish relaxed and happy and before he knows it, you have him cooked." I've used this recipe with success a number of times, though not yet with a fish.

Despite all the shortcomings and general lack of understanding we've endured over the centuries with the Chinese, we're finally making some headway. Early Americans seemed to have no problem with frontier writer Bret Harte seeing "vain tricks" in the "dark ways" of the "peculiar heathen Chinee" in California's gold camps. Of course, the alien Chinese must surely have seen the same qualities in the San Francisco dandies and rough-and-tumble big-nosed miners. It isn't so much a matter of your agreeing with the other guy's point of view. The important thing is that you at least try to understand it.

A contemporary point-of-view story, which illustrates that we *are* developing a better understanding, involves one of the first golf courses to be built in China. This followed close on the heels of the government's reappraisal of its view that golf was a non-productive, hedonistic self-indulgence. (Golfers have always understood this, but we never allow it to throw us off our game.) An American company was called in to design the course and the Chinese were advised to notify the company as soon as they were ready to put in the grass. As Chinese officials at the course gleefully related the story to me, on the Americans' return they were stunned to find the course as flat as a pancake. The designers wanted to know what the heck had happened to all the nice little bumps and dips and undulating fairways. "The idea is to get the ball in the hole, hitting it as few times as possible. Right?" the Chinese asked. The Americans agreed that was the idea.

"Well, we leveled the ground to make it easier," the officials explained.

"But making it easy isn't the idea," the Americans countered painfully. The Chinese, in relating the story, found that very amusing. As things worked out an excellent course was established and both sides learned a little more about each other. Unfortunately, East-West encounters don't always provide much to chuckle about.

They say if you can keep your cool while others are losing theirs, you probably don't grasp the seriousness of the situation. But in China, situations often require keeping cool and making haste slowly. If that seems to have a typically exotic Asian ring, reread Aesop's fable about the tortoise and the hare, which was popular in Athens around 500 BC.

A principle I sometimes invoke when it becomes apparent I may be getting out ahead of the wave is, "Wok, don't run."

This relates to backing off from things that have suddenly gone awry and easing the turmoil onto a back burner for a time, rather than charging ahead. My principle literally calls for picking up some shrimp and setting your mind to other more relaxing thoughts while you steam the shrimp over the wok. It's hard to fret about anything when you're eating steamed shrimp. Or pick up some chicken for the wok and cleaver it to bits. A cleaver can be a particularly cathartic instrument.

The idea of unhurried harmony is an essential Confucian concept. "Be bamboo" means lean with the wind, gracefully. It doesn't mean giving in and making concessions as much as it means moving along together with the other party. Listen closely for the tempo, keep in step and don't get ahead of the herd, where a stumble could prove disastrous. Never tell a newspaper the Chinese are "about to sign" an agreement unless you're prepared to issue a retraction. You may be ready to sign and the Chinese may say (or give you the impression) they are, but wait until they do before you announce it to the world. And it would be well to check with them to make sure they don't mind if you announce it. If the intent of an "about to sign" story is to use the clipping to help float a bank loan or to attract investors or to impress others—who don't know how the system works—that's another matter.

Chinese drive a hard bargain but they're negotiable and we don't always take full advantage of a good negotiating opportunity. We're either moving too fast to spot it or we simply don't know how to recognize it. Don't chase their carrot too fast. Do it the way they do it. In the winter in Beijing's sub-zero weather wear long underwear to negotiations in an unheated room. They do and it gives them an advantage. Rather than saying you're scheduled to leave on a Friday flight, say, "I'll stay as long as it takes." That knocks the edge off their last-day squeeze.

Don't "pluck the feathers of a young bird" by trying to take advantage of a new relationship. Before going into negotiations get a Chinese massage. Notice the technique. Press. Release. Press. Release. There is a negotiating lesson in that. There's another to be found in those little "Chinese puzzles" which are popular with youngsters. You've probably encountered them. The two bent, interlocked nails that can be separated only with a special gentle twist. Or the little woven straw tube, which, with a thumb inserted in each end, grips more tightly as you try to pull your thumbs out. They appear in a variety of forms but the solution is always arrived at in the same manner, logically and without applying force.

If there's a problem it's best never to try go over the head of any official. What often works best is moving down (rather than up) the chain of command. Casual words, properly phrased, to a junior functionary or an interpreter will go right to the top. I've never known anyone who was brash and tried to take a shortcut who got away with it.

It's a different situation when you're dealing with someone you don't know at a counter or over the phone. As helpful or as courteous as service people may be, if you're not making headway with your problem, ask nicely if you could talk with the supervisor. To the supervisor you say, pleasantly, "This person has been very helpful, but I have this problem which you might be able to do something about." Usually, I find they can. What you have to watch for is the possibility you may get someone other than a supervisor. If the person doesn't impress you as someone with authority, ask nicely if you can talk to *their* supervisor. A reasonable, soft-spoken statement of your problem to the person in charge usually works wonders.

Remember the magic words which resolve seemingly insoluble frustrations with hotels, government offices, airlines and such, are, "If you were in my position, what would you do?"

Never lose your composure, despite the frustration. Charles Cross, former US Consul General in Hong Kong and later Director of the American Institute in Taiwan, shared an important diplomatic technique one day. "Take a lesson from the duck," he said. "On the surface, it glides gracefully. Under the water, its feet are paddling like crazy."

If the pressure builds, take a break, buy a kite and go out and fly it. Not only is it hard to fret when you're flying a kite, notice the way a kite stays up by riding the Winds of Change, as well as how it offers just the right amount of resistance. Yes, the kite is a Chinese invention.

Lunching in the coffee shop in my favorite hotel in Beijing, I was disappointed with the quality of the French fried potatoes. They were cold, limp, greasy and overcooked. I've eaten better looking sautéed caterpillars ... and enjoyed them more. The French fries annoyed me for two reasons. First, I eat often at the hotel and would like to have food quality standards upheld reasonably well. Second, being in the food quality business, I am more comfortable with signs of progress than with back-sliding. I slid the offending fries onto my bread plate, and on my business card wrote: "In the history of civilization it's unlikely any potato was treated with less respect." I carried it to the front desk and said softly with a smile, "Give this to the Food and Beverage manager." Then I left for the airport.

Five weeks later, back in Beijing, on being shown to my table the headwaiter said graciously, "I hope you'll try our French fries today." Shocked and amused, I thanked him and when I ordered the waitress said, "Aren't you having French fries?" Wow. I told her I'd try them later in the week. (Chinese don't give up easily.) In a few moments the headwaiter reappeared with a plate of hot, plump, firm, succulent, inviting, golden fries—on the house—and urged me to try them. The fries were excellent and the quality has been maintained since.

That's not the end of the story. A year later, lunching at a hotel in Guangzhou, on the other end of China from Beijing, the headwaiter stopped at my table and said, "I remember you from when I was working in Beijing. You're the one who got them to do the French fries right."

The next day at breakfast with some of the hotel's chefs, one who'd worked in that hotel in Beijing, studied my card and said, "Say, you're that French fry guy."

In telling that story to some people representing US potato interests, they told me about some young Americans lunching at a fast food shop in Korea, who, dissatisfied with their French fries, flung them against the wall. The fries are still terrible. As my editor told me in my early days of sniffing out news stories as a cub reporter, you can catch more flies with fly paper than with a fly swatter. The idea works equally well with flies, fries, and lots of other things. If you really want to get someone's attention in China, try whispering.

Drivers can be particularly challenging. I invariably get one who drives as if he's leading the pack in the Macau Grand Prix. The abandon of their high-speed turns suggests they think Centrifugal Force is a rock band. If implored to slow down, they seem content to do so for roughly .0005 of a mile or two seconds, whichever comes first. Now, after asking them twice nicely to slow down, I hand them a note in Chinese which reads, "Fast driving is bad for my heart so if I pass out please take me to the nearest hospital." It works not because of their concern for my health but because they fear my demise in their back seat would result in their having a haunted taxi on their hands.

Western management is heavily directed toward seeing that problems don't happen. So far, PRC management seems preoccupied with resolving problems which have surfaced. So, what the foreigner often contends with is crisis control or stress management. In some cases you come up against something which is essentially insoluble for a number of reasons. It's not uncommon to discover that you and the Chinese are talking about two entirely different things. But you had no reason to suspect there was a problem until you realized that the "Mr. Stevens" you've been talking about all day is taken by them to mean another, "Stephen" who has nothing to do with the subject at hand. It's a bit like refraction, that distortion of where a fish actually *is* underwater and where you *see* it.

Some blips respond only to a Chinese solution. That is, "action through inaction." As they put it, "The best way to resolve a problem is to do nothing." The trick is in knowing when you're dealing with something in that category. It's the concept of "masterly inactivity" which is common in American board rooms where a decision to do nothing is action, and is so noted in the minutes. It takes good leadership to understand when "action through inaction" should be applied. The *South China Morning Post* has editorialized: "The Americans are often seen as an impatient people, anxious to accomplish today what could be safely left to tomorrow." Americans do have this sense of urgency, seemingly rooted in the idea, "act now, think later." But America's cartoon character "Peanuts" Charlie Brown lives by the (rather Confucian) code that no problem is so big it can't be run away from.

In the early 1960s, wallowing shoulder-high in tub-warm surf near Karachi, I was gripped by an undertow and slurped suddenly out of my depth into the churning sea. Tides are deadly there and drownings common. In that instant it was essential to decide whether to try to fight the Arabian sea or to relax, flatten on top of the water and try to ride the next wave into shore. I chose to catch a ride and on the crest of the next breaker was tumbled unceremoniously into the shallows. China is much like the ocean: a barrier or a bridge, old, vast, challenging, unforgiving, and for many, unfathomable. The odds against China or the ocean gobbling you up are enhanced if you afford them a reasonable degree of understanding and respect, and don't do something dumb.

Recommended reading on this subject is Sun Tzu's *The Art of War* which has been widely translated from the Chinese, appearing in Japanese around AD 600, and was introduced into the West in French in 1772, a version reputedly studied by Napoleon. No one got around to publishing the 2,500-year-old classic in English until 1905. It deals with military strategies which also have application in business and personal relationships and its theme is this basic idea of action through inaction; of winning through power plays and nuances rather than through the use of force or the expending of resources: winning without fighting. It's the philosophy which gave General Stilwell fits when he was trying to marshal Chinese forces to drive the Japanese out of China in World War II. It was at least part of the reason Chiang Kai-shek squirreled away vast amounts of war materiel which the United States provided during the war years. While that may have appalled Vinegar Joe and a broad cross-section of Americans, it was the Chinese way to act in that sort of situation.

One of the most recent renditions of Sun Tzu's work was edited by James Clavell. In his forward, Clavell suggests that if American military and political leadership had studied Sun Tzu, "Vietnam could not have happened as it happened" and "in all probablility, World Wars I and II would have been avoided."

The West has generally missed the significance of all this, favoring instead the suggestion that it is simply through patience that problems are resolved in China. While there is a lot said *about* that approach, there's not a lot to be said *for* it. The importance of patience is overrated and overstated. Patience is one of the great Chinese virtues but a preoccupation with it is best left to buzzards. Problem solving and goal attainment requires proper perspective and pace, passivity, persuasion, pragmatism, perspicacity, prudence, politeness, punctuality, pleasantness, pertinence, performance, practicality, planning, and, perhaps a pinch of pizazz. It takes some time to get the hang of it, rather like learning how to hit a moving target. Patience has its place but don't put all your egg foo yung in that basket.

Working toward bringing about improvements the Chinese want isn't the same as an outsider's setting out to change things. They don't appreciate the latter and it impedes the outsider's efforts. Some foreigners have problems because what they see as being good for China doesn't always mesh with how the Chinese see it. If the advantage is clear—from the Chinese viewpoint—they usually respond quite readily. The key is in your having a good grasp of what their viewpoint is and that's often rooted in their cultural orientation.

Rather than being outright confrontational when problems arise in a business venture, try to develop a position which is in line with their stated national or local policy and/or which enhances the life of the people. That puts you on pretty firm ground. If you have a joint venture food production plant you should not have to endure sanitation standards below those which you maintain for your bathroom at home. Explain your concerns in terms of unsanitary food production being a threat to the health of the people of China. If the quality of delivered raw materials is below standard, it then must follow that the people are receiving sub-standard merchandise. If plant equipment is not properly maintained and cared for it will result in needless economic loss for the country, will discourage further foreign investment and will create hardship for the people through unemployment as abused equipment wears out. Rather than criticizing poor maintenance, be critical of how poor maintenance hurts the people. When you get into areas such as these which clearly impede the country's modernization program, this sort of squeezing can be effective, providing you ease the squeeze onto someone who trusts you and you're careful not to step on anyone's face in the process. But don't expect results overnight.

The first step is to get their mind open and to establish some toeholds of agreement. It's one thing to point out problem areas but you can't expect to get far by lecturing the Chinese about contracts, delays, discrepancies or your frustrations. Keep your strategies and energies within the boundaries of their own orientation and goals and what they can and cannot do. It's easy for foreigners to overestimate just how much authority or freedom of action may be enjoyed by a particular individual or group, even with people at fairly high levels. A reasonable soft-spoken approach may not get you as far as you'd like, but you can take some comfort in knowing that it isn't likely to cause you to lose any ground either. If your strategy needs more work, back off and spend some more time on it. Seek counsel from someone who knows the territory. I've never known anyone with China experience who wasn't happy to share what they've picked up on the winding, bumpier stretches of the China road. In the event people in the home office call for putting a squeeze on the Chinese, tear out this chapter and send it to them. Or suggest they spend some time in China seeing how far they get with that.

In China, the best approach is the Chinese approach. But if you're painted into a corner with no alternative, the next best is to explain your position and remember to smile.

Born in the Year of the Rabbit, I endorse the philosophy:

A wise rabbit doesn't nibble the grass around its burrow

The Sweet and Sour

Assorted Anecdotes and Antidotes

S WEET AND SOUR DISHES testify to the compatibility of properly-blended opposites. This unlikely marriage of vinegar and sugar illustrates a point about "opposites" in human relationships. To reinforce my thesis that people in the same boat should row together, these final pages are devoted to sharing a few personal recollections.

* * *

Back in pre-fax days, I received a cable in my hotel room with the letters, "COLL" in the jumble of coding at the top. Later, I asked the desk clerk, "Was my cable collect?" He said it was. I found that curious. As I pondered he added, "It is *absorutery* collect." In that old Asian inclination to transpose r's and l's, he was assuring me it was correct!

It was the old problem of Asians trying to please, with the answer they presume the foreigner wants. It was also a matter of the clerk not wanting to lose face by saying, "I don't know," in spite of his having no way of knowing whether the telegram was correct or not.

Almost any answer in the Orient is worthy of a little further scrutiny. And if it is correct, it may change.

* * *

With a group of Americans on their first trip to China we were chopsticking through a welcoming banquet when one of our group picked up his camera and pointed it across the table. A Chinese official, who had just taken a bite of roast duck, waved him off.

The American lowered his camera. "You'd rather I do not take your picture?"

"That's OK," the Chinese swallowed. "But you didn't take the cap off your lens."

It never hurts to ask.

* * *

Though desirable, it isn't always essential to speak a foreign language when you work overseas. Few Americans I've encountered put much effort into this. It works for them, but I'm uncomfortable with being totally tuned-out so I've tried to develop my language capability at least to the extent that I can locate my luggage, order a meal, find a bathroom, or get out of any pickle which might arise. An example of how this works occurred the day our daughter Heidi was married at St. Margaret's church in Hong Kong. This was quite a fancy affair and just before things got underway, as guests gathered in front of the church, one of Hong Kong's street people wandered gregariously into the crowd. Barefoot and grubby, he frustrated the photographer who had trouble keeping him out of his viewfinder and Charlene made it clear that resolving such a situation was what the father of the bride was supposed to do. Not wanting to create a scene, I pressed a few banknotes in his palm and said in Chinese, "Run along and get a few beers." Off he toddled. We didn't see him again until midway through the ceremony as he came strolling casually down the entire length of the aisle, an open can in each hand, looking for the guy who'd sent him out to get the beer. Everyone agreed it was a highlight of the wedding.

Always say exactly what you mean.

*   *   *

When Chinese talk of "settling the account" it generally refers to what foreigners call "getting even." It is traditionally accomplished with a finesse which leaves the victim not altogether sure of just what hit him. It is much tidier than the way these things are usually handled in the West. I found myself drawn into this "settling" in connection with a bank transaction in Hong Kong years ago when I was working out of Taiwan. A bank officer, at a branch where we had a sizable and active company account of some twenty-five years standing, declined to cash a US$100 personal check of mine because I did not have a personal account with them. This struck me as indefensible as he knew me and knew where to find me if there was any problem with the check. He was polite but firm. Feeling compelled to make myself feel better about the situation I said, "Well then, would you mind checking the balance on my company account?" He was pleased to provide that service but it took him an unusually long time and when he returned he stammered weakly, "Your company account is overdrawn by US$46,750." I thanked him and left. (What he didn't know was one of our deposits had gone astray in their system and the bank's head office had allowed us a hefty line of credit until the matter was cleared up.)

Losing your temper with the Chinese doesn't get you anywhere, but it's sometimes therapeutic if you can come up with a little something to make yourself feel better.

*   *   *

Differences in the way our business, economic and social systems have evolved will always be a source of some frustration for foreigners who decide to leave home to travel or work in this part of the world. When Charlene and I moved to Taipei from Manila, we arrived with driver's licenses which had just expired. It took us both a full year of struggling through the bureaucratic bramble to finally become licensed. In my case, I'd driven for twenty-five years in nearly fifteen countries. (In some of those places, people drove as if the wheel had only recently been introduced and they hadn't made up their minds whether they really wanted to have it around.) After months of working at it, I finally reached Taiwan's elusive test-drive Disneyland, where I was able to take an examination. The written test was in Chinese. My assistant, Mr. Lu, helped me through it.

Lu, who does not drive, translated, "If you are near a hospital, would you . . . exercise your bugle?" It was a perfect literal translation. "Never," I said firmly. "Near a hospital, I definitely would not exercise my bugle."

I finally acquired the license, and a better appreciation that things go better with the Chinese if they're not rushed.

*   *   *

Along with having some skill with chopsticks, few things make a more immediate affirmative impression on the Chinese than acquiring a good Chinese name. That is, a translation of your name which sounds as if it belongs to a Chinese. The idea isn't necessarily to have a phonetic translation of the name. The name Elwood P. Crunchwaffle, for example, could be rendered phonetically into something like eleven characters, depending on how you do it. What Elwood needs, to have a good Chinese name, is to get it down to two or three characters; three being more common. And, he should be sure to work a real family name into it, which is easily done. Chinese printing shops which do business cards are not noted for their sensitivity to this. It's best to ask a Chinese friend for help and be sure he or she uses the national language rather than one of the dialects. It can be tricky because of the variety of monosyllables. Anyone's name—even a good one—can be inflected for the humor which lingers just under the surface. One American friend has a Chinese name which translates phonetically as "Chinese Virtue." Otherwise inflected, it comes out as "liar." Another American took

"Busy Man" as his Chinese name . . . and is perhaps still unaware that with a slight inflection it can be pronounced as "barbarian."

Talking to an American friend in China about the intricacies of this, he said a Chinese lady at a reception had recently commented that he had "a good Chinese name." But it developed she had mistaken his business card for someone else's. I asked how his name translated.

"Mulberry," he said. "Mr. Mulberry."

"Chinese names are very important," I said. "Yours makes you sound like one of the characters in that parlor game, 'Clue.' Mr. Mulberry and Colonel Mustard." We got out a Chinese dictionary and went to work on his image.

"I don't know," he said, studying the options. "All I can get out of this is: Buddhist monk, funeral, sore throat."

"Let me see that! What do we have over here . . . OK . . . hmmm. Terror stricken, perverse, lose confidence." I checked another possibility. "Here we have, well, harass, gloomy . . . and what's this? Hmmm. The smell of urine."

The solution, I suggested, was to forget the phonics and go for the German meaning of the name.

"OK," he said. "I'll do it later."

"Let's do it now."

"Naw," he said. "I still have 2,000 Mr. Mulberry business cards."

New cards would have been a good investment toward a better image.

*   *   *

When we began receiving prank phone calls in Taipei, although no one would respond when we picked up the phone, I was convinced it was a child, and came up with a plan I was confident would put an end to it.

At the next call, after my saying "hello" three times, the line remained silent. After a long pause, very softly and slowly, I began to sing a kindergarten song, the Chinese version of what we know as *The More We Get Together.* I had a hunch that any youngster, disciplined to their educational system and group orientation, could not remain silent through that song. By the time I got to the chorus, a little wispy voice began to sing along. With the veil of anonymity lifted, we finished the song together and at the end, I said firmly in Chinese, "If you call again I'll tell your father." I had no idea who his father was, but given the father figure's potential for massive retaliation, the phantom ceased his calls.

Chinese aren't inscrutable.

*   *   *

A travel-oriented predictability story involved my checking into a new international hotel in Guangzhou around midday, with a busy schedule for the afternoon. While I prefer to carry my luggage to the room for the sake of expediency, I usually refrain from that because the service is, as they say, somebody's rice bowl. On this occasion, after twenty minutes in my room without my luggage, I phoned the front desk about it and left for a meeting. On returning, the bags still hadn't arrived. I again talked to the front desk, an assistant manager, the concierge and, finally, two bellmen. Repeating this two more times without getting anywhere, it became clear that this wasn't the right approach. I asked to talk with one of the English-speaking Hong Kong supervisors. One was summoned and in soft tones with a smile I explained that I had stayed in some of the worst hotels in the world but never had this much trouble getting my bags before. "I don't want to cause any problem," I said, "and I want you to feel good about today, but your general manager is a friend of mine and I know he is in Hong Kong today. I am going to my room now and call him and tell him I've tried for five hours to get my luggage and I'm going to ask him to help locate it."

Thus, having gotten his attention, I returned to my room and hadn't finished dialing when there was a knock at the door. It was a bellman with my luggage. Waiting five hours for luggage might cause one to get a bit testy, and while feigning annoyance works in some situations in China, if you really get excited it almost guarantees a complete lack of local interest.

What can you do if the hotel manager isn't an old friend?

Use your imagination. Tell them you're a travel writer, syndicated in twenty-three newspapers, and you're in town doing a story about their tourist attractions. Say you've been commissioned to do a survey for the government on weaknesses in the country's tourist industry. Say it's your tenth trip to China and the service has always been very good in all the hotels you stayed in. Say you're meeting the Governor in half an hour and you've a present in the bag for him. Say you have a frozen cheese in the bag which will stink up the whole place when it starts to thaw. Say anything. Nothing is too devious when it comes to getting your luggage back. Or your laundry. Or your composure.

Don't lose your temper and remember you first have to get their attention.

* * *

Depending on the circumstances, feigned histrionics sometimes hasten a desired result. Walking down the lane from our apartment one day, I heard a fiery exchange of agitated Cantonese expletives roiling up through the jungle from Repulse Bay Road. Rounding the corner, I saw long lines of cars waiting bumper-to-bumper while, at a short one-way detour, a bus blocked traffic as the driver and a little flagman screeched at one another. It was another replay of the Old Amateur Roadside Chinese Opera, with the audience (sitting in their cars) waiting patiently while the protagonists, wearing fierce expressions and going through time honored motions, flailed the air to establish that it was the other guy who'd lost face. It was a heck of a show. Always primed to pursue a little cultural research, I was curious to see if I could get traffic moving by stepping in and hollering louder and acting more foolishly than they were. Waving my arms and shaking my head violently to suggest a tinge of instability, I shouted in Chinese, "This is ridiculous! You're creating a nuisance! Get that bus out of here! Go! Now!" The driver blinked once, scampered aboard the bus and sped off. The flagman stepped back, gripping the flag like a club. "No problem," I grinned. "I'm just kidding. With that bus gone, see if you can get this traffic moving again."

Acquiring a little grasp of how Chinese feel about things makes everything easier.

* * *

In feeling our way along together in recent years, China and America both have made fairly good, though uneasy, progress. The transition must have been more difficult for the Chinese, as evidenced by the West's euphoric surge of enthusiasm as soon as the door was opened. But China's door still seems to swing out more than in. They remain protective of their markets and while officially welcoming the fresh air and sunshine through the open door, there are those who remain concerned about what they call, "the flies and mosquitoes" that slip in with it.

In line with that concern, the American weekly, *People* magazine, in March of 1983 carried an item about China's exposure to the American film *Nightmare in Badham Country*. It noted the movie had been seen by some 100 million people in the PRC, and described it as "a tale of two young women who are subjected to false arrest and imprisonment (one gets raped) in a Neanderthal Southern Town." (A folksy tale about what one might expect in a typical small town in America.) With the opening sentence, "Let there be no doubt in anyone's mind that China is becoming Westernized," the item went on to relate how the lovely leading lady, Deborah Raffin, had been recognized "by scores of people" during a visit to Beijing. Figuring there surely would be more to come, I clipped the item.

Sure enough, three months later, *Newsweek* magazine reported on negotiations between Chinese and American television officials, concerning China's interest in acquiring American TV programs to show in the PRC. The visiting delegation had expressed particular interest in such action shows as one "about a private detective in San Francisco's Chinatown" and another titled, *"Muggable Mary: Street Cop* ... in the tough world of the New York City Police Department." The Chinese delegation was quoted as saying such shows "provided an interesting glimpse of American institutions." The *Newsweek* story ended with the question, "If *Muggable Mary* plays Peking, can Alka-Seltzer, Froot Loops and Miller Lite be far behind?" They could, indeed, be far behind. I clipped that one also.

Finally, it all came together in September, when *US News & World Report* followed up with an article under the headline, "China's View of America: Crime, Poverty, Tension." The two-page article questioned the sincerity of China's desire to improve relations, with their official media presenting a picture of the "darker side of American life, often in a heavy-handed manner and with twisted embellishment."

That report may well have served to clear the air, and perhaps should have been considered, at least, for nomination for a Nobel Peace Prize. It's difficult to imagine that the political section of the PRC Embassy in Washington missed either the item or the point it made. Things have mellowed since in that regard, with a generally wider and more objective range of American films now available to viewers. From the misty perspective of those earlier days of our trying to figure out one another, I wonder what discussion that article might possibly have stimulated behind closed PRC Embassy doors in Washington.

"Everyone seen this article saying we're insincere because we're showing movies and TV programs with a seamy, comical view of American life?"

"Right, chief, and we're not sure what to make of it. These are their own films, dealing with what we presume are typical stories about life here. We've researched it, and find that millions of Americans flock to the movies every night or sit around TV at home enthralled with these stories of violence, avarice and lust. We can't figure out why they're upset about our showing this stuff. They're not an easy people to understand, but I've been hearing something about some films with this actor, Mickey Mouse. Maybe we should look into that. . . ." (Up until the late 1970s hardly anyone in China had ever heard of Mickey Mouse, or many other famous Americans for that matter.)

Embassy security being what it is, there's no way to know whether the foregoing conversation actually took place but, in the past few years, Mickey Mouse has become a household name and by now has cavorted across every television screen in China. Things are changing. So much so, foreigners who were working there in the late '70s and early '80s, reflect, "I'm glad I had a chance to see it as it was."

Conversely, it's good that Chinese are traveling outside their country to see the wonders and warts of the West. Two years ago, traveling in America with a group from South China, one of them remarked, "I thought there would be more policemen around." He'd been conditioned by the battalions of men and women in blue in our shoot-em-up mayhem movies which the Chinese probably take to be documentaries.

We've still got a long way to go.

* * *

A weakness common to foreign visitors is their inclination, on a perhaps once-in-a-lifetime trip, to simply jet from one megalopolis to another. They visit the places they've seen on postcards, missing what makes a country what it is. One of the best afternoons I've spent with a Chinese delegation in the US was at a potluck picnic in the town park in Grant, Nebraska. (Population 1,270.) Another group was scheduled to coincide with the Cowboy-and-Indian Pendleton Round-Up in Oregon. And they are still talking about it. Both in Beijing *and* Pendleton. There are a couple of Ministry of Agriculture officials who, from time-to-time, remind me of how I schooled them in the art of selecting a properly-forked willow branch from a beach-side grove where they experienced their very first American wienie roast.

If you have visitors from China, be sure to show them the things *you* do, not just what the tourists do.

*   *   *

In planning a China trip, weigh the options between staying in typically Chinese hotels or the sanitized international jobs, which look like space ships from another planet. They're worlds apart. Shortly after one of Guangzhou's new modern international hotels opened, a diplomat, living in an apartment complex there, related a story about his American neighbor who had a four-year-old. The youngster spent much of his time in the apartment and around the hotel complex and its manicured grounds. The apartment was air conditioned and cozy and the boy had his room, toys and pals. There was the TV and a fridge stocked with imported goodies. He played in the hotel pool and hamburgers and milk shakes were just an elevator ride away. Chopin rippled through the ornate lobby in the evening, from a baby grand. It was cozy. One Sunday morning the father suggested going to the park, to which the four-year-old replied, "Daddy, I don't want to go to China today."

You can't learn much about a country looking at it from your hotel window.

*   *   *

Getting out and around, meeting China on its terms, can do more to broaden your viewpoint than anything else you might undertake. In a little oasis community in Western Gansu Province, staying with an associate in a fairly new but very rural hotel, I stopped at his room on the way to dinner. As he opened the door, I saw a stranger kneeling in the bathroom filling the tub. A boy, about eight, was perched naked on the toilet seat like a little plucked parakeet.

"Who are those people?" I asked.

"I don't know. They just came in. I guess the guy's going to give the kid a bath," he said, with the sage resignation he'd acquired over some twenty years in the Orient.

"In *your* tub?"

"Yeh. Let's have dinner." He paused at the bathroom, waggling his fingers, to convey the idea of closing the door to the room when they finished. There were no keys so there was no question about locking up anyway. The incident wasn't too unusual for a rural setting in an egalitarian society. And, we reasoned, in an oasis, water is an even more communal commodity than it is elsewhere.

Always do things the way the villagers do.

*   *   *

Back when some of this foreign investment was first getting underway in China, I spent some time in Beijing with one of the top executives of a well-known American food company. It was his first trip to the country. He was brimming with that unbridled unwarranted enthusiasm which so often strikes first-timers. In those days it was virtually epidemic. I'd cautioned him about the realities of the market and stressed that it would be some time before his company could expect to do much in China.

Visiting with him on the steps of the Beijing Hotel as we waited for the car to take him to the airport, he asked the interpreter what he'd thought of the company's product which some Chinese had sampled the day before.

"Oh, very good. I like it."

Did he think it would be a good product for China?

"Very good."

Would the interpreter like to be the China representative and introduce the product all over the country?

"Oh, I'd like to do that very much."

The American turned to me with a smug look of vindication and said, "Well?"

"Well, what?"

"Did you hear *that?*"

"Sure. Ask him some more questions."

"There's nothing more to ask," the first-timer replied triumphantly.

"Ask him if he *can* do it."

He blinked, turned to the interpreter and put that to him.

"Oh, no! I couldn't do *that,*" the interpreter sputtered.

A decade later, China still wasn't ready for the product.

It's essential to learn to march to China's drum.

* * *

In the early 1980s, People's Liberation Army guards were stern and unsmiling. Their demeanor suggested the ancient battle command, "Look frightening now!" The only time I ever saw them loosen up in those days was in a railroad station when I happened to be traveling with a cricket in a little bamboo cage. They'd grin and chat about that. But, predictably, things changed and in 1987 when I grumbled at a young PLA guard about a "bothersome" border-crossing procedure he replied softly, "I'm sorry." Following the Tiananmen incident the stern countenances returned. With the Asian Games the following year, the smiles were ordained back.

China changes more often and in more ways than the casual observer realizes.

* * *

While China and the West have learned a great deal about one another in the ebb and flow of recent years, few Chinese have spent much time among Westerners, which is one reason not to try to hurry relationships. As with bread and brew, they're best when given a suitably long ferment. After my assistant, Pansy, had been working for me for some time in sophisticated and international

Hong Kong, I began to notice she carried her briefcase when we went anywhere together. I eventually suggested, "The only reason you carry that is so the Chinese won't think you're dating a Westerner." She smiled and hasn't carried it since. Another small step for Man.

It reminds me of two Chinese proverbs, popular with President Kennedy, "A journey of 1,000 miles begins with a single step" and, "A rising tide lifts all boats." You don't have to have spent a great deal of time in the Far East to realize the tide is rising.

The anchored boat cannot rise with the tide

Epilogue

O N THE EVE of moving from Karachi to Manila in the mid-1960s I called at the Commercial section of our Embassy to see a friend who'd worked in the Philippines.

"Tell me about the Philippines," I said. "What do I need to know?"

"Just remember, *noblesse oblige*," he replied.

"That's just a fancy way of saying, 'Be nicer to people than they expect you to be.' "

"That's it. Remember that and things should go just fine."

As I was soon to learn amidst the manifestations of Filipino hospitality, it is indeed a good thing to keep in mind. A little extra touch of courtesy is extended to important dinner guests in Manila, for example, not by simply walking them to the front door or even the front gate. Departing guests are more properly walked to their car if you want to do it with class and in accord with the time-honored, all-consuming social concept Filipinos call *amor proprio*. Its implications are as strong as face to the Chinese.

From Manila, one of the six countries I traveled regularly in those days was the new island-nation of Singapore. One of my early acquaintances there was a Chinese co-pilot for the (then) Malaysia-Singapore Airlines. On one of my visits he suggested getting together for dinner at what he called, "the best chili crab place in Asia." This turned out to be a little tumble-down hut, not far from the World War II Changi prison camp, where a remote road dead-ended in a bamboo grove at the water's edge. He, his wife and I were knuckle deep into a steaming bowl of huge crimson crab claws when he said, "You know, you really know how to get along with Chinese."

Before I could respond, his wife volunteered an off-handed observation I've never forgotten.

She said, "There's no mystery about getting along with Chinese. All you have to do is be nice."

It isn't quite that simple. But if you'd like to try to get along, keep that in mind and you can't go far wrong. If we ever all get around to working together on that it might help make the world a more fit place to raise kids. That would be nice.

As Confucius said:

Don't do to others what you don't want done to you

About the Author

You can't explain the ocean to a frog ... a Chinese proverb that has never daunted indomitable raconteur Fred Schneiter.

Fred Schneiter lived and worked in Asia a total of 30 years from early 1964, pioneering and directing market development efforts for the US wheat industry in every province of China and a dozen Asian countries. Having had Chinese classmates and neighbors since the first grade, the year Franklin Roosevelt became president, and growing up a short walk from San Francisco's Chinatown with half his high school classmates Chinese, he's acquired a unique understanding and appreciation of the way they see things, and you. For six years he served on the board of Portland's Northwest China Council.

Getting Along With the Chinese was his first book and was on the *South China Morning Post* bestsellers' list for a solid year. While relaunching it with this revised edition, he held to his threat to follow it up with *The Taste of Old Hong Kong—Recipes and Memories from 30 years on the China Coast,* published in 2014 by Blacksmith Books.

EXPLORE ASIA WITH BLACKSMITH BOOKS

From retailers around the world or from *www.blacksmithbooks.com*